LIFE ACCORDI

Christ Pantocrator

Main dome of the Gračanica Monastery, 1318–1321

Gračanica's uniqueness lies in the fact that the icon known as Pantocrator, which inspires liturgical awe, is depicted not just as the God-Man—i.e., God who assumed human nature—but as Co-Man, identifying Himself with man in his suffering and helplessness, with human pain through His suffering on the cross and His humiliating death. Through His philanthropic gaze, the majestic Pantocrator lowers Himself and meets His creation. The eternal and infinite meets the finite in a particular place and time, within history, where they reconcile within the same fate. This composition, with its wrinkles in the forehead, was not repeated in other Byzantine churches, perhaps because its boldness brought it to the threshold of the psychologization of the divine drama. Gračanica's Pantocrator is truly unique, since it was not copied from anyone. It is original and loving, and for this reason it constitutes a portrait of God, as Christ's wonderfully loving eyes have revealed it to human beings. The riddle of human destiny finds its solution in the Pantocrator's theandric gaze.

PATRIARCH PAVLE OF SERBIA

LIFE ACCORDING TO THE GOSPEL

Translated from Serbian by
Aleksandra Petrović

Edited by
Herman Andrew Middleton

Sebastian Press
2017

Published by
Sebastian Press
Western American Diocese of the Serbian Orthodox Church

Edited by
Bishop Maxim (Vasiljević)
and the St. Herman Brotherhood

Prepress & printing
Interklima-grafika, Vrnjacka Banja, Serbia
Contemporary Christian Thought Series, number 37

Address all correspondence to:
Sebastian Press
1621 West Garvey Avenue
Alhambra, California 91803

Email: westsrbdio@gmail.com ∴ Website: http://www.westsrbdio.org

---

Publishers Cataloging in Publication

Names: Pavle, Patriarch of Serbia, author. | Petrović, Aleksandra, translator. | Middleton, Andrew Herman, editor.

Title: Life according to the Gospel / Patriarch Pavle of Serbia ; translated from Serbian by Aleksandra Petrović ; edited by Andrew Herman Middleton.

Other titles: Serbian Patriarch Pavle: a seeker for a dignified solution to the tragic fate of Kosovo and Metohija.

Description: Alhambra, California : Sebastian Press / Western American Diocese of the Serbian Orthodox Church, 2017. | Series: Contemporary Christian thought series ; no. 37. | Includes bibliographical references.

Identifiers: ISBN: 9781936773336 | LCCN: 2017943306

Subjects: LCSH: Pavle, Patriarch of Serbia—Sermons. | Christian life—Orthodox Eastern authors. | Christian life—Sermons. | Spiritual life—Sermons. | Bible—Sermons. | Kosovo and Metohija—Ethnic relations. | Orthodox Eastern Church—Serbia.

Classification: LCC: BX382 .P3813 2017 | DDC: 248.4/819—dc23

Contents

SERMONS ON SAINTS' FEASTS

LITURGICAL HOMILIES AND ARCHPASTORAL LESSONS (1995-1998)

FIRST SERMONS

THE FIRST HIERARCHICAL SERMON, 1957

Your Holiness,
Your Graces Brother-Bishops in Christ,
Brothers and Sisters,

May our first thought, at the start of each new day, and the start of each of our labors, be the remembrance of God. And may our first word, at the start of each new day, and the start of each of our labors, be a word to the glory and praise of Him, One God in Trinity: Father, Son, and Holy Spirit.

Therefore, today, in this solemn moment, when from the hands of His Holiness I have received this staff as a symbol of hierarchical service to God and the Church of God, may my first thought as well rise up to His throne, and may my first word be:

> "Lord, glory to Thee! Lord, help! Lord, bless! Glory to Thee! For glory belongs to Thee alone, to Your greatness alone, to Your wisdom, Your justice; but above all to Your endless goodness, our Father! On account of it, we put our hope also in Your help without which we know not and cannot begin anything good; we also put our hope in Your blessing without which all our effort and work will be nothing more than building a house upon the sand, which will be destroyed as soon as the first rain descends, and the rivers flood, and the winds start blowing" (Matt. 7:27).

Only in such a way then, by binding all of our thoughts, feelings, and deeds to the mighty hand of God will we, brothers and sisters, realize the meaning of our existence in general, and individually: we will always find the right path in all crossroads and wastelands of life, help in trouble, consolation in sorrow, peace when our heart is troubled and frightened amidst the storms of this world. We will find, at last, the heavenly gates opened when the earthly gates close behind us for the last time, and we will hear the blessed voice of the Master and Father, "Well done, good and faithful servant; thou hast been faithful over a few things, I will make thee ruler over many things: enter thou into the joy of thy lord" (Matt. 25:23).

A Christian feels the need for God's help and blessing always, each moment, but especially in times of certain exceptional events, or when one needs to make an important decision, to take on a responsible undertaking that requires attention and strength of the kind one cannot see or find in oneself. Today I find myself in such a position, faced with all the seriousness and responsibility of the hierarchical service, and in such a time as we live in which is not at all easy.

I already knew how exalted the Mystery of the priesthood is, and how exalted a priest should be to be worthy of it. By this Mystery the priest is elevated to the height of a coworker of God in "God's field, God's building" (1 Cor. 3:9). Through this Mystery, the faithful receive the gifts of grace attained through the Lord Jesus Christ and handed over to His Church, without which there is no salvation. For, since no one who is not baptized can enter the Kingdom of Heaven (John 3:5), nor can anyone who does not commune have life eternal (John 6:54), nor can anyone be absolved of sin without the Mystery of confession (Matt. 18:18)—and all this, according to the words of St. John Chrysostom, happens at the hands of a priest–then truly, as this Holy Father states, "that which the priest does down below, God upholds up above, and the Master confirms the decision of His servants."

Still, one can never envision or feel it in all its overwhelming and frightening seriousness until one draws near to the holiness of the Mystery and is standing face to face with it. Then, in an incomparably different manner, one understands the words of the Lord about the Good Shepherd who lays down his life for the sheep (John 10:11); about the love toward Him as the principal condition for shepherding the flock: "Do you love Me?" came first—and then "Feed My sheep" (John 21:13)! Only then one feels what our Lord Jesus Christ expects from us when He says, "Let your light so shine before men, that they may see your good works, and glorify your Father who is in heaven" (Matt. 5:16) because "you are the light of the world, you are the salt of the earth" (Matt. 5:13-14). It becomes clear in itself, then, to what extent we are personally responsible for every evil in the world. Namely, if the name of God is not glorified but blasphemed on earth, is it not because our light is not shining before people, because we are not the light to the world? If every Christian can and should ask himself this question, how much more should a priest ask himself that? And even how much more a bishop? Then one feels in its entirety the weight of all the eyes from heaven and earth directed at the shepherd who alone, before all, has to lead and with his example to show the true but narrow path that leads to life (Matt. 7:14). An example—that is what is asked of him: "Be thou an example of the believers, in word. In life, in love, in faith, in purity" (cf. 1 Tim. 4:12). Only then does he fully realize what sort of knowledge is asked of him, what piety, what care for the souls entrusted to him, what responsibility for each of them. What hands they must be, the hands of one who "offers up sacrifices upon the heavenly altar, who performs the holy Mysteries [ἱερουργεῖν] together with Christ" (St. Gregory the Theologian); "What tongue it must be that speaks the words of God" (St. John Chrysostom).

Most importantly, all these requirements are not an unachievable ideal, unattainable for mortal humans. Behind them stand the endless number of Saints in all generations, in all nations, who have fulfilled it all to the last iota. Let us set aside the divine example of the Heavenly Shepherd, our Lord Jesus Christ, or the sublime examples of the Apostles, especially the Apostle Paul who in his pastoral zeal highly surpassed the requirements he had set before others. Not to mention the multitude of holy hierarchs who, imitating the Great Shepherd, shine as radiant stars from the firmament of the history of the Orthodox Church—such Saints as St. Ignatius the Godbearer, Nicholas of Myra in Lycia, Athanasius, Basil the Great, John Chrysostom, Gregory the Theologian, and so many others; who could count them all? However, out of the multitude of all these "chosen vessels," I will mention a single one, the one whose spiritual image was the most clear to me from the earliest youth and, if I may say, the most radiant. I believe it is to you as well. Even as a very small child, before entering elementary school, I heard about him, I saw his image, and in my soul I felt his workings. I believe that happened to you as well.

It is the feast of St. Sava, which at this time over thirty years ago was celebrated in church and in school. School children and elders would first attend the entire church service, and then they would come to school with chanting, with the cross and banners. Our old grandmas, with their trembling hands, would pull us little children out from the church a little earlier and take us to school. The winter was bitter: we, the youngest ones, and they, the oldest ones, needed to get warm. The school is decorated with evergreens and white embroidered towels. In the front, high up on the wall, is a great icon with an ivy wreath. On it is the Saint in gold-woven vestments; he holds an open book in one hand, and blesses with the other. A wide golden circle is around his head. "Who is that, grandma?" one of us children would ask. "That is St. Sava, my son," grandma would answer. "And why does he have such clothes?" we would continue tirelessly with our questions. "Because he was a bishop." "And why does he have that shiny circle around his head?" "Well, that is because he is a Saint. Only Saints have that." "Well, then! That is St. Sava. That is the bishop. The bishop, then, in golden clothes high above everyone blesses with one hand, holds the Gospel with the other, and around his head a golden saintly halo is shining," we would conclude with our child's mind. Our questions and our thoughts would be interrupted. The school would fill up. The priest blessed the water and wheat, students sang and recited, but I heard and saw little of it. All my attention was fixed on the icon of St. Sava, adorned with the green wreath, and on his wondrous image. At one moment the sun shone and fell on the Saint's icon. The golden halo flashed and, it seemed to me, lit up our entire village covered in snow, the school and all of us in it. And from that light emanating from the holy head of the holy bishop, on that gloomy and frosty winter day, all of us gathered there under his icon felt bright and warm and joyous.

Later I heard and found out much more about St. Sava and his manifold works. All of it spoke to me: only through him did the Serbian people truly find themselves—because through him they truly found Christ; through him they were brought to Christ, and through him they stand before Christ to this day. The people feel and know this: even now they spiritually live from the spiritual heritage of St. Sava; under his pastoral guidance they overcame all the misfortunes that befell them, and they will overcome those that befall them now and are yet to come. Only such a shepherd can they understand and desire. Therefore, in their Orthodox mind, they always prepare the same kind of welcome for each new pastor and hierarch. They humbly bring to him the icon of their Saint with the words of Holy Scripture engraved underneath "For such an high priest became us, who is holy, harmless, undefiled, separate from sinners" (Heb. 7:26). Such, whose service to God and Church means a blessing to the people; who firmly holds the Gospel and steadfastly keeps the Gospel; who with the holiness of his life shines and enlightens, thus professing Christ even when he stops professing him with his mouth. Yes, we need such a high priest!

Faced with such spiritual leadership and with such shepherds, and thus compelled to use this measure to measure one's own soul, who can feel anything but sorrow, fear, and despair, that the measure had been taken, that one had been weighed, and had been found light—light and poor in all that with which they richly adorned the bright priestly vestments that they wore. If many of these luminaries, when placed before the holy Mystery of priesthood, felt "inadequate to be elevated to such a degree" (St. Sava), feeling their soul "weak and insignificant" (St. John Chrysostom), and considering themselves "much lower than the holy act of serving the Lord" (St. Gregory the Theologian), wherein can I put my hope, what can I look to in order to console and strengthen myself? Certainly not to my own self and my own weaknesses (if I had had the thought to put my hope in myself, I would have never taken this service upon myself). However, only by faith in the Lord Jesus, the Good Shepherd, Who willingly took up the cross for each of us, therefore, for me as well. Will He, then, leave me without His help, He Whose strength is made perfect in weakness (2 Cor. 12:9); will He leave me without His guidance and blessing when, according to Holy Scripture, this is precisely what good shepherding of His people depends upon?

Furthermore, with faith in the help of St. Sava who always took care to enlighten his entire nation with Christ's truth; how, then, could he forget a part of his nation, us, his faithful flock in the region where he was born and where he grew up? And, likewise, with faith in the help of the Holy "Honorable Prince" Lazar of Kosovo, who, in that same region as well, fought and won that terrifying and glorious spiritual battle for the heavenly kingdom. Even to this day, the people who with their prince were then "joined unto the heavenly kingdom" have magnificently resisted the temptation: to gain the world and to lose the soul. I believe that the Holy Prince, with the rest of the Saints whose relics and graves lie in the region where I am to go, will know how to bring wisdom even unto us, and strengthen us so that, in the battle between the temporal and the eternal, we would not suffer defeat where they gained victory.

I put my hope also in the wise counsel of Your Holiness and the other older hierarchs and brothers in Christ, in the support of you brother priests, concelebrants of the Church of Christ. Likewise, I hope in the prayers of all the rest of you brothers and sisters. If the Holy Apostle Paul more than once had need of the prayers of the faithful, how am I not to beseech you to "strive together with me in your prayers to God for me" (Rom. 15:30)? Even if only today, even with only one prayer made up of only three words: "Lord, have mercy!" And may the merciful Lord Jesus, by the prayers of His Saints, bless you "with all spiritual blessings in heavenly places" (Eph. 1:3), so that "with one mind striving together for the faith of the gospel; and in nothing terrified by your adversaries" (Phil. 1:27-28), "ye might walk worthy of the Lord unto all pleasing" (Col. 1:10); "blameless and harmless, the sons of God, without rebuke" (Phil. 2:15); so that "on that day" (2 Tim. 1:18) the fearful day, when the Lord comes, we would remain steadfast and join the chorus of Saints from our nation in Christ's heavenly kingdom. Let that be my first blessing to you and all the faithful sons and daughters of the God-protected Diocese of Rashka and Prizren.

And may our last thought, at the end of each day, and at the end of each of our labors, be the remembrance of God. And may our last word, brothers and sisters, at the end of each day, and at the end of each of our labors, of all our conversations and our whole life, be: "Lord, glory and praise to Thee for all things!"

THE FIRST PATRIARCHAL SERMON

At the enthronement in the cathedral church in Belgrade, December 1990

"In the day of salvation have I succored thee" (2 Cor. 6:2).

These words of the Holy Apostle Paul are addressed to all Christians, even to us gathered here today, most reverend and right reverend brothers and hierarchs, venerable and reverend fathers, and dear brothers and sisters, faithful people of the Living God. Indeed, with the help of God we become what we are, and we acquire what we have. We, too, feel this evangelical truth, in a unique way, in what is for us a fateful moment, when upon our weak shoulders we receive the burden of apostolic service on the throne of St. Sava, the burden that—we feel it with our whole soul and, here, publicly we confess it to you all—far surpasses our more than modest powers and abilities. At the same time, however, we feel and confess, together with the same Holy Apostle, "I can do all things through Christ Who strengtheneth me" (Phil. 4:13).

The grace-giving help of God is the foremost need of the people of God, called and gathered into the holy, theanthropic unity of the Church as the Body of Christ; in this sense, it is also the most pressing need, today perhaps more than ever, of our faithful and cross-bearing Orthodox Serbian people as well. After all, this is the only real need of the entire world, whether the world is aware of it or not. Especially in this time of frightful, apocalyptic divisions among people, rising out of man's suicidal schism by which he split from the only Peacemaker, from the One who is our peace—the God-Man Christ, One of the Holy Trinity. However, every historical time, ours included, the way it is, is transformed in the Church into the hour of Christ, into "the agreeable time" and "the most suitable time," into "the day of salvation"—now and here (2 Cor. 6:2). Furthermore, that means that all of us Christians are called to be the coworkers of God in Christ's act of our salvation and the salvation of the world. "But in everything let us show ourselves as the servants of God; in long-suffering, in misfortunes..." but also, if not more, "in vigils, fasts, in purity, in wisdom ... with the weapon of righteousness" (2 Cor. 6:4-7). For only then will we be like unto those who possess nothing, yet have everything, the poor who enrich many with Christ (cf. 2 Cor. 6:10).

On this long path of cooperation with the Savior, Lord Christ, working on our own and the salvation of our neighbors, we see our modest place. In order to walk this path, and so that our patriarchal service on the throne of St. Sava would not be to the detriment and disgrace of the Church, we need, dear brothers and sisters, the prayerful help of all of you, all the faithful; therefore, we humbly beseech you for it.

Ascending the throne of St. Sava as the forty-fourth Serbian patriarch, we do not have any personal platform of patriarchal action. Our platform is the gospel of Christ, the good news about God among us, and the Kingdom of God within us—if we accept it with faith and love. We consider it our holy duty, however, to point out at this time just a few of the theanthropic dimensions of the gospel, which are of vital importance to us, and especially relevant.

In the Orthodox Church of Christ, all people are one body and one spirit in the Lord (cf. 1 Cor. 10:17 & 12:12-27; Eph. 1:23 & 4:4; Col. 1:18 & 3:14, and elsewhere), inseparably united by holy love, the source of which is the true faith, as is the case with any other virtue and genuine human act. Only in Christ, as the children of God and the brothers of Christ, we humans are brothers amongst each other as well. It is exactly to such brotherhood and unity, founded on theanthropic love, that we will, God willing, unceasingly call people, from our own, as well as from other nations, near and far, and we will emphasize that it is the only alternative to the false "fraternity and unity," based on godlessness, or more precisely, on idolizing man as god. Love and unity, however, are not possible without fundamental repentance and true spiritual rebirth, on a personal as well as on an all-encompassing level. For indeed we are all to blame for all things! Therefore, from now until our last breath, brothers and sisters, we summon and will summon each and every one, starting with ourselves, to repentant spiritual restoration, as the foundation and precondition of every other renewal and transfiguration; we will call people to forgiveness and peacemaking, to love and unity, to fraternal oneness of mind instead of selfish single-mindedness and greed, to love for God and love for mankind. To this holy endeavor, the only endeavor worthy of any man and any nation, we call every Serbian brother and sister in the fatherland and in the diaspora; all our brothers and sisters in faith in the Orthodox universe and the Christian world in general, as well as all people and nations of good will. We personally nurture love toward all without distinction, and we bless all the descendants of St. Sava, wherever they may be, all Christians and all people, without distinction.

As the Serbian Patriarch, we understand our primacy among the equals, and any primacy among people, as the primacy of service, sacrifice, and the cross. It is not our words, but Christ's, that state, "Whosoever will be chief among you, let him be your servant" (Matt. 20:27). Sacrifice is the foundation of unity, both in ecclesiastical and in national conciliar life, as well as in all other areas of human endeavor, and the cross is the only unending glory of man. We remind you of this twofold truth, beloved children of God, because we are at the threshold of a sacrificial and penitent year, the year in which our holy Church will prayerfully commemorate the fifty-year anniversary of the tremendous suffering of the Serbian people (1941-91), but also the gift of mercy and glory that our people have received in Christ through this suffering. Let us not forget: on the humble and mutual sacrificial spirit of all God builds the true greatness and dignity of all. This is the teaching of Christ, the teaching of our martyrs and new-martyrs! Therefore, let us listen to the Holy Apostle Paul, and let us each honor one another above ourselves!

We will endeavor to justify, before God, this holy assembly, and all people, the trust and hopes that are placed in our humility. In the end, which is not an end, but rather only a beginning, we wish to send a message to all our beloved faithful in the diocese of Rashka and Prizren, on the sacrificial field in Kosovo, which is the field of the true Serbian glory and eternal predisposition, in Metohija and ancient Serbian Ras, to the witnesses of the cross of Christ and penitents, in many ways, to all Serbs: that our new responsibilities do not in any way signify a parting, but rather an even tighter unity with them, and an even more zealous service to their salvation, our own and the salvation of all the people, to the glory of the One True God and Lord, glorified in the Holy Trinity.

SERMON IN THE PATRIARCHATE OF PECH

At the induction onto the Throne
of the patriarchs of Pech, May 2, 1994

Your most revered and right reverend Graces, brothers in Christ, priests, monastics, dear brothers and sisters.

We have served today the Divine Liturgy of the Body and Blood of our Lord Jesus, and so we came into full unity with Him, the Son of God, and with each other. Let us always remember and remind ourselves that we today represent the Serbian people and the Serbian Orthodox faith. As His Eminence, the most reverend Metropolitan Amphilochius said, let us always be reminded that our holy ancestors believed in this faith, and lived by it, and represented it, led by St. Sava and all holy hierarchs, martyrs, and new martyrs to this day. And this faith—it is the faith in our Lord Jesus Christ, the evangelical faith throughout the ages. The Lord Jesus cautions us that the meaning of our life is holiness; holy life according to the holy Orthodox faith. This is the will of God—your holiness. Let us always keep that before our eyes, above all and before all we, the priests—who were given much, therefore much will be asked of us—followed by the monastics, and then by all the faithful as well; for we are all one in the Lord Jesus Christ.

Particularly in these difficult times let us be witnesses, by faith and by life according to that faith, to all those who have eyes to see and ears to hear, as the words of the Lord proclaim, "Let your light so shine before men, that they may see your good works, and glorify your Father who is in heaven" (Matt. 5:16). At the same time, this will be the best way to help our people in the misfortunes of this civil war. It will be a way to help our enemies as well, so that they too can grasp the truth of God and the Holy Gospel, and that they will stop persecuting and torturing innocent people, and destroying holy temples, ours and those belonging to others.

However, on the path of God, troubles and suffering are inevitable. Our Lord Jesus Christ cautions us about this as well, "Whoever wants to be my disciple must deny themselves and take up their cross and follow me... If they have persecuted me, they will also persecute you" (Matt. 16:24; John 15:20). However, He also says, "Do not be afraid that you are to suffer. I am the first and the last; I was dead and here I am alive unto ages" (Rev. 1:17-18). Moreover, He says that He will be with us always even unto the end of the world. Our people knew from the beginning that on the path of God, on the evangelical path, it pays to lose one's head; our people, upon receiving the faith, confessed it as the teaching confirmed by the faith of their holy ancestors.

Didn't the Lord Jesus say, "Do not be afraid of those who can kill the body, but subsequently cannot do anything more; but be afraid of the one who has the power to throw you into the fires of hell" (Matt. 10:28)? Was this not the same teaching of mother Yevrosima from Serbian epic poems, by which she counseled her son, "Son, do not speak falsely, according to the father or the uncles, but according to the justice of the true God." "It is better for you to lose your head than to defile your soul with sin." Were not those evangelical words of our Lord also the words of the Holy Prince in Kosovo, that "the earthly kingdom is temporary, while the heavenly kingdom is forever?" The Holy Prince warns us also of this lesson, brothers and sisters, who are in this holy family, in this holy temple. He cautions us that, as we represent the Serbian people and Orthodox faith, we should be and remain human, as our ancestors were. For they knew the word of the Holy Scripture about the nations who should know that they are human. However, we too should know this teaching, and know how to live by it; only, always as humans, never as non-humans, not at any price.

Brothers and sisters, we pray today to our Lord, and to His and our St. Sava, and to all the Saints and the newest holy martyrs who gave their lives for the Orthodox faith and their holy name—we pray that they would help us, their descendants, today to not disgrace our holy name, and not to lose our souls. For, before us, too, stands our true fatherland and the Kingdom of Heaven where all our holy ancestors await us. I repeat to myself and to all of us, when we stand before them, let them not be ashamed of us, nor we be ashamed before them. May we not be ashamed before their Lord and ours, but may He recognize us as His own, so that we also may hear those blessed words, "Come, ye blessed of my Father, inherit the kingdom prepared for you from the foundation of the world" (Matt. 25:34). That is the meaning of our faith and of Christian life.

May the Lord, by our prayers, help all of us to live our lives honorably and uprightly, witnessing to Him, the Son of God, in these times which lie in evil.

God bless you and grant you every good thing.

SERMON AT LITURGY

In the cathedral church on the occasion
of the overcoming of the Schism, February 15, 1992

"This is the day that the Lord has made; let us rejoice and be glad in it" (Ps. 117:24). "How good and how pleasant it is for brethren to dwell together in unity" (Ps. 133:1), when brothers feel that they are brothers and act like brothers. When they know and firmly believe that there is "One Lord, one faith, one baptism, One God and Father of all, who is above all, and through all, and in you all" (Eph. 4:5-6). When they gather together in the name of Christ, pray together there where He is, and together they approach the same chalice of the Body and Blood of the Lord. And thus they attain unity with the entire universal Orthodox Church, both militant on earth, and triumphant in the heavens, with the Saints of God and those from our own nation, St. Sava and the Holy Prince of Kosovo, holy martyrs, and new martyrs.

All those innumerable goods, which we awaited and desired all these, almost thirty, unfortunate years, we have lived to see here on this day and in this hour. May the Lord hear our joint prayers, that the united and never again divided Church of ours, in word and example, may be the teacher of peace, unity, brotherly love, and harmony, to act in such a way upon the reason, feelings, and conscience of our people that they may be united in all that is good and honorable, in all that is Christian and evangelical; that they may remain the people of God.

In such fateful circumstances as these in which our people find themselves we, and they, need more than anything else to grasp all the misfortune that arose from wandering in the wilderness through which they were led, from the horrifying coldness of spiritual frost and darkness in which they found themselves. The Church of Christ—who else—should provide them with the light, to point them to the path that they should take, which our ancestors walked for over a thousand years, and thus arrived at the Kingdom of Heaven.

In the spiritual darkness into which the world was plunged, and we were in this world, there is only one sure way to come out of that darkness—it is the way that the Lord points to, "Let your light so shine before men, that they may see your good works, and glorify your Father who is in heaven" (Matt. 5:16). In this all-encompassing darkness, the light of one little candle means a lot, let alone the flame of the candles of faith, and the holy life according to the faith, of the multitude of faithful people, first of all the monastics and the priests of God. As wise maidens with lighted lamps we are called to lighten, brothers in Christ, for ourselves and for our neighbors, the path that leads to the wedding feast of the Son of God.

On today's feast day of the Meeting of our Lord, Jesus Christ was brought to the Jerusalem temple, on the fortieth day after His birth, so that He and His mother, the Holy Theotokos, might fulfill that which is according to the law that He gave through Moses the prophet. There in the temple, His divinity was seen and announced by two holy souls, the Elder Simeon and the Prophetess Anna. Today, brothers and sisters, on this great feast day we have also fulfilled that which we should have according to the law of God. Therefore, when in peace and joy we leave this temple may we continue, in peace and brotherly love, our walk throughout our whole life.

And today, and tomorrow, and in the future, whatever has happened—it happened and it has passed. Let it remain behind us. Let us leave it up to God and His wisdom to weigh that which has happened, and to repay everyone justly. As for us, may we always have harmony and evangelical love before our spiritual eyes, and may we in mutual forgiveness keep these as the apple of our eye. To the one, though, who maliciously asks us who will remain the winner in all this, and who the loser, we should know how to give a peaceful and clear answer, to him as well as to ourselves: Here brothers have met, who were and who remained brothers, not one the winner and one the loser. There is but one victor—the God of peace, harmony, and love. And with God and in God, the victor is St. Sava, the one who reconciled and reunited his brothers, and who in the service of peace went to the enemies and brought peace to them and to his people.

One is the loser also—the demon of discord, disharmony, and unrest, who always sets a brother against a brother, Cain against Abel. May none of us ever set out to follow Cain's path, and may we never walk upon it at any price.

The Church of Christ, the Church of the God-Man, the Lover of mankind and the Peacemaker, the Reconciler of heaven with earth, of all people and all nations, the Church of St. Sava, the Christ-loving and brother-loving one, today goes out to meet her Lord and her brothers, showing an example of meeting and peacemaking to all children of St. Sava, all brothers here, and in Krajina, and in the diaspora, as well as to all people of goodwill.

That is the message of today's feast and of this joyous act that we have performed with God's blessing.

May we be with the Son of God, the Peacemaker, the Conqueror of death, sin, and demons, and may He be with us, today, always, and unto ages of ages. Amen.

SERMONS ON THE LORD'S FEASTS AND THE FEASTS OF THE THEOTOKOS

ON CHRISTMAS EVE

Sermon at the Divine Liturgy on January 6/December 24, 1996, in the church of the Protection of the Mother of God in Belgrade

May this festive day be a blessing to you on the eve of the birth of the Son of God, and may tomorrow's day be blessed, the Nativity, the day of the birth of the Son of God!

Dear brothers and sisters, let us have before our spiritual eyes this endless love of God, the Son of God, Who for us sinners descended into this world, was born as a man, endured all persecutions, sufferings, and finally the cross and death for us and for our salvation, out of love for us. Let us respond with our love toward Him, too, although we are not rich kings who brought Him gold, incense, and myrrh—let us bring unto Him pure hearts and pure souls, so that, when we come before Him, He will recognize and identify us as His own; and—I always repeat this to myself, to you, and to all who have ears to hear—so that our ancestors may rejoice when we stand before them, and recognize us as their closest kin. Merry Christmas to you, and all the following days! God bless you!

ON THE FEAST OF THE SYNAXIS OF THE MOTHER OF GOD

Sermon at the Divine Liturgy
on January 8/December 26, 1996,
in the church of the Holy Prophet
Elijah in Mirievo, Belgrade

"And when they were departed, behold, the angel of the Lord appeared to Joseph in a dream, saying, 'Arise, and take the young child and his mother, and flee into Egypt, and be thou there until I bring thee word: for Herod will seek the young child to destroy him.' When he arose, he took the young child and his mother by night, and departed into Egypt: and was there until the death of Herod: that it might be fulfilled which was spoken of the Lord by the prophet, saying, 'Out of Egypt have I called my son.' Then Herod, when he saw that he was mocked of the wise men, was exceeding wroth, and sent forth, and slew all the children that were in Bethlehem, and in all the coasts thereof, from two years old and under, according to the time which he had diligently inquired of the wise men. Then was fulfilled that which was spoken by Jeremiah the prophet, saying, 'In Rama was there a voice heard, lamentation, and weeping, and great mourning, Rachel weeping for her children, and would not be comforted, because they are not.' But when Herod was dead, behold, an angel of the Lord appeared in a dream to Joseph in Egypt, saying, 'Arise, and take the young child and his mother, and go into the land of Israel: for they are dead which sought the young child's life.' And he arose, and took the young child and his mother, and came into the land of Israel. But when he heard that Archelaus did reign in Judaea in the room of his father Herod, he was afraid to go thither: notwithstanding, being warned of God in a dream, he turned aside into the parts of Galilee: And he came and dwelt in a city called Nazareth: that it might be fulfilled which was spoken by the prophets, 'He shall be called a Nazarene.'"

Matt. 2:13-23

In these days, brothers and sisters, we celebrate the birth of the Son of God, His coming into the world, His birth in the flesh, so that He Who is from eternity the Son of the Heavenly Father, could be the Son on earth of the Holy Virgin; so that He, the Son according to divine nature, could be Son according to human nature as well, while simultaneously the hypostatic properties of the Holy Trinity are not commixed. And He Who played the main role in the creation of the world and man, He was the One Who saved people. All of us, brothers and sisters, are objectively saved by His sacrifice, by His act of salvation in general. To be actually and personally saved depends on us, whether we adopt, with our faith and our life according to the faith, His salvation that He gave to us as a gift.

In the Orthodox Church it is a custom, on the great feasts of the Lord and of the Mother of God, to celebrate on the first day the person who is the most important for that feast. For the birth of the Son of God, certainly, He is the most important person. And the next day, that is, here today, we celebrate the person second in importance for this event, and that is the Holy Theotokos, who gave birth to Him. So it is with the other feasts of Christ and the Theotokos.

We should keep in mind, brothers and sisters, that the Holy Theotokos was chosen since the creation of the world to be the mother of the Son of God for her holiness of life, for her purity, and especially for her humility.

And in the song that she had sung unto God, when the Archangel Gabriel announced that she would be the mother of the Son of God, she among other things says, "...For he hath looked upon the humble state of his handmaiden: for, behold, from henceforth all generations shall call me blessed" (Luke 1:48).

Humility, therefore, brothers and sisters, is the mother of all evangelical virtues, because God opposes the proud, and gives grace to the humble. The one whom God opposes, because in fact that sinner opposes God, cannot have any grace, any prosperity in anything. He will obtain eternal ruin, if he does not repent. Humility, then, is the base and the foundation of all evangelical virtues. This does not mean to be passive; it is not spiritual lethargy. On the contrary, humility requires a great strength to conquer pride within us, the sin that turned an angel into a devil. Such was the humility that the Holy Theotokos possessed, and those traits that made her worthy to be the mother of the Son of God were precisely those spiritual traits, spiritual qualities that she with the help of God's grace attained, but attained them herself. For this reason St. John Chrysostom cautions Christian parents about the importance of making an effort to develop those qualities in their sons and daughters. "You," he says, "take efforts to prepare rich gifts for your daughter, to clothe her in silk and velvet, to adorn her with golden jewelry; but look upon her who was chosen to be the mother of the Son of God!" "The king's daughter is all glorious within," the Prophet David says (Ps. 45:13). This is where the efforts should go: into ensuring that the daughter and son attain and preserve inner beauty. This should be the fundamental and chief duty of parents, especially mothers! This does not mean, of course, that parents should not concern themselves with their children's material needs as well, to create opportunities for them to be able to initiate and lead an independent life. But above all is the effort to conduce, by their lives and their Orthodox faith, the attainment of those inner virtues in their children, starting with humility and all the way to love, which is the bond of perfection, the most perfect of all virtues.

May our Lord Jesus Christ and His Most Holy Mother help us attain those virtues and so save our souls, keeping holy and pure the honor of our family and our people, and thus help our enemies as well, so that they might repent also, that they might see which path one should take—the path of God, so they might be saved, too. This is also our duty according to the word of the Lord, "that they may see your good works," He says, "and glorify your Father who is in heaven" (Matt. 5:16). May today's feast be blessed and a blessing unto you. Christ is Born!

ON HOLY THEOPHANY

Sermon at the Divine Liturgy on January 19/6, 1997,
in the church of the Birth of the Most Holy Mother of God
in Zemun

"Then cometh Jesus from Galilee to Jordan unto John, to be baptized of him. But John forbad him, saying, 'I have need to be baptized of thee, and comest thou to me?' And Jesus answering said unto him, 'Suffer it to be so now: for thus it becometh us to fulfill all righteousness.' Then he suffered him. And Jesus, when he was baptized, went up straightway out of the water: and, lo, the heavens were opened unto him, and he saw the Spirit of God descending like a dove, and lighting upon him: And lo a voice from heaven, saying, 'This is my beloved Son, in whom I am well pleased.'"

Matt. 3:13-17

In the name of the Father, and the Son, and the Holy Spirit! We have prayed to God, brothers and sisters, on today's great feast of Theophany, the feast that initially in Church signified the manifestation of the divinity of the Son of God in this world. It signified at the same time His birth, and His baptism in the Jordan, and the beginning of His ministry and His miracles, for us and for our salvation.

On this day also, a multitude of those who had been preparing for it were baptized, originally Jews or Gentiles; they had prepared for this act of being grafted onto Christ the Vine, for entering the holy Church, which is the pillar of truth, and in which we are saved; in which we become members of the Body of the Son of God, to also suffer together with Him, and to be resurrected with Him; that is, by His resurrection, and His suffering, to be saved.

Likewise, from ancient times, there was a blessing of the waters on this day, which—you know yourself, not to repeat myself—this blessed water does not spoil for a year or even longer. Thus, in this way, we are all sanctified by the power of God, which is given here unto us as well as a sign of blessing and the grace of God, which acts even today, and always.

May today's feast be blessed—God has revealed Himself! God bless you!

ON HOLY THEOPHANY
SECOND SERMON

Sermon at the Divine Liturgy on January 19/6, 1996,
in the church of the Holy Apostles Peter and Paul
in Topchider, Belgrade

We have prayed, brothers and sisters, on today's great feast of Theophany, the baptism of the Lord Jesus Christ in the river Jordan when He, in His thirtieth year, came to the Holy Prophet "to fulfill all righteousness," (Matt. 3:15) as He Himself says, and saving all people from Adam unto the end of the world, to be baptized and to begin His public ministry, His public work and the Economy of salvation. For He was hitherto an unknown carpenter, and then He begins, as I said, His public work and His ministry.

By His action, God's action, brothers and sisters, the water is sanctified even today, and you know—I do not have to point it out to you—that it remains unspoiled for a year or more. Through this as well, the Lord shows unto us His might and His power so that we also, striving in our faith and our life according to that faith, may be worthy of the name we carry: the Orthodox name, Serbian and Orthodox. In this way, may we be His witnesses in this world that lies in wickedness.

May the Lord help all of us to live like our ancestors, according to this teaching, and to quietly preach this teaching to all those who have ears to hear and eyes to see, so that when we come before the Lord, and His and our Saints from our nation, we may walk with our head held high and not be ashamed before them; furthermore, that we may hear the word of the Lord that we are His faithful servants, and that we will receive the kingdom He has prepared for us since the beginning of the world.

May the Lord bless you all, now and ever and unto ages! Amen.

ON THE MEETING OF OUR LORD

Sermon after the Divine Liturgy and Parastos
on February 15/2, 1996, in the Ruzhitsa church
in Kalemegdan, Belgrade

"And when the days of her purification according to the law of Moses were accomplished, they brought him to Jerusalem, to present him to the Lord; (as it is written in the law of the Lord, 'Every male that openeth the womb shall be called holy to the Lord';) and to offer a sacrifice according to that which is said in the law of the Lord, 'A pair of turtledoves, or two young pigeons.' And, behold, there was a man in Jerusalem, whose name was Simeon; and the same man was just and devout, waiting for the consolation of Israel: and the Holy Spirit was upon him. And it was revealed unto him by the Holy Spirit, that he should not see death, before he had seen the Lord's Christ. And he came by the Spirit into the temple: and when the parents brought in the child Jesus, to do for him after the custom of the law, then took he him up in his arms, and blessed God, and said, 'Lord, now lettest thou thy servant depart in peace, according to thy word: for mine eyes have seen thy salvation, which thou hast prepared before the face of all people; a light to lighten the Gentiles, and the glory of thy people Israel.' And Joseph and his mother marveled at those things which were spoken of him. And Simeon blessed them, and said unto Mary his mother, 'Behold, this child is set for the fall and rising again of many in Israel; and for a sign which shall be spoken against; (Yea, a sword shall pierce through thy own soul also,) that the thoughts of many hearts may be revealed.' And there was one Anna, a prophetess, the daughter of Phanuel, of the tribe of Aser: she was of a great age, and had lived with an husband seven years from her virginity; and she was a widow of about fourscore and four years, which departed not from the temple, but served God with fastings and prayers night and day. And she coming in that instant gave thanks likewise unto the Lord, and spake of him to all them that looked for redemption in Jerusalem. And when they had performed all things according to the law of the Lord, they returned into Galilee, to their own city Nazareth. And the child grew, and waxed strong in spirit, filled with wisdom: and the grace of God was upon him."

Luke 2:22-40

We have prayed to the Lord on this great feast day by serving the bloodless Mystery of Holy Communion. We have prayed to the Lord and the Holy Theotokos for all of us, brothers and sisters; to Him Who, according to His law, on the fortieth day after His birth, was brought to the Jerusalem temple by His mother—we prayed that He would help us in these times, in troubles and misfortunes, to survive as the people of God, as it should be, and as is the only meaningful way to be. Even our coming into this world, amidst these troubles and misfortunes that befall us, has meaning, as well as our departure from this world. The body departs for the earth, from which it was taken, and the soul goes to the immortal God, Who created it immortal.

We have prayed to God for our ancestors, too, and for the latest victims of these wars and battles for faith and freedom. Our ancestors, taught by the evangelical teaching of the Lord Jesus, knew throughout the centuries to defend their freedom, their faith, and their homes, never taking what belonged to others, and never imposing their faith on others. Let this be the teaching we should always keep, and hand it over to those who come after us to represent the Serbian people and the Orthodox faith. It was never easy to be a man of God in this world that lies in evil, let alone in such troubles and misfortunes, with such enemies—those who here, and in the whole world, have risen up against our people, and have accused us of being responsible for all the misfortunes in this civil war. For all the atrocities, they accuse us alone. If it were not for the all-seeing Eye of God, and His all-knowing Mind, and His justice, and His just way, it would really be unbearable. But, no one will be justified by falsehood, or injustice, or crime. Then, with our Lord, Who was crucified and died on the cross, yet resurrected, may we endure whatever troubles we have to deal with, and those that may come our way! His suffering for us and for our salvation purifies all suffering on the path toward Him, the suffering for His truth and His justice.

May the Lord grant rest to the souls of all those who died for their faith and their fatherland, defending their homes and loved ones! May the Living God help those who remained invalids in the best years of their life. May He also strengthen us to truly be His people both now and forever! God bless you and grant you every good thing!

ON THE ANNUNCIATION OF THE MOST HOLY THEOTOKOS

Sermon at the Divine Liturgy on April 7/March 25, 1997, in the Monastery of the Entry of the Most Holy Theotokos into the Temple, in Belgrade

"And after those days his wife Elisabeth conceived, and hid herself five months, saying, 'Thus hath the Lord dealt with me in the days wherein he looked on me, to take away my reproach among men.' And in the sixth month the angel Gabriel was sent from God unto a city of Galilee, named Nazareth, to a virgin espoused to a man whose name was Joseph, of the house of David; and the virgin's name was Mary. And the angel came in unto her, and said, 'Hail, thou that art highly favored, the Lord is with thee: blessed art thou among women.' And when she saw him, she was troubled at his saying, and cast in her mind what manner of salutation this should be. And the angel said unto her, 'Fear not, Mary: for thou hast found favor with God. And, behold, thou shalt conceive in thy womb, and bring forth a son, and shalt call his name Jesus. He shall be great, and shall be called the Son of the Highest: and the Lord God shall give unto him the throne of his father David: And he shall reign over the house of Jacob for ever; and of his kingdom there shall be no end.' Then said Mary unto the angel, 'How shall this be, seeing I know not a man?' And the angel answered and said unto her, 'The Holy Spirit shall come upon thee, and the power of the Highest shall overshadow thee: therefore also that holy thing which shall be born of thee shall be called the Son of God. And, behold, thy cousin Elisabeth, she hath also conceived a son in her old age: and this is the sixth month with her, who was called barren. For with God nothing shall be impossible.' And Mary said, 'Behold the handmaid of the Lord; be it unto me according to thy word.' And the angel departed from her."

Luke 1:24-38

In the name of the Father, and the Son, and the Holy Spirit. Today, brothers and sisters, we have prayed to God on this great feast of the beginning of our salvation, as it says in the church hymn. You know as well that today's feast is the day when the Holy Archangel Gabriel, on the order from God, appeared to the Most Holy Theotokos and announced to her that she would give birth to the Son of God. She immediately accepted the will of God, and only asked, "How shall this be, seeing I know not a man?" Whereas, when the same Holy Archangel appeared to the high priest Zacharias, announcing that his wife Elizabeth will give birth to a son whom he should name John, Zacharias expressed disbelief, because he knew that his wife was barren and already old, and that he himself was already old as well. And then he asked "what would be the sign of this" (Luke 1:18) and for that he was punished with muteness—he became mute until the day when all that would happen. On the other hand, the Holy Theotokos, when the Archangel said that the "Holy Spirit shall come upon thee, and the power of the Highest shall overshadow thee," humbly said—"Behold the handmaid of the Lord; be it done unto me according to thy word."

The Lord never commits violence over man to whom He grants freedom, neither over the angels, of course. He upholds and respects the freedom that He has given. If a man does not want to walk on the path of God, to be saved, God will not save him by force, because that would be violence, and God cannot commit violence, just as He cannot commit sin either, because sin and violence are not power, but lack of it. Indeed, God is Almighty, but almighty in good, of course.

I would like to mention this as well. We often have difficulty with the reasoning of this world, which seeks for a man and woman not to be one in Christ the Lord, but to be the same. For, in fact, the feminist movement in the world today, the feminist lobby as they say, wants that precisely. Or, as Otto Weininger says it better, "the feminist movement today seeks, in fact, the emancipation of a prostitute in a woman, not the emancipation of the person and mother, the person within." One should keep in mind that the Holy Theotokos, and all womanhood along with her, was elevated to the highest degree. To her we sing every day, and we read that she is "more honorable than the Cherubim, and beyond compare more glorious than the Seraphim," because she alone was chosen above all mankind to be the mother of the Son of God. This is what elevates every woman to the greatest heights if, of course, she continues to strive, just as the Holy Theotokos had done, and was chosen on account of those qualities to be the Mother of God.

"The king's daughter is all glorious within," (Ps. 45:13) it says in the psalm. It is with this beauty, this inner beauty, that the woman radiates and shines. If women in the world had that in mind, this world would be completely different. However, such are these present times, and it will become even harder, because the Lord Jesus said that, the closer we get to the end of the world, the harder and harder it will be for the true faith in this world. But He told us this in advance, so that we could prepare ourselves. In such a way, both males and females, are to be witnesses of the Son of God in this world.

Today we have a joyous opportunity to receive a new servant in the Lord, a new deacon.

The Greek word *diakonos* means exactly that: an attendant, servant. Let us keep in mind the words of the Lord, "Whosoever will be chief among you, let him be your servant, for even the Son of Man," that is, He Himself, "did not come to be served, but to serve, and to give His life as a ransom for many" (Matt. 20:27-28). Let us never forget that the Son of God was a carpenter up until His thirtieth year on earth; He had blisters on His hands, and He was not ashamed to extend His hand to receive compensation for all those yokes and plows that He had made, as it says in the time of St. Justin the Martyr. One such intellectual, one such person as the Holy Apostle Paul, was not ashamed to work by night, while he preached by day. Out of goat hair he made sacks, rugs, and tents, as was customary at that time in the East. St. Basil the Great, St. Gregory the Theologian, and other Saints also worked. Therefore, we should not be ashamed or embarrassed of any labor. We should only be ashamed and afraid of that which is sinful. Then we will truly, by our faith and our life according to that faith, realize the meaning and aim of our life in this world, that is, we will attain blessedness in our real fatherland in the heavens, the Kingdom of Heaven.

We pray today to the Holy Theotokos to strengthen us in all that is holy and honorable, especially all the maidens and women in this world. And that our nation, and all the nations in the world, be preserved from the misfortunes that have befallen us, and that at present come upon us. Most Holy Mother of God, pray to your Son and our God, to help us to stay human, the people of God, His people, His children, in this world and the next. God bless you, and happy feast day!

ON THE SECOND DAY OF PASCHA

Sermon at the Divine Liturgy
on April 15/2, 1996, in the Monastery of the Holy Archangel Michael,
in Rakovitsa near Belgrade

> "No man hath seen God at any time, the only begotten Son, who is in the bosom of the Father, he hath declared him. And this is the record of John, when the Jews sent priests and Levites from Jerusalem to ask him, 'Who art thou?' And he confessed, and denied not; but confessed, 'I am not the Christ.' And they asked him, 'What then? Art thou Elias?' And he saith, 'I am not. Art thou that prophet?' And he answered, 'No.' Then said they unto him, 'Who art thou? That we may give an answer to them that sent us. What sayest thou of thyself?' He said, 'I am the voice of one crying in the wilderness, "Make straight the way of the Lord," as said the Prophet Esaias.' And they which were sent were of the Pharisees. And they asked him, and said unto him, 'Why baptizest thou then, if thou be not that Christ, nor Elias, neither that prophet?' John answered them, saying, 'I baptize with water: but there standeth one among you, whom ye know not; He it is, who coming after me is preferred before me, whose shoe's latchet I am not worthy to unloose.' These things were done in Bethsaida beyond Jordan, where John was baptizing."
>
> John 1:18-24

I congratulate you on today's feast, the second day of the resurrection of the Son of God, which is celebrated for seven days, that is, for a whole week, and every Sunday throughout the year, because the resurrection of the Son of God is the most important event in the Economy of our salvation that He established. With His whole life on earth as God-Man, He established the Economy of our salvation.

Already, with His coming into this world as the Almighty God, He had no other place to be born in, not in any house, nor in any home, but in a cave. His suffering began when Herod persecuted Him, and He had to flee to Egypt with His mother and His stepfather Joseph. Likewise, as a carpenter, for thirty years until His baptism in the Jordan, He lived just like us, with hands covered in blisters. And so on, from the time He was baptized in the Jordan to His going into the desert where He was tempted by the devil, and furthermore, during His ministry, when the faithful did not accept Him as the Son of God, even though they had seen both His works and His miracles. In the end, they seized Him and crucified Him on the cross, and He died on it. He does everything for our salvation, and out of love for us, so that we too may be saved, and earn on this earth a blessed life in our true fatherland, that is, the Kingdom of Heaven. Furthermore, out of His infinite love, He endured all for our sake, but also due to His endless divine power, He was resurrected. He alone is the One Who raised Himself from the dead, and thus secured eternal life for us as well—if we make ourselves worthy of it with our faith in Him, and our life according to that faith; not only in words, then, but also in deeds, to strive each day as God expects and asks from us.

The Holy Apostle Paul says that the resurrection is the chief event in the history of our salvation. "And if Christ be not risen, then is our preaching in vain, and your faith is also in vain" (1 Cor. 14:15). But Christ did rise, and here the Apostle Paul and the other Apostles were ready to lay their lives down for this faith that they preached to all people, and that is preached to us today as well. By this faith may we live and be made worthy of the Kingdom of God. Of course, it is not easy for us humans to believe this. The way we are in our families: how much hatred, how much animosity, how much misery is found in the family where loved ones are bound by blood to each other; not to mention in international affairs, and the misfortunes of war that have befallen us, too! God so loved the world, us humans the way we are, that He gave His Only-Begotten Son that anyone who believes in Him would not perish, but have life eternal. And the Son of God came willingly to suffer for us, the way we are. Therefore, always keep in mind His death on the cross for us and for our salvation, and His glorious resurrection. We will come before Him, and He will determine whether we have deserved eternal blessedness in the kingdom of heaven, what "eye hath not seen, nor ear heard, neither have entered into the heart of man, the things which God hath prepared for them that love him," (1 Cor. 2:9) or we deserved eternal torments, where "their worm dieth not, and the fire is not quenched" (Mark 9:44). Let us keep this before our eyes always, and we will preserve ourselves from all evil toward our loved ones, and our people, and the whole world. Thus, indeed, we will be found worthy of the Kingdom of God for which He created us.

Happy feast day to you and all the following days. Christ is Risen!

ON THE ASCENSION OF CHRIST

Sermon at the Divine Liturgy on May 24/11, 1996,
at the church of the Ascension in Belgrade

In the name of the Father, and the Son, and the Holy Spirit! We have said prayers, brothers and sisters, on this great feast of our Lord in this holy temple dedicated to this feast. We have glorified Him, the Son of God together with His Father and the Holy Spirit, praying to one God in Holy Trinity to be merciful to us, and to our entire nation, and to all people of goodwill in the world. We prayed on this day that signifies the feast—*slava*—of this temple, this parish, and the entire Orthodox Belgrade.

After His glorious resurrection, the Lord was with the Holy Apostles for forty days, speaking to them about the Kingdom of God. According to the interpretation of the Holy Fathers, He spoke to them about the organization of the holy Church, His Church on earth, and on the fortieth day He ascended in front of them in glory up to the Kingdom of Heaven. Before that, He said, "Wherever I am, there will my servant be also" (John 12:26)—and the Lord is in heaven and in the heavenly kingdom. That is, then, the purpose and the meaning of our life here on earth, to be made worthy and able to enter the Kingdom of God, too. Indeed, as servants of God, to be where He is, in the Kingdom of Heaven. We can attain this goal, brothers and sisters—just as our ancestors did, just as all the Saints in the Church of Christ from the beginning to today, and until the end of the world—only by holy faith, and by a holy life according to that faith. That has always been the message of the holy feast and of every Saint. If they, the Saints, could attain this goal, and we are of the same body, of the same strength that God has given us, why would we not be able to do the same? We can, only if we want, and if we strive for it. For whatever surpasses our strength—

according to the word of God—the Almighty God will accomplish in each instant, because His grace, His holy help is always present, always at our side, if we do not cast it away, if we deserve it.

Wishing a happy feast—*slava*—to the parish priests of this temple, the parishioners of these parishes, the entire Belgrade, and all Orthodox, I wish all of you, all of us, brothers and sisters, to arrive to the Kingdom of Heaven following the path of God—to be where our Savior is, according to His word. May the Lord help us to achieve this at all times! God bless us!

ON PENTECOST TUESDAY

Sermon at the Divine Liturgy
on June 13/May 31, 1995, in the Monastery of the Entry
of the Most Holy Theotokos into the Temple, in Belgrade

"And there followed him great multitudes of people from Galilee, and from Decapolis, and from Jerusalem, and from Judaea, and from beyond Jordan. And seeing the multitudes, he went up into a mountain: and when he was set, his disciples came unto him: And he opened his mouth, and taught them, saying, 'Blessed are the poor in spirit: for theirs is the kingdom of heaven. Blessed are they that mourn: for they shall be comforted. Blessed are the meek: for they shall inherit the earth. Blessed are they which do hunger and thirst after righteousness: for they shall be filled. Blessed are the merciful: for they shall obtain mercy. Blessed are the pure in heart: for they shall see God. Blessed are the peacemakers: for they shall be called the children of God. Blessed are they which are persecuted for righteousness' sake: for theirs is the kingdom of heaven. Blessed are ye, when men shall revile you, and persecute you, and shall say all manner of evil against you falsely, for my sake. Rejoice, and be exceeding glad: for great is your reward in heaven: for so persecuted they the prophets which were before you. Ye are the salt of the earth: but if the salt have lost his savor, wherewith shall it be salted? It is thenceforth good for nothing, but to be cast out, and to be trodden under foot of men.'"

Matt. 4:25; 5:1-13

Today we celebrate the Third Person of the Holy Trinity—the Holy Spirit, because we believe in One God, but Triune in Persons. Our enemies say that this faith is unreasonable and incongruous. They claim that we say that one is the same as three. Surely they do not want to know, or do not want to understand that these are the categories of our mind within which we reason, because we cannot do it any other way; that is the way we were created. These categories, such as time, space, numbers and the rest, they apply to us, created beings. There could be three of us, or ten, or more, but God as He is, He cannot be numerous—He cannot be many gods. One interpreter cautions us kindly—when we say One in essence, and Three in Persons, we are thinking of numbers, categories of the mind, but they do not apply to God. Then He could not be even One, if we are referring to the numbers as such. He alone exists and from Him everything else receives existence. One cannot conceive it any other way.

But God is not solitary. He is Triune in Persons. Father Unbegotten, begets the Son, and the Holy Spirit proceeds. What does that mean? What is essentially begetting and proceeding? What is the difference between them? We as created beings, and our minds, created by God, are not capable to comprehend it fully. St. Gregory the Theologian answers this question of what is procession, and what is generation, thus, "You tell me what is un-begetting, and I will tell you what begetting and proceeding means." But if we carry on like that further and further, we will reach a point where our mind will leave us, that is, our mind cannot grasp the infinitude of God's being. It was revealed to us that God is One, Triune in Persons, and this is what we believe. Further examinations than what I just said would be according to the categories of our mind that do not apply to God, because God does not exist in time; we live in time, and this applies to us, as well as all created beings. He lives in eternity, and time is something utterly different from eternity. Time is that which has a past; it has a future and a present. There is really no past—it has already been. Likewise the future—it will come. And what exists? The present exists. But what is present? By the time the clock strikes, it is future, and when it has already struck, it is past. What, then, is present?

For God, there is no past, nor future; for Him there is only present. This is the fact of the matter. And God does not need any space. We, created beings, need space, but God transcends the categories of space.

Before the war, a man who was not a believer asked his son when he came back from school, "What have you learned about today?" "I was," he said, "in religion class, and the priest was explaining our faith to us, the dogma of the Holy Trinity."

"He must have told you how Father and Son are One in essence, and that they are one entity, that is, identical in nature both the Father and the Son. My son, do you see how impossible that is, because I am the father, and you are the son—which one of us is older, and which one is younger?" And the son replied, "Father, surely you are older as a man, but as a father, you are not older than me as a son. The moment you became a father, I became a son. And if God is the Father from eternity, then the Son of God is from eternity as well."

Our faith is surely accessible to our mind to an extent, but the essence of God—God's Being—surpasses us, it is incomparably higher and wider than our mind. This does not mean that our mind is unnecessary, that we should not act according to our reasoning, because the Lord says, "examine the Scriptures" (John 5:39). However, our mind is but one organ of our spiritual being, and the other ones are the heart, the will, and freedom. We do not negate the necessity of the mind in any way, but according to the word of the Lord, we know that other faculties are needed as well. Therefore He says, "Now that you know these things, you will be blessed if you do them" (John 13:17). You are not blessed if you know, nor blessed if you do, but when you know and do. How will you do something, if you do not know it? However, we are perfectly capable of learning and knowing, yet we do exactly the opposite. And in another place, He says, "Be ye therefore wise as serpents, and harmless as doves" (Matt. 10:16)! Hence, we need wisdom and reason, to develop them continuously, under the condition that we simultaneously develop goodness, the heart, and meekness—then will the man of God be perfect.

May the Lord, One in the Holy Trinity, grant us to remain His people, in all that is holy and honorable and good, and thus to help our brothers as well, who today are fighting and dying. Likewise unto our enemies, that they be human, and to see what they are doing; to give up their hostility, because that is a misfortune both for us and for them. And may the Lord send peace to our country, to our people, our enemies, and the entire world. God bless you!

ON THE TRANSFIGURATION OF THE LORD

Sermon at the Divine Liturgy on August 19/6, 1996, in the church of the Holy Apostles Peter and Paul in Topchider, Belgrade

> "And after six days Jesus taketh Peter, James, and John his brother, and bringeth them up into a high mountain apart, and was transfigured before them: and his face did shine as the sun, and his raiment was white as the light. And, behold, there appeared unto them Moses and Elias talking with him. Then answered Peter, and said unto Jesus, 'Lord, it is good for us to be here: if thou wilt, let us make here three tabernacles; one for thee, and one for Moses, and one for Elias.' While he yet spake, behold, a bright cloud overshadowed them: and behold a voice out of the cloud, which said, 'This is my beloved Son, in whom I am well pleased; hear ye him.' And when the disciples heard it, they fell on their face, and were sore afraid. And Jesus came and touched them, and said, 'Arise, and be not afraid.' And when they had lifted up their eyes, they saw no man, save Jesus only. And as they came down from the mountain, Jesus charged them, saying, 'Tell the vision to no man, until the Son of man be risen again from the dead.'"
>
> Matt. 17:1-9

In the name of the Father, and the Son, and the Holy Spirit! Today, brothers and sisters, we celebrate the feast of the Transfiguration of the Lord on Mount Tabor. The Son of God, when He began His ministry, did not begin immediately with the fact that He is the Son of God and that He will suffer, die, and rise from the dead, but with His sermon, with His works, and His miracles, He proclaimed to the Apostles and all those who had eyes to see and ears to hear that it is Him, and that He is the Son of God.

However, when He told them that He needed to suffer too, that the Prophets themselves had foretold it, for the salvation of men, neither the people of that time, nor even the Apostles could understand it. They expected the Savior to come as the king of this world, the mightiest one, who would bring down the Roman Empire, and raise up the kingdom of the people of Israel; that He would subdue all people to that kingdom, and then spread His teaching to the whole world in that way. There are also writings by certain chroniclers of that time that convey how they understood the coming of the Savior. He will, hence, come as the mightiest one: wherever He casts His gaze, there everything bows to Him; wherever He goes, everyone gathers there; He is the one to follow, and He alone is the one Whom the whole world recognizes. However, I say, His message is that He will suffer, and die on the cross, but also that He will rise from the dead; but this was not clear to these people, not even to the Apostles.

Among other things, He also showed His divine glory to the three disciples whom He took up the mountain. "His clothes and face were brighter than the sun." And two Old Testament prophets appeared before Him: Moses and Elijah. Moses, as the writer of the five books of the Old Testament and the Laws given on Mount Sinai, and Elijah, who was an unsparing prophet, who fearlessly preached one God, fearing neither King Ahab nor his wife Jezebel. Thus the two greatest prophets of the Old Testament appeared at that time, showing that they are servants of the Son of God, and they "spoke to Him about His suffering in Jerusalem." Then light shone upon them, and out of that light, the voice of God the Father was heard, "This is my beloved Son, in whom I am well pleased; hear ye him." The Apostles fell down in fear, and when they opened their eyes, they saw Jesus alone, because the Holy Prophets had already ascended into heaven.

This faith, brothers and sisters, sustained the Holy Apostles as well, that they were prepared to give up their lives for the teaching and the truth of the Son of God and His Gospel. That faith sustained our ancestors as well and all the Saints. With such faith, they even laid down their lives, and never renounced their Orthodox faith and their holy name. In this time of ours, so many have laid down their lives in Croatia, Bosnia, and Herzegovina, not taking away what belonged to others, but defending their homes and their graves, and their freedom, not imposing their faith on anyone, but defending their own faith, just as our ancestors had done throughout the centuries.

On this day, there was a great assembly at the Krka Monastery, and here with us are some of those people who were exiled and who fled from there. Together with them, we prayed to God for those who remained there, for the wounded, for invalids, for all mothers, parents without children, and children without parents, and for the departed. We prayed to the Lord Almighty to lead them into the heavenly kingdom, to help us that we may be made worthy of this unending heavenly kingdom, so that together with them we can be numbered with our holy ancestors throughout eternity.

Lord Jesus Christ, Son of God, help us to also transfigure our souls from sinful to righteous, from earthly to heavenly, from being sons and daughters of earth, to being sons and daughters of God, and that we may find ourselves in Your kingdom together like this, together with all Your Saints. Happy feast day, and God bless you!

ON THE ENTRY OF THE MOST THEOTOKOS INTO THE TEMPLE

Sermon at the Divine Liturgy
on December 4/November 21, 1995,
at the feast of the Vavedenye Monastery in Belgrade

> "Now it came to pass, as they went, that he entered into a certain village: and a certain woman named Martha received him into her house. And she had a sister called Mary, which also sat at Jesus' feet, and heard his word. But Martha was cumbered about much serving, and came to him, and said, 'Lord, dost thou not care that my sister hath left me to serve alone? Bid her therefore that she help me.' And Jesus answered and said unto her, 'Martha, Martha, thou art careful and troubled about many things: But one thing is needful: and Mary hath chosen that good part, which shall not be taken away from her...' And it happened, as He spoke these things, that a certain woman from the crowd raised her voice and said to Him, 'Blessed is the womb that bore You, and the breasts which nursed You!' But he said, 'Yea rather, blessed are they that hear the word of God, and keep it.'"
>
> Luke 10:38-42; 11:27-28

In the name of the Father, and the Son, and the Holy Spirit! We have gathered, brothers and sisters, in this holy temple to celebrate the temple feast—*slava*—the Entry of our Most Holy Sovereign Lady, the Mother of God, into the Temple. Her parents brought her to the temple to be instructed in the divine teaching. This should act as our constant guidance as well, and something to pursue. In the temple of God we are taught the words of God; this should be the food for our soul, as the Lord says, for man does not live on bread alone, but on every word that comes out of the mouth of God. That is precisely what is preached in the temple of God: the words of God, God's teaching, the path one should take to arrive to the Kingdom of Heaven, into unending life, where all the Saints are. One can enter the Kingdom of Heaven only by taking the path of God, that is, by the holy Orthodox faith and a holy life according to that faith. The first of the fundamental Christian virtues, which enables us to attain all the other ones, is the holy virtue of humility. Even in the song that the Holy Theotokos uttered after the Annunciation, after the conception of the Son of God, when she met her cousin Elizabeth, She spoke the words, "My soul magnifies the Lord." Thereupon she said that the Lord had looked upon the humility of His servant, and "from now on, all generations will call me blessed" (Luke 1:46-48). The humility of the Holy Theotokos, in addition to her other virtues, especially made her elect to be and become the mother of the Son of God. St. John Chrysostom cautions the Christians of that time. "You," he says, "take efforts to prepare rich clothes for your daughter, to adorn her with gold and pearls; but look upon her who alone was chosen out of all generations to be the mother of the Son of God!" "The king's daughter is all glorious within," the Prophet David says (Ps. 45:13), and indeed, she was truly radiant in beauty in her outward humility and modesty.

Let us keep that in mind always. Pride is the sin that turned an angel into a devil. Humility, as you can see, is the virtue that made the daughter of man to be the mother of the Son of God. I constantly need to remind both myself and you, brothers and sisters, to acquire this primary Christian virtue by fighting the pride within us and around us. The virtue of humility is not lassitude. It is a virtue that is difficult to acquire, because pride has been thriving within us since our mother's womb, from our forbearers on. It means not to desire, as a prideful man does and desires, to appear before people as something great and important. Other people of this world waste energy on deceiving others by appearing good, honorable, all sorts of cultivation and cleverness. Unlike them, we should rather strive to use this energy to truly be like that, to truly be good, holy, honorable, not according to human measure, but according to the measure of God. And then we will fulfill the meaning and purpose of our existence, of our being on this earth. And then we will, I repeat, do the most to help our nation in these misfortunes that have befallen it, and even our enemies, and all the people of goodwill in the world. For everyone profits from a good man, and the one who profits the most is, of course, that man himself, because he realizes the purpose of his life and obtains for himself an eternal place in the other world.

We have also communed today, brothers and sisters, at the beginning of this fast before the Nativity of our Lord Jesus before His coming into this world. I wish both to you and to myself that Holy Communion may be unto us for the forgiveness of sins, and for growing in goodness, unto our help and life eternal.

I particularly beseech all of you, brothers and sisters, as we approach Holy Communion, to strive to prepare beforehand with all the virtues, and especially with humility. In the Old Testament, one noble husband speaks of his pious wife, and among other qualities and virtues he says, "In you there is no false virtue." I beseech you all, and you Christian women, to keep this in mind, to cultivate your beauty within: "The king's daughter is all glorious within" (Ps. 45:13). At least on that day, when you approach Holy Communion, abstain from beautification, and especially from using lipstick, because one is to receive Holy Communion, and thus you must consider this matter! At least on that day, take care to leave behind false beauty. This is the thing I repeat constantly—we need inner spiritual beauty, and the virtues of the heart and soul of a true Christian.

I congratulate the Mother Abbess and the sisters of this holy family on the occasion of their temple feast—*slava*—I pray to God that He may grant them every true good, and that they may come out of this fast restored, spiritually better and healthier than they were when they entered the fast. And this I desire, brothers and sisters, for all of you, as well as for myself, for all people of goodwill, and for all Orthodox Christians. May the Holy Theotokos, as the paragon of our life, be our helper and intercessor before her Son, our Lord and God and Savior, likewise for our long-suffering nation. God bless you and grant you every good thing!

ON THE HOLY TRINITY

Sermon at the Liturgy on April 24/11, 1996,
on the Wednesday after Thomas Sunday,
in the patriarchal chapel of St. Simeon
the Myrrh-gusher, in Belgrade

"But Jesus answered them, 'My Father worketh hitherto, and I work.' Therefore the Jews sought the more to kill him, because he not only had broken the sabbath, but said also that God was his Father, making himself equal with God. Then answered Jesus and said unto them, 'Verily, verily, I say unto you, the Son can do nothing of himself, but what he seeth the Father do: for what things soever he doeth, these also doeth the Son likewise. For the Father loveth the Son, and sheweth him all things that himself doeth: and he will shew him greater works than these, that ye may marvel. For as the Father raiseth up the dead, and quickeneth them; even so the Son quickeneth whom he will. For the Father judgeth no man, but hath committed all judgment unto the Son: That all men should honour the Son, even as they honour the Father. He that honoureth not the Son honoureth not the Father which hath sent him.'"

John 5:17-23

Brothers and sisters, we believe in one God in essence, but Triune in Persons. We believe in the Father, Son, and the Holy Spirit. They are identical in nature, and they are different only in that the Father is Unbegotten, the Son is Begotten, and the Holy Spirit proceeds.

What generation (begetting) and procession (proceeding) means, we cannot fully comprehend. We believe in what was revealed to us by God: in the Father's being unbegotten, in the begetting of the Son, and the procession of the Holy Spirit. Granted, at the beginning of John's Gospel, the Holy Evangelist says, "In the beginning was the Word, and the Word was with God, and the Word was God" (John 1:1). All things that were made were made through Him. Just as a word is born of our mind in a dispassionate, and not a physical way, in a similar manner—not quite the same, of course; I say we cannot grasp this fully—the Son is begotten of the Father, non-fleshly, and the Holy Spirit proceeds. And they are co-equal, I said, in being; there was never a time in eternity when the Son and the Holy Spirit did not exist. For God does not live in time, that is, to Him the category of time does not apply as is the case with us created beings. Rather, He is in eternity, in the eternal present.

Once, a child, a son, came home from school and his father asked him what he had learned. He said that they had religion class that day—because this was before the war, when they still had religion in schools. He said that the priest, the catechist, spoke about the Holy Trinity. "The catechist must have told you how the Father and Son are co-equal in being, and that there was never a time when there was no Son. My son, look at how illogical that is! Here, I am your father, and you are my son—who, then, of the two of us is older?" The son replied, for the catechist spoke to them about that precise matter in class, "Father, you are older than me as a man, but as a father, you are not older than me. For, the moment you became a father, I became a son."

Likewise, as much as is possible, and within the reach of our mind and our human logic given to us by God, we should awaken our faith in us and others, because it is under attack from all sides—by the devil through our mind, and by the enemies of the Gospel, enemies of Christians, and by atheists and other sectarians. Therefore, we need to awaken our faith, but also to strengthen it by our life. May the Lord help everyone, you and me as well, and may God bless you!

ON THE MOST HOLY THEOTOKOS

Sermon at the Divine Liturgy on the feast
of St. John Damascene, December 17/4, 1996,
in the patriarchal chapel of St. Simeon
the Myrrh-gusher, in Belgrade

"And Jesus went with him; and much people followed him, and thronged him. And a certain woman, which had an issue of blood twelve years, and had suffered many things of many physicians, and had spent all that she had, and was nothing bettered, but rather grew worse, when she had heard of Jesus, came in the press behind, and touched his garment. For she said, 'If I may touch but his clothes, I shall be whole.' And straightway the fountain of her blood was dried up; and she felt in her body that she was healed of that plague. And Jesus, immediately knowing in himself that power had gone out of him, turned him about in the press, and said, 'Who touched my clothes?' And his disciples said unto him, 'Thou seest the multitude thronging thee, and sayest thou, "Who touched me?"' And he looked round about to see her that had done this thing. But the woman fearing and trembling, knowing what was done in her, came and fell down before him, and told him all the truth. And he said unto her, 'Daughter, thy faith hath made thee whole; go in peace, and be whole of thy plague.' While he yet spake, there came from the ruler of the synagogue's house certain which said, 'Thy daughter is dead: why troublest thou the Master any further?' As soon as Jesus heard the word that was spoken, he saith unto the ruler of the synagogue, 'Be not afraid, only believe.' And he suffered no man to follow him, save Peter, and James, and John the brother of James. And he cometh to the house of the ruler of the synagogue, and seeth the tumult, and them that wept and wailed greatly. And when he was come in, he saith unto them, 'Why

> make ye this ado, and weep? The child is not dead, but sleepeth.' And they laughed him to scorn. But when he had put them all out, he taketh the child's father and mother, and them that were with him, and entereth in where the child was lying. And he took the child by the hand, and said unto her, 'Talitha cumi;' which is, being interpreted, 'Little girl, I say unto thee, arise.' And straightway the girl arose, and walked; for she was of the age of twelve years. And they were astonished with a great astonishment. And he charged them strictly that no man should know it; and commanded that something should be given her to eat."
>
> Mark 5:24-43

In this Gospel reading, we see the power of faith in the example of the woman who was ill for so many years, "If I just touch his clothes," she said, "I will be healed. ... And the Lord felt that power had gone out from him." The power of God was what heals both now and always. Great was the faith of the woman: "if I just touch his clothes, I will be healed." We should keep it in mind, and to have faith ourselves, and not be afraid of anything except sin. And, on account of sin, we should be afraid of God Himself, because every sin is a sin against God.

I would mention this as well, and you heard it in the Epistle reading, where the Apostle calls the Holy Theotokos a woman. In the eyes of the law and the people, she really was a woman, the wife of St. Joseph. In fact, she was betrothed to him, and to the Jews that was equivalent to marriage. According to the words of St. John Damascene, whom we celebrate today, this was in order to confuse and mislead that devil who knew the words of the Prophet Isaiah that the Virgin will conceive and give birth to a son (cf. Is. 7:14). Thus, the devil was looking out for a virgin, and he left the Holy Theotokos aside, because he knew she was a "woman." According to the words of St. John Damascene, as I said, this is why she is called woman here and in other places in the Epistle, because she was in the eyes of the law "the wife of Joseph." You know yourselves that she conceived of the Holy Spirit. She was a virgin before birth (of Christ), in giving birth, and after birth. That much you should know to answer to yourself and others alike, because there are Protestant sects that do not teach it that way.

MOST HOLY MOTHER OF GOD "OF THE THREE HANDS"

Sermon at the Divine Liturgy on the Sunday of the Holy Fathers, June 8/May 26, 1997, in the temple of St. Sava in Vrachar, on the occasion of the visitation of the icon of the Mother of God "Of the Three Hands"

"These words spake Jesus, and lifted up his eyes to heaven, and said, 'Father, the hour is come; glorify thy Son, that thy Son also may glorify thee: As thou hast given him power over all flesh, that he should give eternal life to as many as thou hast given him. And this is life eternal, that they might know thee the only true God, and Jesus Christ, whom thou hast sent. I have glorified thee on the earth: I have finished the work which thou gavest me to do. And now, O Father, glorify thou me with thine own self with the glory which I had with thee before the world was. I have manifested thy name unto the men which thou gavest me out of the world: thine they were, and thou gavest them me; and they have kept thy word. Now they have known that all things whatsoever thou hast given me are of thee. For I have given unto them the words which thou gavest me; and they have received them, and have known surely that I came out from thee, and they have believed that thou didst send me. I pray for them: I pray not for the world, but for them which thou hast given me; for they are thine. And all mine are thine, and thine are mine; and I am glorified in them. And now I am no more in the world, but these are in the world, and I come to thee. Holy Father, keep through thine own name those whom thou hast given me, that they may be one, as we are. While I was with them in the world, I kept them in thy name: those that thou gavest me I have kept, and none of them is lost, but the son of perdition; that the scripture might be fulfilled. And now come I to thee; and these things I speak in the world, that they might have my joy fulfilled in themselves.'"

John 17:1-13

Father Abbot of Vatopedi monastery, other brothers, venerable monks from Mount Athos, we are always aware—we, the Serbian people—of that which we received upon receiving Christianity from the mother Church in Constantinople. We have received both literacy and literature, and other capacities enhanced by the Holy Gospel of Christ. Christianity, therefore, ennobled our natural capacities, so that we could be, and remain, the people of God. All this while being aware that it is better to lose one's head than to defile one's soul with sin, because life on earth and the earthly kingdom is temporary, whereas life in the Kingdom of God is eternal.

We were always, therefore, aware that we have received this from the holy brothers Cyril and Methodius, who were from Thessaloniki, and who were the enlighteners of the Slavic people. We always knew that our enlightener, teacher, and spiritual father, St. Sava, was a disciple of Mount Athos. He had acquired and learned his Orthodox faith in the home of his pious parents; however, he deepened that faith in knowledge and mind, as well as with his heart and life on Mount Athos. He also obtained both the autonomy and autocephaly of our Church from the Patriarch of Constantinople. For this reason, we are always grateful to the mother Church and to the noble Greek Orthodox people.

I thank the entire Greek nation for their spiritual and material help that they have extended to us in the misfortunes of this civil war that has befallen us. Our people know well the quality and quantity of that help in medical supplies, food, clothes, and money. Brother Greeks realized early on to what extent our enemies in the world portrayed us as inhuman; falsely, for selfish reasons. The Greeks presented the truth about our people to the world, not because we are brothers in faith and historical misfortunes and troubles, but they did it because of the truth. For us Orthodox Christians, truth is always God, and from God. Therefore, serving the truth, justice and love, and all that is holy and honorable, means serving God.

That love of yours, and of all Mount Athos, is likewise revealed here today in your bringing the holy Icon of the Three Hands, the Abbess of Hilandar, to our country, that she may always be and remain our protectress and helper in this life and in the one that is to come.

Thanking you, again and once more, we pray to the Holy Theotokos to be the protectress of the Greek people as well, of all Orthodox people, and all people of goodwill in the world. In the end, let us pray together with one mind, one heart, and one mouth, and exclaim to the Holy Theotokos: Most Holy Mother of God, Most Holy Theotokos, save us. Amen.

SERMONS ON LENTEN THEMES

ON FASTING

Sermon at the Divine Liturgy on February 3/January 21, 1997,
in the patriarchal chapel
of St. Simeon the Myrrh-Gusher, in Belgrade

"Then came his disciples, and said unto him, 'Knowest thou that the Pharisees were offended, after they heard this saying?' But he answered and said, 'Every plant, which my heavenly Father hath not planted, shall be rooted up. Let them alone: they be blind leaders of the blind. And if the blind lead the blind, both shall fall into the ditch.' Then answered Peter and said unto him, 'Declare unto us this parable.' And Jesus said, 'Are ye also yet without understanding? Do not ye yet understand, that whatsoever entereth in at the mouth goeth into the belly, and is cast out into the draught? But those things which proceed out of the mouth come forth from the heart; and they defile the man. For out of the heart proceed evil thoughts, murders, adulteries, fornications, thefts, false witness, blasphemies: These are the things which defile a man: but to eat with unwashed hands defileth not a man.'"

Matt. 15:12-20

The matter here is the regulation of the law of Moses that God gave Hebrews, who were spiritually not yet developed; they were still like children who needed to be given certain commands: do this; do not do that, and so on.

We Christians who are grown and matured are given general principles: love for God and our neighbors. If we love God, we will of course not bow down to idols, nor refuse to listen to His word. If we love our neighbors, we will fulfill all that the Law of Moses prescribes, and even far more than that. Hence, God through Moses gave them rules not to eat certain foods, and these foods were enumerated, so that the Hebrews could differentiate themselves from the other pagan people in food as well. This was the principle. And so, if they ate pork, for example, or of any unclean animals, who do not have cloven hooves—it was listed, as I said, in detail in the Law which foods were unclean—they would be committing sin. We, however, by abstaining from certain foods during fasts, do not do so because these foods are unclean in themselves—in that case, we could not eat those foods even outside of fasts—but we do it because, according to the words of St. Basil, "The institution of fasting was established in Paradise, not to eat of it, in order to strengthen one's will." Since plant-based food is Lenten, it is not that strong, so we are afforded an opportunity to further consider our spiritual state, and correct ourselves, renouncing bad habits, and acting according to what is virtuous.

One more word on this; so, you understand what the difference is between our fasting and the Hebrew law. The Lord says, "out of the heart come forth those things which proceed out of the mouth, and those are: evil thoughts, evil words, deeds, and so on. And that is what makes man unclean." Furthermore, He says that the Hebrews and Pharisees were scandalized, although He said, "Woe unto the world because of offences." "For it must needs be that offences come," He says, "but woe to that man by whom the offence cometh!" (Matt. 18:7). However, He pays no heed to this, because He did not say anything that was scandalous. Because of their bad habits, which they had already acquired, on account of which they did not accept the Lord as Savior, they—Pharisees, Sadducees, and the rest—were offended by whatever He said. And so He says, "They are blind guides leading the blind, and if the blind lead the blind, both will fall into a pit."

Strive, therefore, to be those who have pure eyes, so that we may see not only this world, to look upon it with all the other living things, but also to keep our spiritual eye pure, which is the mind, that we may see the other world, and the essence of all things and all commandments. Therefore, to be those who have ears to hear what is good, and who have eyes to see what is good. Do not gaze upon evil. We can also turn around when we see something evil, and walk away, and of course, we can also close our eyes, so that whatever is evil does not attract us.

Christ, as I said, condemned temptation unto sin the most, that is, when we who are given more do what is evil and scandalize, entice to sin, those who are weaker. He condemned that the most. But there is no word of His anywhere that blessed are those who are tempted into sin. We all have the mind, the reason, and the strength to resist temptation, and in this way to avoid its devastating power that drags people into sin. God bless you!

BEFORE THE BEGINNING OF GREAT LENT

Sermon at the Divine Liturgy before the beginning of Great Lent, March 8/February 23, 1997, in the patriarchal chapel of St. Simeon the Myrrh-gusher, in Belgrade

"Take heed that ye do not your alms before men, to be seen of them: otherwise ye have no reward of your Father which is in heaven. Therefore when thou doest thine alms, do not sound a trumpet before thee, as the hypocrites do in the synagogues and in the streets, that they may have glory of men. Verily I say unto you, They have their reward. But when thou doest alms, let not thy left hand know what thy right hand doeth: That thine alms may be in secret: and thy Father which seeth in secret himself shall reward thee openly. And when thou prayest, thou shalt not be as the hypocrites are: for they love to pray standing in the synagogues and in the corners of the streets, that they may be seen of men. Verily I say unto you, They have their reward. But thou, when thou prayest, enter into thy closet, and when thou hast shut thy door, pray to thy Father which is in secret; and thy Father which seeth in secret shall reward thee openly. But when ye pray, use not vain repetitions, as the heathen do: for they think that they shall be heard for their much speaking. Be not ye therefore like unto them: for your Father knoweth what things ye have need of, before ye ask him. After this manner therefore pray ye: Our Father which art in heaven, Hallowed be thy name. Thy kingdom come, Thy will be done in earth, as it is in heaven. Give us this day our daily bread. And forgive us our trespasses, as we forgive those who trespass against us. And lead us not into temptation, but deliver us from evil: For thine is the kingdom, and the power, and the glory, for ever. Amen.

All things are delivered unto me of my Father: and no man knoweth the Son, but the Father; neither knoweth any man the Father, save the Son, and he to whomsoever the Son will reveal him. Come unto me, all ye that labor and are heavy laden, and I will give you rest. Take my yoke upon you, and learn of me; for I am meek and lowly in heart: and ye shall find rest unto your souls. For my yoke is easy, and my burden is light."

Matt. 6:1-13; 11:27-30

We are at the threshold of the great and honorable Lent, which God established as early as in the Old Testament; and the Lord Jesus, with His example of fasting forty days in the desert, and with His words, instructed us why and how we should keep the fast.

Fasting is—as I have said before, and as you no doubt have already heard—both physical and spiritual. There is a need for both, because we are both bodies and souls. Surely, the soul is weightier than the body, and the body, as they say, more significant than the clothes we put on it. For this reason, the spiritual fast is more important than the physical one. This does not mean that the physical fast is not important, but only inasmuch as it is helpful for keeping the spiritual fast. St. John Chrysostom asks what use will it be to you to keep the fast and eat no meat, if you devour your brother by evil words, spite, and other?

Moreover, "And you," the Lord says, "when you pray, go into your room, close the door and pray to your Father, who is unseen. Then your Father, who sees what is done in secret, will reward you openly." This word is about our private, personal prayer, for our own needs. However, in the Church of Christ, there is a communal prayer, too, just like we have gathered here today. This prayer has a higher level, a higher meaning. Beside these words in which the Lord addresses every need of each person, He also says about the communal prayer, "For where two or three are gathered together in my name, there am I in the midst of them." And how can He not be here, where so many of us are gathered today, certainly, in His name.

Likewise, when we give alms, do not do it publicly, showing off before people so they could praise us. Rather, do it to help a brother in need, because we know we are brothers, so that he too might be raised up and enabled to support himself on his own.

As for those who are in troubles, in misfortunes, we should help them to survive, because that is truly the love that God expects us to show our neighbors, of course, as much as it is in our capacity. In today's circumstances, when many can barely make ends meet, we should help as much as we can, no more, certainly, nor less; most important, not to do this so that people can laud us, because that is hypocrisy, vanity, and pride.

This day today, the Saturday before Cheesefare Sunday, right before Lent, is dedicated by the holy Church, to the holy monastics. To those, then, who dedicated their lives to God, and spent them in prayer, fasting, divine contemplation, exaltation of soul, and strengthening of their souls. As it says in the church hymns, "Those who knew to subdue what is less important to that which is more important," that is, to subdue the body to the soul. In that way, they have cleared for us the path we should take in these Lenten days, keeping the fast according to our abilities, in terms of strictness, I mean.

The Church prescribed for those who are seriously ill, with tuberculosis, diabetes, and suffering from other chronic diseases, that they may keep the mildest fast, including fish and oil, for the entire duration of Lent; likewise, pregnant and nursing women, those working in hard labor, and the elderly. Therefore, one should not overdo it; I mean, in the sense that if a man is too weak to keep too strict a fast, he should not do so to weaken himself even more.

God gave us common sense—we are co-workers of God—to do what we reasonably can, and, of course, what is according to reason enlightened by God. Naturally, those who can, and especially who have too much in excess, should keep a stricter fast, which is to eat without oil, except on Saturdays and Sundays, and to partake of wine on Annunciation and Palm Sunday.

May the Lord help, and the Holy Fathers who knew how to keep the fast as it should be, both physical and spiritual. May they help us as well, so that in these times, we too might know how to work for our salvation, and to help all people of goodwill. There are so many heretics today who do not keep any fast at all, and who condemn us for keeping it. Let us pray to God for them as well, that the Lord may enlighten their inner mind and heart, and that they also might take the path they should. Of course, we can quietly point to that path, as it is meet and right. God bless you!

SUNDAY OF THE PRODIGAL SON

Sermon at the Divine Liturgy
on February 11/January 29, 1996,
in the church of the Ascension of the Lord,
in Zharkovo, near Belgrade

"And he said, 'A certain man had two sons: And the younger of them said to his father, "Father, give me the portion of goods that falleth to me." And he divided unto them his living. And not many days after the younger son gathered all together, and took his journey into a far country, and there wasted his substance with riotous living. And when he had spent all, there arose a mighty famine in that land; and he began to be in want. And he went and joined himself to a citizen of that country; and he sent him into his fields to feed swine. And he would fain have filled his belly with the husks that the swine did eat: and no man gave unto him. And when he came to himself, he said, "How many hired servants of my father's have bread enough and to spare, and I perish with hunger! I will arise and go to my father, and will say unto him, 'Father, I have sinned against heaven, and before thee, and am no more worthy to be called thy son: make me as one of thy hired servants.'" And he arose, and came to his father. But when he was yet a great way off, his father saw him, and had compassion, and ran, and fell on his neck, and kissed him. And the son said unto him, "Father, I have sinned against heaven, and in thy sight, and am no more worthy to be called thy son." But the father said to his servants, "Bring forth the best robe, and put it on him; and put a ring on his hand, and shoes on his feet: And bring hither the fatted calf, and kill it; and let us eat, and be merry: For this my son was dead, and is alive again; he was lost, and is found." And they began to be merry. Now his elder son was in the field: and as he came and drew nigh to the house, he heard music and dancing. And he called one of the servants, and asked what these things meant. And he said unto him, "Thy brother is come; and thy father hath killed the fatted calf, because he hath received him safe and sound." And he was angry, and would not go in: therefore came his father out, and entreated him. And he answering said to his father, "Lo, these many years do I serve thee, neither transgressed I at any time thy commandment: and yet thou never gavest me a kid, that I might make merry with my friends: But as soon as this thy son was come, which hath devoured thy living with harlots, thou hast killed for him the fatted calf." And he said unto him, "Son, thou art ever with me, and all that I have is thine. It was meet that we should make merry, and be glad: for this thy brother was dead, and is alive again; and was lost, and is found."""

Luke 15:11-32

On this second preparatory Sunday, brothers and sisters, before the beginning of the great and honorable Lent, the holy Church prescribed the Gospel reading of the prodigal son, in order to point out to us what is sin, and what true repentance. This story, the interpreters say, contains the entire evangelical teaching. They say that, if the whole of Holy Scripture of the New Testament were lost, and only this story preserved, that it would deliver to us in a nutshell the entire evangelical teaching, that is, what is sin, what is true repentance, what straightening one's life means, and what is salvation.

In this story, you heard how a man had two sons, and how the younger told his father, "Father, give me my share of the estate, so that I may live how I desire and want." His father certainly dissuaded him from this; according to the laws of that time, and the present, he was not obliged to give him the estate—for as long as he was alive, it belonged to him. But when he saw that it was no use, he set aside for him a portion of his estate. The son sold it all, took the money, turned his back on his father and his father's house, on his brother, too, and he went in the opposite direction.

Around such a frivolous man with money like company gathered, and soon he spent all his possessions in debauchery, drunkenness, and hedonism. The money was gone, and the friends disappeared. They went to look for another such gullible fellow, but with money, and the other one was now like a strained lemon—without interest. So he was left to starve, and he came to a point where he was going to die of starvation unless he did something about it; so he was hired by a man as a swineherd. Now this prodigal son was Jewish, and was forbidden by Mosaic Law to come in contact with the swine, for it would make him unclean, not only physically, but ritually as well. They would have to pray, and wash in a particular manner, in order to be able to pray to God. And it says, "He joined himself to a man to keep his swine." When a Hebrew man reaches that state—just like Muslims, you know, they are also forbidden to come in contact with the swine for ritual reasons—and he had reached that state: it is either death, or watching the swine. And he wanted to fill his belly with the husks, the acorns that the swine ate, and was not given even as much.

Then, it says, "he came to his senses." Hence: up until then he was not in his senses. True, he was roaming around this world, his eyes pulled him to and fro, and this is what he came to. "Then," it says, "he came to his senses." And he said: "How many servants are in my father's house, and none of them are starving, and I—the son—am dying. I know what I will do. I will return to my father and tell him, 'Father, I have sinned against heaven and against you, and I am not worthy to be called your son; but I beg you, accept me at least as one of your servants.'" And he carried out his plan. "And the father," it says in the Gospel, "saw him from afar." The heart of the father was expecting him—if only he would return; if only he would come back! And when he saw him, he ran out to meet him, embraced him, and kissed him, ordered his servants to bring him new clothes, and sandals for his feet; and he gave him a ring for his hand—a sign that he was restoring him to his previous filial state. And the son said what he had intended, "Father, I am not worthy to be called your son; but I beg you, accept me at least as one of your servants." And the father then told the servants to kill a fatted calf, because, "This my son was lost, and is found; he was dead, and is alive again." You see that it is sin that destroys a man, where a man is lost, going in the opposite direction, going toward his ruin; and sin is what brings death.

And they began to rejoice and celebrate. That man also had an older son who was working in the fields. And when he came to the house, he heard the sounds of celebration, and called over one of the servants. "What is this?" he asked. And the servant explained, "Your younger brother has returned, and your father ordered us to kill a fatted calf." And the son was mad, and did not want to enter the house. They told the father about this, and he came out. And the son said, "Father, I have fulfilled every commandment of yours, and you never gave me as much as a goatling, so I could celebrate with my friends. And when this son of yours came, who had wasted your estate, and squandered it with all kinds of good-for-nothings, you ordered that a fatted calf be killed." And the father said, "Son, you are always with me, and all that is mine is yours; was it not right that we should be glad, when this brother of yours came back, who was lost and is found, was dead and is alive again."

In this story, brothers and sisters, as was said by those who know it better, is the entire essence of evangelical teaching. You see what sin is, and what repentance is—what salvation is. Sin is, therefore, turning one's back on God, our heavenly Father, and going in the opposite direction from Him, from the Kingdom of Heaven, from our true fatherland, our true home. What is repentance? Repentance is realizing that we are moving toward an abyss, to ruin; that we are going to the enemy of our heavenly Father, to the devil who desires for us the same ruin that he had created for himself. And then: turning around 180 degrees in the opposite direction, and now walking toward the heavenly Father, toward our home, moving toward God; and then, admitting the sin; not self-justification, as it happens with many of us. That son does not say to the father, "All kinds of good-for-nothings talked me into doing this and that." No! "I am guilty; I have sinned." And then, a prayer, a plea, "Forgive me, father; I am not worthy to call myself, nor to be called, your son anymore; but I beg you, accept me from now on as one of your servants." And the father mercifully took his son back; again he gave him festive clothes, a ring on his hand, sandals on his feet; he embraced him and restored him to filiality.

What I just said, you understand, is also our duty during this honorable Lent, and throughout our whole life: to know what sin is. That sin is that which distances us from God, which brings death unto us; and that repentance is this realization that wherever He is not, we are moving toward eternal ruin, and then: turning around to our heavenly Father, admitting our sin, and amending our lives. It happens nowadays among us, too, that those who have not sinned, sin daily, but they have not so sinned, and consequently consider themselves innocent; that is, they consider themselves above everything, and judge all those who repent. Let us beware of this sin as well. Let us always, brothers and sisters, sincerely rejoice if one sinner is sincerely repenting; let us pray to God that we may know what sin is, that we may know what sin means for a sinful man: that it leads him to eternal ruin. The sorrow that this unrepeatable, unique person, in such a way is ruined for eternity; this sorrow, and the prayer to God that He too may help, and make this sinner sincerely repent, change his life, earn the Kingdom of Heaven, and be saved—this should be our continual prayer! For the Lord Jesus Christ said, "I have not come to call the righteous, but sinners to repentance" (Luke 5:32).

May our Lord Jesus help us as well to be sincere penitents, to also approach our heavenly Father in sincerity, Him and the Son of God, and with sincere repentance and correction of life to earn the Kingdom of Heaven, and to enter our real fatherland, our Father's house, and the communion with all the Saints. May this day be blessed, and may God help both myself and all of you to enter this honorable Lent sincerely, and to come out of it better than we were upon entering.

ON MEATFARE SUNDAY

Sermon at the Divine Liturgy
on February 18/5, 1996, in the church
of the Holy Trinity in Zemun

"When the Son of man shall come in his glory, and all the holy angels with him, then shall he sit upon the throne of his glory: And before him shall be gathered all nations: and he shall separate them one from another, as a shepherd divideth his sheep from the goats: And he shall set the sheep on his right hand, but the goats on the left. Then shall the King say unto them on his right hand, 'Come, ye blessed of my Father, inherit the kingdom prepared for you from the foundation of the world: For I was hungry, and ye gave me meat: I was thirsty, and ye gave me drink: I was a stranger, and ye took me in: Naked, and ye clothed me: I was sick, and ye visited me: I was in prison, and ye came unto me.' Then shall the righteous answer him, saying, 'Lord, when saw we thee hungry, and fed thee? or thirsty, and gave thee drink? When saw we thee a stranger, and took thee in? or naked, and clothed thee? Or when saw we thee sick, or in prison, and came unto thee?' And the King shall answer and say unto them, 'Verily I say unto you, Inasmuch as ye have done it unto one of the least of these my brethren, ye have done it unto me.' Then shall he say also unto them on the left hand, 'Depart from me, ye cursed, into everlasting fire, prepared for the devil and his angels: For I was hungry, and ye gave me no meat: I was thirsty, and ye gave me no drink: I was a stranger, and ye took me not in: naked, and ye clothed me not: sick, and in prison, and ye visited me not.' Then shall they also answer him, saying, 'Lord, when saw we thee hungry, or athirst, or a stranger, or naked, or sick, or in prison, and did not minister unto thee?' Then shall he answer them, saying, 'Verily I say unto you, Inasmuch as ye did it not to one of the least of these, ye did it not to me.' And these shall go away into everlasting punishment: but the righteous into life eternal."

Matt. 25:31-46

We have prayed, brothers and sisters, on this day, on this holy Sunday, the day of the week when we commemorate the resurrection of the Lord Jesus, on this Meatfare Sunday, when the holy Church prepares us to enter the honorable and great Lent. This is done by the gradual abandonment of usual food, and by introducing the kind of food that was the first food of the people in paradise. St. Basil the Great also says that, "The mark of the Orthodox fast is just that, the difference in food, as God had ordained for our forbearers, not to eat of the fruit of the tree of knowledge of good and evil, but that they may eat the fruits of all other trees." Hence, fasting entails food of mainly plant-based origin, and that is, he says, the mark of the Orthodox fast.

Fasting, then, is an institution of God, God's resolution; it has a divine source. It was established so that, abstaining from certain foods, we could thereby think more intensely about the soul, consider our spiritual state, contemplate upon what constitutes sin, what needs to be cleansed and weeded out of the soul; also, to plant the opposite virtue in replacement. Likewise, on this Sunday, as you have heard from the Gospel reading on the Last Judgment, the Church reminds us that we are to come before God's righteous judgment, and that we should direct our whole life toward this: to be in words, deeds, and thoughts the way God expects and wants us to be. In a word, to move ever closer to Him, walking on His path toward the Kingdom of Heaven, and the communion with all the Saints in that kingdom in which He is, our Master and righteous Judge. Hence, we should always keep in mind, brothers and sisters, that we are to face God's righteous judgment. You also heard from the Gospel how the Lord affirms the freedom He gives people. For those who walk toward God in their life according to faith, the Lord accepts that freedom of theirs and tells them, "Come, ye blessed of my Father!" You are walking toward me: come! That path, the Lord explains, means to do good toward our neighbors, our brothers: to feed the hungry as much as we are able, to give drink to the thirsty, to cure the sick, to visit the imprisoned, and to clothe the naked. "When you have done it," He says, "you have done it unto Me. Inasmuch as you have done it unto one of the least of my brethren, you have done it unto Me." The Lord also affirms the freedom of will of those other ones, who walk away from Him, in the opposite direction, as a matter of fact, toward eternal torment, into the abyss for soul and body. And He says, "Depart from Me... Depart." The Lord is not indifferent.

The Son of God ascended the cross, endured sufferings, and died for all of us. He is not indifferent, of course. However, He does not take away the freedom He has given people. As the Saints say, "God could have created us without *us*, but He cannot save us without *us*" [i.e. *without our cooperation—T.N.*]. We have to take part as His co-workers in the act of our salvation, that is, to adopt that salvation that He brought about for all, with our faith, with our life and actions according to faith—to walk, thus, the path of God into the Kingdom of Heaven.

May the Lord help all of us, brothers and sisters, to always consciously live our lives the way God wishes, because that is absolute good, above all for us, and then for our nation as well, and for all people of goodwill in the world. "That they may see," as He says, "your good works, and glorify your Father who is in heaven" (Matt. 5:16).

All-merciful Lord, help us also to be worthy of the name of Orthodox Christians, Orthodox Serbian people, just as our ancestors were, and that together with them, when we come before Your righteous judgment seat, we may hear that voice, "Come ye blessed of my Father," and to enter into the kingdom of blessedness, where there is no sickness, nor sorrow, nor sighing. May this day be blessed, and may the beginning of Great Lent be blessed, its duration, and completion. May we all come out of this Lent better than we were upon entering it, spiritually better and healthier, both in soul and in body. God bless you! Amen.

THE FIRST SUNDAY OF LENT—SUNDAY OF ORTHODOXY

Sermon at the Divine Liturgy on March 16/3, 1997,
in the church of Sts. Constantine and Helen in Belgrade

> "The day following Jesus would go forth into Galilee, and findeth Philip, and saith unto him, 'Follow me.' Now Philip was of Bethsaida, the city of Andrew and Peter. Philip findeth Nathanael, and saith unto him, 'We have found him, of whom Moses in the law, and the prophets, did write, "Jesus of Nazareth, the son of Joseph."' And Nathanael said unto him, 'Can there any good thing come out of Nazareth?' Philip saith unto him, 'Come and see.' Jesus saw Nathanael coming to him, and saith of him, 'Behold an Israelite indeed, in whom is no guile!' Nathanael saith unto him, 'Whence knowest thou me?' Jesus answered and said unto him, 'Before that Philip called thee, when thou wast under the fig tree, I saw thee.' Nathanael answered and saith unto him, 'Rabbi, thou art the Son of God; thou art the King of Israel.' Jesus answered and said unto him, 'Because I said unto thee, "I saw thee under the fig tree," believest thou? thou shalt see greater things than these.' And he saith unto him, 'Verily, verily, I say unto you, Hereafter ye shall see heaven open, and the angels of God ascending and descending upon the Son of man.'"
>
> John 1:43-51

In the name of the Father, and the Son, and the Holy Spirit. Today, brothers and sisters, we celebrate the first Sunday of the holy, great, and honorable Lent, which is called the Sunday of Orthodoxy, because in the ninth century, in 852, when Orthodoxy defeated Iconoclasm, it was determined that this Sunday should be the one when we would celebrate precisely that: Orthodoxy.

Specifically, there have been kings and bishops, and other people, who thought that icons are unbecoming in the Orthodox Church. I suppose it was out of the desire to make it easier for Muslims, as well as Jews—both of whom have no icons at all—to come to Christianity. Thus, under this pressure, these bishops and kings wanted them removed from the Church. However, brothers and sisters, icons have been in the Church since the beginning. True, in the Old Testament the Lord commands in God's Ten Commandments, "You shall not make for yourself any graven image; you shall not bow down to them or worship them" (Deut. 5:8). But the words of the Lord also include this: He tells Moses not to make any images nor statues, because he says, "You have not seen God manifest." What does that mean? St. John Damascene says: this means when you have seen Him, God in the flesh, then you can make icons, clearly. Hence, the Church of God, after the birth, that is, the incarnation of the Son of God, His suffering and resurrection, began to paint icons, and to venerate them. According to the word of St. Basil and of all the Saints, we bow down, brothers and sisters, neither to the material, nor the paint, the gold, the silver, and the metal used to craft the icon, but we bow down to the person whom the icon represents. Likewise, we would not throw away a picture, a photograph, of our father or mother somewhere—but put it in a visible place, because they represent the image of our parents, which is not insignificant—let alone the image of God and His Saints.

May the holy icons remind us also of this: as we celebrate them, may we also strive to enter the glory of the Kingdom of God, to be and become sons and daughters of God, to enter the blessedness of that kingdom and be holy. That is the meaning of icons in the Church and our homes. To be a reminder of the holy ancestors, both ours and of all Orthodox. If they, being human and people of flesh and blood just like us managed, through their efforts and with God's grace, to deify their souls and truly be heavenly citizens, we can and should do that as well, if we want. Otherwise, if we do not want it, but we make our soul unworthy of the Kingdom of God, and we ruin it, make ready for eternal torments—we are responsible for it. Hence, in the Orthodox Church, icons are there to represent those historical persons who have succeeded in becoming heavenly. You know also that, in the contemporary world, especially in the Roman Catholic church, their icons are in fact like portraits of people of this world, very beautiful, male and female, but too much like an image of this world, of earthly bodies. Here as well, icons represent people, but more like people from hell, than paradise. As another example, take for comparison a Western icon of an El Greco or of any other great Western artist, and you will see there a woman with the charms of this world. On the other hand, that beautiful icon from Dechani of the Holy Theotokos with the Divine Child in her hands—an icon whose image traveled around the world, and is for me a most beautiful thing to behold—the Holy Theotokos embodies a virgin before birth (of the Lord), in giving birth, and after giving birth. She represents the One who alone was chosen of all generations to be the mother of the Son of God because of her qualities, that is, her purity of soul and holiness, just as it says in the psalm, "The king's daughter is all glorious within," (Ps. 45:13).

This inner beauty is expressed in the face and the whole appearance of the Holy Theotokos and all the Saints. You should differentiate between an icon before which one can pray, and an icon as a painting that is evocative of this world, but before which one cannot pray, as one great Russian theologian says, who was once a pagan, unbeliever, and atheist. Namely, when he was at the Sistine Chapel and saw, I think, Raphael's painting of the Mother of God, he admired the work of that artist. In the meantime, he became a believer, and rose to the rank of an Orthodox priest, and archpriest, a great name in theology. Next time he was at the Roman Sistine Chapel and saw that painting-icon, he wrote the following, "I cannot pray in front of this painting. Here we see a pretty woman who is treading on clouds as if they were snow, holding a child, and who perhaps is not even a virgin, a maiden. I cannot pray." You understand what the matter is. An icon is supposed to depict for us a historical person of this world, whether the Lord Jesus, the Holy Theotokos, or holy people who are heavenly. According to the word of Christ, "Where I am, there will my servant be" (John 12:26). And where is the Lord? In the Kingdom of Heaven. Let us prepare, therefore, for the Kingdom of Heaven, for the blessedness of that kingdom, now in this world. That is the "only thing needful," as the Lord says to Martha in that sermon of His in her home. Let us attain that. Of course, we despise neither the body nor this world, but our true fatherland and our true life is in the heavenly kingdom.

May the Lord help us to keep this Lent so as to come out of it incomparably better and healthier in soul and body than we were when we entered. God bless you and grant you every good thing.

I beseech you to endure this honorable Lent, even in its milder form, with oil and fish; and let us leave off the meat for when Pascha comes. According to the word of St. Basil, "just as when a man is thirsty, how much more tasty water is to him; so when he is hungry, how much more flavorful the food is to him." Thus, if we abstain from non-Lenten food, how much more flavorful will it be to us, and naturally, how much better our organism will be able to use it. God bless you!

THIRD SUNDAY OF LENT—VENERATION OF THE HOLY CROSS

Sermon on March 26/13, 1995, in Zheleznik

> "...Whosoever will come after me, let him deny himself, and take up his cross, and follow me. For whosoever will save his life shall lose it; but whosoever shall lose his life for my sake."
>
> "For what shall it profit a man, if he shall gain the whole world, and lose his own soul? Or what shall a man give in exchange for his soul? Whosoever therefore shall be ashamed of me and of my words in this adulterous and sinful generation; of him also shall the Son of man be ashamed, when he cometh in the glory of his Father with the holy angels. And he said unto them, 'Verily I say unto you, that there are some of them that stand here, who shall not taste of death, till they have seen the kingdom of God come with power.'"
>
> Mark 8:34-38; 9:1

Today, brothers and sisters, we celebrate the third Sunday of Lent, the Veneration of the Holy cross, in which we particularly venerate the honorable cross that the Church brings out before us all. It is to strengthen us in the middle of this honorable Lent, that we may endure until the end on this evangelical path, the path of God, having in mind the honorable cross of Christ, and its might and power that come from the Son of God Who was crucified on it. For we kiss the honorable cross, we bow down in worship before it, and we venerate it, not because it was a means of punishment and death of criminals in those olden times, but because the Lord Jesus was crucified on it, for us and for our salvation. It was so that He would remove the sins that for centuries have been loaded onto mankind's shoulders, beginning with Adam the forefather. Furthermore, so that He would thereby prepare us that we may enter the heavenly kingdom, if we lead our lives the way He commands and ordains.

You know yourselves, without my reminding you, that there are Christian sects who call themselves Christian, but who do not worship and venerate the cross of Christ. Adventists, Jehovah's Witnesses, Baptists, and so on—all these Western sects that separated from the Orthodox Christian Church. They even scold us for bowing to the honorable cross and kissing it. I had an occasion to hear an Adventist say, "You are completely unreasonable, you Orthodox Christians. You bow down to the cross; that would be the same as if someone took a gun and killed your son, and you took that gun, and bowed down before it and kissed it." This person does not understand, as I said before, that we do not worship the cross as the weapon of death, but the cross our Lord was crucified on. Not any cross. Not the crosses of the two thieves who were crucified with our Lord for their crimes, but the honorable cross of Christ, upon which He, the Righteous One—who took upon Himself our sins, and the consequence of those sins, that is, death, for our sake and for our salvation—suffered torments and death, out of His endless love for us. Then, by His infinite divine power He rose on the third day, to enable us to rise on that last day, and enter the heavenly kingdom, the blessedness of that kingdom, where there is no sickness, nor sorrow, nor sighing—if we earn it.

In the Gospel reading, the Lord cautions us that there is no other way to follow Him, to be His faithful, but to willfully take upon yourself your cross, that is, the cross as the symbol of suffering, the cross of struggle in this world, on the path of truth, justice, and love of God. Denying these difficulties on this path of God means denying Christ. It also means that we are denying Him not only in words, with our tongue, but with evil deeds, sins, as well. For this reason, when our soul comes before Him as the Righteous Judge, and before the multitude of all those departed up until that moment, He will deny us and say, "I do not know you!" An Orthodox Christian, hence, knows that there are two unavoidable sufferings in this world: either suffering on the path of God, or the suffering on the opposite path. So he willfully accepts struggles and suffering on the path of God as his cross, following Christ.

In these days, brothers and sisters, our people are suffering in Croatia, and Bosnia, and Herzegovina. They suffer in this civil war that was imposed upon our nation; they suffer on the path of God. I know that even here there are a certain number of those who commit crime, and who return crime for crime. However, the majority are those who consciously fight for the freedom of their homes, to preserve the graves of their ancestors, and the land where they had lived for centuries; and they are fighting for God's justice. In a word, they fight for the honorable cross, and for golden freedom. The way our ancestors set out for the Kosovo field with the Holy Prince: not to plunder what belonged to others, nor to repress the freedom of other nations, nor to impose their faith on others, but to defend their own.

May the Lord look upon us and our enemies alike, and grant both to us and to them peace that is so much needed, although they are not aware of it.

Let us pray to the Lord, crucified on the cross and resurrected, to also help us today to keep our faith in Him, and to preserve our honor, the honor of our family and our nation, pure and bright, and to grant peace to us and to our enemies. For everyone is suffering, and those who are innocent and powerless suffer the most. God bless you!

FIFTH SUNDAY OF LENT—ST. MARY OF EGYPT

Sermon at the Divine Liturgy
on April 13/March 31, 1997, in the Monastery
of the Holy Archangel Gabriel in Zemun

"And they were in the way going up to Jerusalem; and Jesus went before them: and they were amazed; and as they followed, they were afraid. And he took again the twelve, and began to tell them what things should happen unto him, saying, 'Behold, we go up to Jerusalem; and the Son of man shall be delivered unto the chief priests, and unto the scribes; and they shall condemn him to death, and shall deliver him to the Gentiles: And they shall mock him, and shall scourge him, and shall spit upon him, and shall kill him: and the third day he shall rise again.' And James and John, the sons of Zebedee, come unto him, saying, 'Master, we would that thou shouldest do for us whatsoever we shall desire.' And he said unto them, 'What would ye that I should do for you?' They said unto him, 'Grant unto us that we may sit, one on thy right hand, and the other on thy left hand, in thy glory.' But Jesus said unto them, 'Ye know not what ye ask: can ye drink of the cup that I drink of? and be baptized with the baptism that I am baptized with?' And they said unto him, 'We can.' And Jesus said unto them, 'Ye shall indeed drink of the cup that I drink of; and with the baptism that I am baptized withal shall ye be baptized: But to sit on my right hand and on my left hand is not mine to give; but it shall be given to them for whom it is prepared.' And when the ten heard it, they began to be much displeased with James and John. But Jesus called them to him, and saith unto them, 'Ye know that they which are accounted to rule over the Gentiles exercise lordship over them; and their great ones exercise authority upon them. But so shall it not be among you: but whosoever will be great among you, shall be your minister: And whosoever of you will be the chiefest, shall be servant of all. For even the Son of man came not to be ministered unto, but to minister, and to give his life a ransom for many.'"

Mark 10:32-45

In the name of the Father, and the Son, and the Holy Spirit! On this fifth Sunday of great and honorable Lent, brothers and sisters, the Church commemorates St. Mary of Egypt who, as many other Saints before her, was first a sinner, but then she realized that her life was leading her into spiritual ruin, into an abyss. She repented, and for years she spent her life as a monastic, sanctifying her soul and body.

True repentance, brothers and sisters, as we can see from the life of St. Mary of Egypt and all the Saints, is the correction of life; furthermore, it is not justification of oneself and one's sins, self-justification, but admitting one's sins, the way it was clearly expressed by the prodigal son. He did not justify himself for living the way he did after he left his father's house: Some people talked me into it. Rather, he admitted his sin, "I have sinned against heaven, and in thy sight, Father" (Luke 15:21). I have sinned according to God's and the human law; for if another is guilty of my sin, he should repent. If I am not guilty, there is no reason for me to repent. But, in fact, it is I who am guilty. If someone entices me and forces me to sin, and I consent to it, I am guilty. True, he provoked me, coaxed me, forced me, but I assented to the persuasion and the force. He can kill me even, but to force me—no way, if I strive to endure with God's grace, which is always present. I am not justifying my sin, because that is running away from true repentance.

On the other hand, the Lord counsels us in today's Gospel reading about humility. The brothers James and John, His Apostles, asked Him to give them priority: that they might sit at His right and left hand in the heavenly kingdom. But the Lord cautions them, "It is not for Me to give that, but it will be given to those for whom it was prepared." And it is prepared for those who ready themselves. How? By serving God and their neighbor, "For the Son of God did not come to be served, but to serve," and to serve unto death, even unto death on the cross. You know from the Gospels what His life was like. How persecuted He had been when still a child, and how much in Nazareth and in other places; how humiliated He had been. "Why are you listening to him?" they said; "An unclean spirit is in him" (cf. Mark 3:30), evil people said. And He suffered all this for our sake and for our salvation. In the end, He prayed on the cross, while the entire crowd mocked Him under the cross, "If you are the Son of God, descend now from the cross that we may see and believe!" (cf. Mark 15:32). And He prayed, feeling sorry for them more than for Himself and His suffering, "Father, forgive them, for they know not what they do" (Luke 23:34).

There, you see, is the tragedy of sin, that man becomes a slave; he turns away from the heavenly kingdom, from God, from the Son of God in the Kingdom of Heaven, and goes in the opposite direction; yet he does not even realize, does not know what he is doing. Therefore, if and when we know what that person is doing, we should see that he is going toward ruin, and feel sorry for him. For we know that our love toward our enemies means to feel compassion for that unrepeatable, unique person, and to pray to God to do what He can, so that the vain man may snap out of it. Indeed, God Almighty can do anything, but He cannot commit violence over a man who does not want to be saved [that is, violate his free will, T.N.], for force is not power. While God is Almighty, violence and every evil is not might, but weakness. Nonetheless, God is the Almighty; He is Almighty in everything that is good and holy. May He help us that, with His help and our efforts, we may imitate all the Saints and St. Mary of Egypt. Furthermore, to do one of the two goods, according to the words of St. Gregory the Theologian: either not to sin, because then it would be easy to endure what follows, or, if we have sinned, to immediately repent and correct ourselves.

May the Lord help both you and me to find ourselves in the heavenly kingdom, together like this, on that side where the Lord will recognize and acknowledge us as His own. God bless you!

SECOND SERMON ON THE FIFTH SUNDAY OF LENT—ST. MARY OF EGYPT

Sermon at the Divine Liturgy on March 31/13, 1996, in the church of the Ascension of our Lord in Zheleznik

On the fifth Sunday of Lent, the holy Church brings before us the example of St. Mary of Egypt, initially a sinner, and then a penitent, and a Saint. What sin can do to a man, this we can see in our times as well, and in any time in history. However, what true repentance can do, the correction of life, and entering the Kingdom of Heaven, what blessedness they bring, this we can see from the lives of all the Saints. Hence, we are all called, as we are all sinners, to be sincere penitents, and to enter into the blessedness of the heavenly kingdom. That is the meaning and purpose of our existence and of endeavors on this earth, the aim of our entire life and the struggles we endure.

In this world, troubles and sufferings are unavoidable. We have them in abundance in our times, but our ancestors had them, too, and all the people in the world have their own struggles and difficulties. We Orthodox Christians willfully take upon ourselves the cross of our Lord for which He said, "Whosoever will come after me, let him deny himself, and take up his cross, and follow me" (Mark 8:34). However, the One Who points us to this first took up His own cross and carried it to Golgotha, was crucified on it, and died on it. But, as Almighty God, He also resurrected.

On this fifth Sunday of Lent, when we have only two weeks left until the resurrection of our Lord, let us endure, brothers and sisters, on the evangelical path of Christian life. The meaning of physical fasting is to give us an opportunity, and to help us to cleanse our soul from every sin. Likewise, to plant in it all that is holy, and pure, and good, so that we can thus reach the days of Lord's Passion, and with Him, carrying our own cross, to celebrate His glorious resurrection—the greatest event in the Economy of our salvation. "And if Christ be not risen, then is our preaching in vain, and your faith is also in vain" (1 Cor. 15:14). Christ's resurrection is the guarantee, brothers and sisters, that we will rise also, and that we will enter the heavenly kingdom, into the blessedness of that kingdom, if we earn it.

"Fear not, little flock," the Lord said, "for it is your Father's good pleasure to give you the kingdom" (Luke 12:32). No matter how many of us there are, let us strive to be in this small number that will enter the heavenly kingdom. Likewise, with our lives, our faith and life according to the faith, to show others as well, if they want to see, according to the word of the Lord and His commandment, what the path of God is, and the destination of that path.

Looking up to our holy ancestors as models, who were capable of enduring all difficulties and struggles, may we also thereby be human, enter into the Kingdom of Heaven, and be numbered with our Saints, martyrs, and new-martyrs. God bless you!

ON LAZARUS SATURDAY

Sermon at the Divine Liturgy on April 6/March 24, 1996,
in the cathedral church in Belgrade

> "Now a certain man was sick, named Lazarus, of Bethany, the town of Mary and her sister Martha. (It was that Mary which anointed the Lord with ointment, and wiped his feet with her hair, whose brother Lazarus was sick.) Therefore his sisters sent unto him, saying, 'Lord, behold, he whom thou lovest is sick.' When Jesus heard that, he said, 'This sickness is not unto death, but for the glory of God, that the Son of God might be glorified thereby…' Jesus therefore again groaning in himself cometh to the grave. It was a cave, and a stone lay upon it. Jesus said, 'Take ye away the stone.' Martha, the sister of him that was dead, saith unto him, 'Lord, by this time there is a stench: for he hath been dead four days.' Jesus saith unto her, 'Said I not unto thee, that, if thou wouldest believe, thou shouldest see the glory of God?' Then they took away the stone from the place where the dead was laid. And Jesus lifted up his eyes, and said, 'Father, I thank thee that thou hast heard me. And I knew that thou hearest me always: but because of the people which stand by I said it, that they may believe that thou hast sent me.' And when he thus had spoken, he cried with a loud voice, 'Lazarus, come forth.' And he that was dead came forth, bound hand and foot with graveclothes: and his face was bound about with a napkin. Jesus saith unto them, 'Loose him, and let him go.'"
>
> John 11:1-4, 38-44

I congratulate you with today's feast, on the Saturday when our Lord raised Lazarus of the Four Days from the dead, and thus showed that He is the Almighty God; but He showed this especially by His own resurrection from the dead. There had been other holy people who by the power from God had raised others from the dead, such as the Prophet Elijah, for example. However, there is only One, only He, our Lord Jesus Christ, Who by His divine power personally rose from the dead. Glorifying Him, the Almighty Lord, in a few days we will commemorate His ascension on the cross, His death and resurrection, out of love for us, and His desire to save all those who wish to be saved. He brought salvation to all of us, in fact, objectively performed an act of salvation, and we adopt that salvation, with our faith and our life according to that faith, only if we want.

I would like today, on the feast when He raised Lazarus, to point out to you the words of the Holy Apostle Paul, that we Christians are co-workers of God. He endowed us with certain capacities, and He expects us to use these capacities for good. What in time, and in the tasks of that time, surpasses our powers, He will accomplish as the Almighty God. An Indian man, who at first was a pagan and used to tear the Holy Scripture when he would read it, but later became a Christian, remarks on the passage we listen to and read so many times: how the Lord, in the act of raising Lazarus also showed that we people are His co-workers. When He came to the tomb, He said, "Remove the stone!" We people can do that. When the people removed the stone from the tomb, then comes He, the Almighty God, "Lazarus, come out!" "And the dead man came out," it says, "wrapped in linen strips." How many times have I read that passage and, surely, you as well—that passage, that fact—but it never occurred to us that therein is shown, illustrated, how we are co-workers of God. The Apostle Paul, too, who spoke the word, paints a picture for us as well, saying, "I have planted, Apollos watered; but God gave the increase… Now he that planted and he that watered are one: and every man shall receive his own reward according to his own labor" (1 Cor. 3:6,8).

This we should know, and keep the words of St. Basil always in mind, that, "what distinguishes a good man from the bad, a righteous man from the sinner, human from inhuman, is this: a good man uses for good what God gave him unto good." There is the difference between heaven and hell, between human and inhuman; this seemingly small, but essential difference. We should always know, and strive to use all those traits that God has endowed us with for good. In that way, we will be great before Him, and earn the Kingdom of God which is our true fatherland, and which awaits us. Likewise, we will be numbered with our holy ancestors who look upon us from the heavens, and who expect to recognize and acknowledge us as their own in all that is holy and honorable. Thus we will be of greatest benefit to ourselves above all, to our nation, and to all the people in the world.

To those who on this day celebrate their family patron day—*slava*—I congratulate, and to all of you a happy feast of the resurrection of Lazarus, the pledge of our resurrection as well. God bless you!

SIXTH SUNDAY OF LENT—PALM SUNDAY

Sermon at the Divine Liturgy on April 7/March 25, 1996, in the Monastery of the Holy Archangel Gabriel in Zemun

"On the next day much people that were come to the feast, when they heard that Jesus was coming to Jerusalem, took branches of palm trees, and went forth to meet him, and cried, 'Hosanna: Blessed is the King of Israel that cometh in the name of the Lord.' And Jesus, when he had found a young ass, sat thereon; as it is written, 'Fear not, daughter of Sion: behold, thy King cometh, sitting on an ass's colt.' These things understood not his disciples at the first: but when Jesus was glorified, then remembered they that these things were written of him, and that they had done these things unto him. The people therefore that was with him when he called Lazarus out of his grave, and raised him from the dead, bare record. For this cause the people also met him, for that they heard that he had done this miracle."

John 12:12-18

In the name of the Father, and the Son, and the Holy Spirit! Brothers and sisters, on this day of the entrance of our Lord Jesus Christ into Jerusalem, we have approached the week of His passion and His death, but also His resurrection. At the raising of Lazarus, which was seen by so many people, when the Lord came to the tomb and ordered that it be open, the sister of Lazarus said: "It has been four days now, and there is a stench already." She had already seen the death of her brother, and had felt that the body had already started to decay. And the Lord raised Lazarus in front of all those people. But this was of no consequence to His enemies. They decided to kill Him, and in the end to kill Lazarus, too. This is why there are so many who do not believe in the Lord Jesus, and who say, "Let us see ourselves, too, and then we will believe!" However, that is clearly not enough either; such people will always find an excuse. Even so, man is a free being. Our Lord performed this miracle in front of such a great crowd, as was the case with His other miracles as well, yet—Judas remained Judas, the traitor, and that holds until the end of the world.

We believe those who saw this, who felt His wounds after His death, and after His resurrection. These were the ones who, having seen Him, having heard the teaching from His mouth, and having seen all His works, were prepared to lay down their lives for Him, and for their faith. "How can you believe," says St. John the Evangelist, "since you accept glory from one another but do not seek the glory that comes from the only God?" (John 5:44). Only by life according to the Gospel can our faith become stronger and stronger, more and more firm; and when we cleanse our heart from sin, so that God may be reflected in it, we will see God. For blessed are the "pure in heart," they will "see God" (Matt. 5:8). The way we are, sinful as we are, we are like a mirror that is covered in char and dust; it cannot reflect anything until we clean it. Such is our heart. Seeking to see God the way we are, it would be forced if God were to appear to us.

May the Lord Jesus Christ, the Son of God, Who raised Lazarus, the son of the widow of Nain, and Jairus' daughter, and Who healed so many others, help us as well, and raise our souls for all that is holy, honorable, and pleasing to God! Likewise, that in this time, difficult as it is, we would be witnesses of the truth of His teaching, by our faith and our life, and so prepare for ourselves a blessed place in the heavenly kingdom, in communion with all the Saints from our nation, who look upon us from heaven, and expect that we, too, act as it becomes those who are Orthodox.

Lord Jesus, be merciful to us sinners; through faith in You—died, yet resurrected for us—help our souls to enter the blessedness of Your kingdom! To You be glory and praise forever! God bless you! Amen.

SERMONS
ON SAINTS' FEASTS

ON THE FEAST OF THE SYNAXIS OF ST. JOHN THE BAPTIST

Sermon at the Divine Liturgy in the church
of the Birth of St. John the Baptist, on January 20/7, 1995,
at the Central Cemetery in Belgrade

"The next day John seeth Jesus coming unto him, and saith, 'Behold the Lamb of God, which taketh away the sin of the world. This is he of whom I said, "After me cometh a man which is preferred before me: for he was before me. And I knew him not: but that he should be made manifest to Israel, therefore am I come baptizing with water."' And John bare record, saying, 'I saw the Spirit descending from heaven like a dove, and it abode upon him. And I knew him not: but he that sent me to baptize with water, the same said unto me, "Upon whom thou shalt see the Spirit descending, and remaining on him, the same is he which baptizeth with the Holy Spirit." And I saw, and bear witness that this is the Son of God.'"

John 1:29-34

St. John the Baptist, brothers and sisters, is celebrated the day after Theophany, because it was so determined in the Church of Christ—that on the great feasts of the Lord and the Mother of God, the first day we celebrate the main person and the second day, the person second in importance who participated in that event. Hence, the main person in yesterday's Theophany is the Lord Jesus, Who in His thirtieth year came to the Jordan and was baptized, and then began His ministry. The second person who participated in this event was, of course, St. John the Baptist, and we celebrate him today, that is, we celebrate his synaxis (assembly).

It is needful always to mention, brothers and sisters, to ourselves and to all others who want to listen and hear, that every man comes into this world in his own time. God sends him in his own time to perform those tasks that, in his time, are laid out before him. Performing these tasks with the best of will and the best of strength, and so fulfilling the will of God, we realize the meaning and purpose of our life. Therefore, whether we will accomplish what God had in mind when He sent us out in our own time, or we will live in opposition to that purpose—this fact determines whether we will be human or inhuman, whether we will be great before God, people, and ourselves, or we will be worthless.

At the annunciation of the Archangel Gabriel to the father of St. John the Baptist, the priest Zacharias, the Holy Archangel, acting on the order from God, notified Zacharias that his wife Elizabeth would give birth to a son, and that he should name him John. And the Archangel said,

> "[A]nd many shall rejoice at his birth. For he shall be great in the sight of the Lord, and shall drink neither wine nor strong drink; and he shall be filled with the Holy Spirit, even from his mother's womb. And many of the children of Israel shall he turn to the Lord their God. And he shall go before him in the spirit and power of Elias, to turn the hearts of the fathers to the children, and the disobedient to the wisdom of the just; to make ready a people prepared for the Lord" (Luke 1:13-17).

There is the entire program of the life of St. John the Baptist, the way the Lord, having created him, sent him into this world to fulfill his tasks. And we know that St. John the Baptist fulfilled what God had intended for him. He lived in the desert, unknown to people, but as you heard from the Gospel, here the Lord told him to go to the Jordan to baptize. And he fulfilled this duty. Moreover, he was told, "Upon whom thou shalt see the Spirit descending, and remaining on him, the same is he which baptizeth with the Holy Spirit" (John 1:33). And St. John testifies, "...And I saw, and bear witness that this is the Son of God."

How few words, how modest the words that St. John spoke about himself and his mission! And how fearless was he to defend the truth of God before Herod and all the mighty ones of this world! Also, you know that he laid down his life for this truth of God.

I repeat both to myself and to you, we were also sent by God in our own time and put to tasks that each of us is to accomplish, in our families, and in society, in the Church, and with all mankind. I say this again, whether we will perform these tasks with the best of the strength that God has given us, and the best of will—that depends on us. We often make up excuses for ourselves: had we been born in a happier and better time, we would have been better, too. That is just an excuse! When He placed us in this time, God gave us the powers that we need, in addition to the help of His grace, to endure, to resist, and to accomplish our tasks. If we waste our powers on worthless things, we will not have any left for what matters the most! And besides, living in a manner opposite to what God commands, subsequently we will not want to follow His way. So, we will go in the opposite direction and deserve eternal torments. Either the blessedness of the heavenly kingdom — "What eye hath not seen, nor ear heard, neither have entered into the heart of man, the things which God hath prepared for them that love him" (1 Cor. 2:9), or the eternal torment, "Where their worm dieth not, and the fire is not quenched" (Mark 9:44).

Praying to St. John today, and always, and to his and our Lord, we pray, brothers and sisters, that we who today represent the Serbian people and the Orthodox faith, may know what we are doing at all times. Likewise, that we may use the powers that God has given us for our good, and the good of our nation, even for the benefit of our enemies, that they too may see the path they should walk, and the goal they should reach, to repent and be saved. God bless you!

ON THE FEAST OF THE SYNAXIS OF ST. JOHN THE BAPTIST—SECOND SERMON

Sermon at the Divine Liturgy held on January 20/7, 1996, in the church of the Birth of St. John the Baptist at the Central Cemetery in Belgrade

We see, brothers and sisters, from the Gospel reading (John 1:29-34), the greatness of St. John the Baptist, whom God sent as His angel to witness and to indicate the coming of the Son of God. We also see how St. John carried out his mission regardless of all the difficulties and dangers; you know that he even laid his life down for the word of God, to be a steadfast witness of this word, and of the truth and justice of God.

For 400 years, there were no prophets in the Hebrew nation, from the Prophet Malachi up until the appearance of St. John the Baptist. And then, when he began baptizing in the Jordan, people all started flocking to him. They all thought he was the savior, the anointed one of God, *Christos* in Greek, in Hebrew—the Messiah. However, here he clearly and openly speaks, and above all witnesses:

> "Behold the Lamb of God, which taketh away the sin of the world. This is he of whom I said, 'After me cometh a man which is preferred before me: for he was before me. And I knew him not: but that he should be made manifest to Israel, therefore am I come baptizing with water.' And he said, 'I saw the Spirit descending from heaven like a dove, and it abode upon him. And I saw, and bear witness that this is the Son of God.'" (John 1:29-34)

St. John is, according to the word of the Lord, the greatest born of woman. His greatness is in that he is a prophet of God, that he is the bond between the New and the Old Testaments. He was still an Old Testament prophet, because the Lord had not yet suffered and resurrected, and He had not yet completely established His Church. However, here John with his own hand points to the Lamb of God Who takes upon Himself the sins of the world, that is, he points to the Lord Jesus, and he places his hand on Him at His baptism in the Jordan—not because the Lord needs John's baptism, but as He Himself says, "to fulfill all righteousness" (Matt. 3:15). Indeed, considering his birth, and his miraculous conception by childless, aged parents, his strict ascetic life, and his mission to baptize people and even the Lord Himself; finally, considering his death for the truth, and for the Kingdom of Heaven, St. John truly was the greatest born of woman.

May the Lord Jesus and His Forerunner and Baptizer St. John, also our St. John, help all of us to be worthy of the name we carry, the Christian name, the name of Orthodox Serbs. To all who celebrate St. John as their family patron Saint—*krsna slava*—blessings and help in all that is holy and honorable! God bless you!

SERMON AT THE VIGIL ON THE EVE OF ST. SAVA

Sermon at the festal vigil on January 26/13, 1996, in the chapel of St. John the Theologian, in the new building of the Faculty of Orthodox Theology in Belgrade

I offer my congratulations to the esteemed Dean, and the professors, to all students, and to all you brothers and sisters, on the occasion of the feast of St. Sava, our first archbishop and enlightener, whom we should always keep in our thoughts, emulating him and the way he elevated his soul, and earned the heavenly kingdom with the holiness of his life. For this reason, he was able to accomplish all those great and glorious things, both for the earthly and the heavenly kingdom.

However, in the present time of misfortune that has befallen us, our nation and others, the act of our St. Sava, his act of peacemaking, is the greatest. He reconciled his brothers; he made peace between our country and others. It was in the service of peace that he went to Jerusalem, too, to the East, to gain approval from all other eastern patriarchs for the newly-restored Bulgarian Patriarchate. Then he hurried to relay this joyous news to the Bulgarian church and people. In spite of winter, he arrived there, but there he also departed from this life.

Looking up to him who was able to abandon all glories of this world, riches and power, and to dedicate his life to God and his neighbors—this should be the program of our life both now and always: to serve God out of love for God, and to serve one's nation out of love for it. This is the means to acquire greatness, that is, by serving. And he, as so many Saints from our nation, acquired that precisely—holiness; meaning, a benefit for his nation and for all the people of goodwill in the world.

We pray to him to help us to endure as the people of God, and when we come before him, not to be ashamed because our deeds that are not the ones he, and his and our Lord, expect. I congratulate you on the occasion of your patronal feast of St. Sava, and I pray to him to help us to fulfill the meaning and purpose of our life, which is the heavenly kingdom, and the blessedness of that kingdom. May we all find ourselves there together as we are now. God bless you!

ON THE FEAST OF ST. SAVA

Sermon at the Divine Liturgy on January 27/14, 1995, in the cathedral church in Belgrade

> "I am the door: by me if any man enter in, he shall be saved, and shall go in and out, and find pasture. The thief cometh not, but for to steal, and to kill, and to destroy: I am come that they might have life, and that they might have it more abundantly. I am the good shepherd: the good shepherd giveth his life for the sheep. But he that is an hireling, and not the shepherd, whose own the sheep are not, seeth the wolf coming, and leaveth the sheep, and fleeth: and the wolf catcheth them, and scattereth the sheep. The hireling fleeth, because he is an hireling, and careth not for the sheep. I am the good shepherd, and know my sheep, and am known of mine. As the Father knoweth me, even so know I the Father: and I lay down my life for the sheep. And other sheep I have, which are not of this fold: them also I must bring, and they shall hear my voice; and there shall be one fold, and one shepherd."
>
> John 10:9-16

I congratulate you on the occasion of today's feast day, and I pray together with you to St. Sava, and to his and our Creator and Maker. We pray, before and above all, to his and our Lord and all the Saints, and to him as the peacemaker who reconciled his brothers, and brought peace to other nations as well, to send much needed peace to us and to all who are afflicted by the misfortunes of this war. And, as the Church prescribed, I ask you, brothers and sisters, to spend this day in fasting. Let us spend these upcoming days, until Saturday, February 4th, in humility, fasting, and prayer to God. May He look upon us and all those who are suffering, for we are all sufferers.

The Lord and His Saints will always be with us, brothers and sisters, if we remain with them in everything that is holy, honorable, and well-pleasing to our merciful God.

As we pray to God daily, let us thus beseech Him to look upon us and our enemies, and to touch the hearts of us all in repentance, in reason, that all this bloodshed may cease; then, let everyone discuss in peace all those issues that had always existed among people and among nations. And, as one of the people with an understanding of these matters has said, it does not matter whether this democratic discussion in peace will last for one day or for five years. It is important that the bloodshed ceases, and for all this misfortune to end.

Therefore I beseech you, brothers and sisters, to spend these days in fasting and prayer, praying to God for peace and blessings. I congratulate you on the occasion of today's feast, and I wish both for you and myself, and for all people of goodwill, every good thing from the Lord.

ON THE FEAST OF ST. SAVA — SECOND SERMON

Sermon at the Divine Liturgy on January 27/14, 1996, in the church of the Birth of the Mother of God in Zemun

I wish you a happy feast today of the first Serbian enlightener and Saint, St. Sava. I congratulate the children especially, the students who look up to St. Sava. He is the protector and founder of all our schools, teachings about God, teachings that we are human, and that we should remain human and the people of God; that we are bodies, too, that we are earthly, but that we are heavenly as well, and that we are souls.

This is what sustained our ancestors in slavery, and after being freed from slavery, up until the present day; to take care of the body as much as it is needed, and to take care of the soul as much as it needs care. In a word, to serve God out of love for Him, and out of love for our people, to serve them, and our families, and all people of goodwill. By serving God and our neighbor, one acquires greatness before God.

This is the message and the teaching of St. Sava: to know our faith, but to also live by it, because this is the teaching of our Lord Jesus. That is the precise message of St. Sava. It is not enough to live honorably; one should have the true and holy faith; both one and the other. This is what is needful always, and especially in this time.

May St. Sava help us brothers and sisters, to live in unity and love! He reconciled his brothers, and made peace between the surrounding nations; likewise, for peace and the welfare of his neighbor, he laid down his life in Bulgaria. He was on a trip to obtain acceptance from all other patriarchates in the East for the newly-restored Bulgarian Patriarchate. As he was hurrying to notify the Bulgarian church of his success in this endeavor, he died in Bulgaria, as you know. It was out of love for his neighbor, his brothers, for his nation and other nations. God bless you, and may the blessing of St. Sava be with you always!

ON THE FEAST OF THE THREE HOLY HIERARCHS

Sermon at the Divine Liturgy
on February 12/January 30, 1996,
in St. Mark's church in Belgrade

"Ye are the light of the world. A city that is set on an hill cannot be hid. Neither do men light a candle, and put it under a bushel, but on a candlestick; and it giveth light unto all that are in the house. Let your light so shine before men, that they may see your good works, and glorify your Father which is in heaven. Think not that I am come to destroy the law, or the prophets: I am not come to destroy, but to fulfil. For verily I say unto you, Till heaven and earth pass, one jot or one tittle shall in no wise pass from the law, till all be fulfilled. Whosoever therefore shall break one of these least commandments, and shall teach men so, he shall be called the least in the kingdom of heaven: but whosoever shall do and teach them, the same shall be called great in the kingdom of heaven."

Matt. 5:14-19

In the name of the Father, and the Son, and the Holy Spirit! Having prayed, brothers and sisters, in this holy temple on the feast of the holy, great Orthodox Saints and teachers, St. Basil the Great, St. Gregory the Theologian, and St. John Chrysostom, I wish you help from them in all that is holy, honorable, and well-pleasing to our merciful God. Especially today, I congratulate, and offer best wishes from the holy Orthodox hierarchs, to the Society of Metalworkers in Belgrade, who celebrate this day as the patronal feast of their guild.

All three are great luminaries of the Orthodox Church, both in teaching and in fighting the heretics for the Orthodox truth, and in their holy lives according to the Gospel of the Lord Jesus. We should always keep in mind that our faith was founded so that we could know it, but to know it in order to live by it in this world. Nothing bears greater witness to the Lord and to His evangelical teaching than the holy evangelical life of all believing Orthodox Christians. St. Basil the Great cautions and teaches us, "What distinguishes a good man from a bad one," he says, is this: "A good man puts to good use everything that God has given him, and by which He designated him for good things. A bad or sinful man is the one who turns to evil that which God has given him to use for good."

Furthermore, the Saints instruct us by the teaching of the Lord, and by the example of the Lord Jesus, that our every labor should be honorable; likewise, that we should know that no work, even the filthiest one, stains us in a spiritual, moral sense. What does defile us, and makes us unclean before God, are our deeds. This teaching of the Lord is confirmed by the Three Holy Hierarchs, and by the example of Him Who as a carpenter up until His thirtieth year had worked with His own hands. This is also confirmed by the Holy Apostle Paul, and is reflected in the life of all the Saints. St. Gregory the Theologian writes about himself and St. Basil, "I still have on my hands the traces of our work, when we were clearing the rocks in the garden in Cappadocia, and when we were pushing the cart." Those luminaries of the Orthodox Church did not shy away from any honorable work. We should always have this before our eyes! Thus, as Christians, we should be witnesses of the evangelical teaching, by our words, and our honorable life, striving to provide for ourselves with our efforts and labor, both intellectual and physical.

Therefore, I congratulate all of you on the occasion of today's feast, and especially the Society of Metalworkers in Belgrade on their patronal feast of the Three Holy Hierarchs, and I pray to the Lord that these Saints be role models, both to them and to all of you, in all that is holy and honorable, and that they grant us help so that we, too, may reach the heavenly kingdom, in which they reign with the Lord and all the Saints. God bless you and grant you all that is good!

ON THE HOLY UNMERCENARIES CYRUS AND JOHN

Sermon at the Divine Liturgy on February 13/January 31, 1996, in the patriarchal chapel of St. Simeon the Myrrh-Gusher in Belgrade

> "And when he had called unto him his twelve disciples, he gave them power against unclean spirits, to cast them out, and to heal all manner of sickness and all manner of disease.
>
> Now the names of the twelve apostles are these; The first, Simon, who is called Peter, and Andrew his brother; James the son of Zebedee, and John his brother; Philip, and Bartholomew; Thomas, and Matthew the publican; James the son of Alphaeus, and Lebbaeus, whose surname was Thaddaeus; Simon the Canaanite, and Judas Iscariot, who also betrayed him. These twelve Jesus sent forth, and commanded them, saying, 'Go not into the way of the Gentiles, and into any city of the Samaritans enter ye not: But go rather to the lost sheep of the house of Israel. And as ye go, preach, saying, "The kingdom of heaven is at hand." Heal the sick, cleanse the lepers, raise the dead, cast out devils: freely ye have received, freely give.'"
>
> Matt. 10:1-8

Today we celebrate the Holy Unmercenaries Cyrus and John, doctors who were unmercenary; they did not heal people for money, but in order to help them, and God then found a way for them to sustain themselves—the faithful supported them.

This urge to do good to our neighbors, to serve one's neighbor, has been present in the Church since the Lord's words, "by serving one's neighbor one becomes great before God." It is the desire for the loved one to be saved, even the wish and prayer to God for our enemies, that they may be saved, too. This is love toward our enemies: the feeling and knowledge that they are going toward eternal ruin, because they are not aware of it; yet we know it. This sorrow in our heart, that this person will perish and be in eternal torments, prompts us to pray to God, and to do what we can that they may snap out of it, repent before God, change their life, and be saved.

The Apostle Paul urges us as well, "Honor one another above yourselves" (Rom. 12:10). However, vanity within us causes us to condemn our neighbors. We are not forbidden; rather, it is our duty when we see someone doing evil, to likewise recognize that as evil. However, there is also our prayer to God for the man to correct himself; and when our feelings settle down in a few days or months, we should tell this brother that what he was doing was not good. St. Basil the Great exhorts us, "Do not be a fratricide on account of false brotherly love." By not doing what you can, not warning him in a peaceful way, you will in this manner help him to lose his soul.

However, when we condemn our brother, we do not exalt ourselves with actual effort to be lifted up, morally and spiritually; rather, we push him down, so that the distance between us is to his detriment, and so that we can appear in the eyes of the world as higher and better than him; just like that Pharisee, from the Gospel reading a couple of Sundays ago, who lauded himself, "I am not like other people; I do more than You asked of me" (Luke 9:11-12). The Lord Jesus teaches us about this in another place in the book of Revelation, speaking about the angel of the church in Ephesus, "But you have this in your favor: You hate the practices of the Nicolaitans, which I also hate" (Rev. 2:6). He hates these deeds of Nicolaitans; He does not hate either man or sinner. Likewise, we are commanded to love our enemies.

And from the cross He prayed, "Father, forgive them, for they know not what they do" (Luke 23:34). Therefore, we should strive and know that we will give answer before God for every empty word, let alone for sinful words. We should condemn sin, evil, for if we do not internally discern that it is evil, how will we ourselves abstain from it? However, let us not condemn our neighbor, but feel sorry for him that he will perish if he does not repent; and let us pray to God that he may be saved, too; this means, read "Rejoice, O Virgin Theotokos," or the "Our Father" for him, and pray to God for his salvation, but refrain from condemning your brother. God bless you!

ON THE HOLY MARTYR TRYPHON

Sermon at the Divine Liturgy on February 14/1, 1996,
in the church dedicated to this Saint,
at the cemetery in Topchider, in Belgrade

"He that heareth you heareth me; and he that despiseth you despiseth me; and he that despiseth me despiseth him that sent me. And the seventy returned again with joy, saying, 'Lord, even the devils are subject unto us through thy name.' And he said unto them, 'I beheld Satan as lightning fall from heaven. Behold, I give unto you power to tread on serpents and scorpions, and over all the power of the enemy: and nothing shall by any means hurt you. Notwithstanding in this rejoice not, that the spirits are subject unto you; but rather rejoice, because your names are written in heaven.' In that hour Jesus rejoiced in spirit, and said, 'I thank thee, O Father, Lord of heaven and earth, that thou hast hid these things from the wise and prudent, and hast revealed them unto babes: even so, Father; for so it seemed good in thy sight.'"

Luke 10:16-21

In the name of the Father, and the Son, and the Holy Spirit! We prayed to God today, brothers and sisters, as we should do every day and every hour—to pray to Him for all that we need in this life, that which is needful for our nation, and for all people of goodwill in this world, and that is: peace, unity, and brotherly love, which have been, are, and always will be in short supply in the world.

Nonetheless, how others will act depends on them alone—it is in their hands; but how we act is in our hands. God, as well as our holy ancestors, expect us to always act as the people of God, as people who are aware, who know what they are doing. For there are those who know not what they are doing, according to the word of the Lord that He spoke from the cross about those criminals who were mocking Him under the cross. He prayed, "Father, forgive them, for they know not what they do" (Luke 23:34). Hence, brothers and sisters, let us always be the ones who know what they are doing, and do what we should, likewise acting according to the evangelical teaching. For Christianity is this precisely: the knowledge of the evangelical teaching, the teaching of our Lord Jesus Christ, and living according to that teaching every day, every hour, and every minute.

That is the lesson of today's Holy Martyr Tryphon, who suffered for the Christian faith. He was aware that there is, besides this world, the other timeless world, that besides the body, there is also the immortal soul, and that the body is only a home in which the soul resides. When that home is destroyed, the host remains; the soul remains alive and is immortal. We should keep this in mind at all times, brothers and sisters, and remind ourselves of it, as well as all others who have ears to hear. We should not impose it upon them, but constantly put it out there, if they want to hear it: that we are in this world only temporarily, and that we should not waste all our time and all our energy on that which is transitory, on the things of this world. Rather, we should give the body and the earth as much as belongs to them—no more; equally, we should give the soul and the heavenly kingdom what belongs to them—no less. Likewise, according to the word of the Lord, we should give unto Caesar what is Caesar's, to the authorities what belongs to them, and unto God what belongs to God. Neither more unto Caesar than what is his, nor less unto God than what belongs to Him. That was, and still remains, the teaching of St. Sava as well, and before him, dating to the third century, of St. Tryphon, all the way to the present day.

I congratulate you on the occasion of today's feast and I wish you, from St. Tryphon, all that is holy and honorable; that he may support us in all that is good, so that we may find ourselves in the heavenly kingdom, on the side that the Lord will recognize and acknowledge as His, leading us into the kingdom of blessedness, where there is no sickness, nor sorrow, nor sighing. God bless you and grant you all that is good!

ON ST. SIMEON THE MYRRH-GUSHER

Sermon at the Divine Liturgy on February 26/13, 1995, in the church of St. Sava in Vrachar

> "All things are delivered unto me of my Father: and no man knoweth the Son, but the Father; neither knoweth any man the Father, save the Son, and he to whomsoever the Son will reveal him. Come unto me, all ye that labour and are heavy laden, and I will give you rest. Take my yoke upon you, and learn of me; for I am meek and lowly in heart: and ye shall find rest unto your souls. For my yoke is easy, and my burden is light."
>
> Matt. 11:27-30

In the name of the Father, and the Son, and the Holy Spirit! Today we celebrate, brothers and sisters, St. Simeon the Myrrh-Gusher, Stephan Nemanya, the father of our statehood and our freedom—the one who knew throughout his life to glorify God, and to do good for his people. How many difficulties and battles he endured! And when the Byzantines defeated him and his army, he was willing to go before the Byzantine emperor with a rope around his neck, but also, being freed, to fight for freedom once again. Furthermore, at the end of his life he handed over power to his younger son, making sure it would be well-established during his lifetime, and under his supervision, so to speak—that the Serbian state would be well-established. Then he became a monk, going to Mount Athos, to his son Sava, in order to build Hilandar together—the monastery that is the foundation of our ecclesiality, our Orthodoxy, our faithfulness to the Gospel. Throughout centuries, a multitude of monks from our nation have submitted themselves to ascetic feats here. It was the highest school of theology wherein many archbishops and bishops prepared to serve God, their Church, and their people. To the present day, Mount Athos is the pillar and the fortress of truth; it is the ladder leading from earth to heaven—the bastion of Orthodoxy.

May the Lord and St. Simeon, St. Sava, and all the Saints, help us, as we defend freedom and our faith, to always be and remain the people of God, as is right and meet. We should always have in mind that we are to come before the face of God, before His judgment, to receive from Him the recognition that we have been and have remained on His path, fulfilling His will, as it should be, and for which purpose He created us. Let us have this before our spiritual eyes at all times, to truly be worthy both of our ancestors and of our Orthodox name.

Blessed and happy patronal feast—*slava*—to the Singing Society, to all its members, and to all of you, brothers and sisters. God bless you, and grant you every good thing!

ON ST. SIMEON THE MYRRH-GUSHER SECOND SERMON

Sermon at the Divine Liturgy
in the patriarchal chapel, on February 26/13, 1996

I congratulate you, brothers and sisters, on the occasion of the patronal feast of this holy temple, praying to God, to His and our St. Simeon the Myrrh-gusher, and to all the Saints headed by St. Sava, all the Saints from our nation—that they help us to be and to remain the people of God, for which purpose God created us, because He wants all people to be saved and to come to the knowledge of truth. Therefore, in this time, difficult as it is, let us be witnesses of the Son of God, of the faith in Him, and of the strength of our faith. Let us endure everything, even the temptations that befall us so profusely in this time!

I also congratulate all the societies who celebrate St. Simeon and Stephan Nemanya as their patron. God bless you, and grant you every good thing!

ON ST. SIMEON THE MYRRH-GUSHER
THIRD SERMON

Sermon given in 1995

We have gathered, brothers and sisters, on this feast of the resurrection of our Lord, and the feast day of our father, and the father of our statehood, our freedom, and our Orthodoxy—St. Simeon the Myrrh-gusher, Stephan Nemanya.

He is certainly someone to celebrate, because St. Stephan Nemanya, St. Simeon the Myrrh-gusher, by his life and works truly celebrated the One we also celebrate today; in the end, he dedicated his life, his last days, to Him in a monastery. Indeed, he is the father of our statehood, and the father of the unity of our people. His life according to the Gospel, and according to God, was such that this teaching, both in words and in life, and in his deeds, was felt in the depths of the soul of his youngest son, St. Sava. For this reason, being thus brought up in the home of his parents, Sava could dedicate his whole self and all his strength to God and his people.

Praying to God today, in this time that is so difficult for all our people, for our statehood and unity, we turn to St. Simeon the Myrrh-gusher for help, asking that he pray for us before the throne of God, so that we may endure all hardships as the people of God, in unity and accord, in Orthodoxy—in all to which he had dedicated his life. Thus, that we may be worthy descendants of our holy ancestors, by praying to God, to other Saints from our nation, and to all other Saints in the Orthodox Church.

In all the centuries that our people have been present in the Balkans, they have had many struggles and difficulties. How much strife and internal battles with our own people, as well as externally with enemies! Our people endured everything through their Orthodox faith, knowing that sufferings are unavoidable on the path of God, but also that one should endure these sufferings until the end in order to enter the Kingdom of Heaven, and so that we do not have to lower our head in shame before our ancestors. We have the same duty today: to do whatever is necessary and possible, by our faith and our life according to that faith, so that we and our enemies would obtain peace—for we all need it so much, although they are not even aware of it, and know not what they do. We should remain the people of God, on the path that our ancestors have walked, so that we may find ourselves with them in the heavenly kingdom.

Let us pray therefore, today and always, to St. Simeon and St. Sava, our spiritual father, that they support and sustain us on the path of God, and grant much needed peace to us and to others in these misfortunes that have befallen us.

Merciful Lord! Help everyone, and us as well! St. Simeon, our father, and St. Sava, our spiritual father, help and bless us!

ON THE HOLY GREAT-MARTYR GEORGE

Sermon given on May 6/April 23, 1995

In the name of the Father, and the Son, and the Holy Spirit! We have prayed, brothers and sisters, to the Lord God, One in Holy Trinity, Father, Son and Holy Spirit, and we have offered a bloodless sacrifice of the Body and Blood of Christ. We also prayed, brothers and sisters, to St. George as we celebrate today his feast day and the patronal feast of this temple; for he is the patron of this temple and of many families in our nation, a family patron Saint—*slava*. Praying to God and to His Saints, we ask that they sustain us in these difficult times, so that we may truly be worthy descendants of our ancestors. Both in freedom and in slavery, our ancestors knew how to be and remain a people of God, by fighting for justice and truth, for the honorable cross and golden freedom; they knew how to always endure as humans, preserving their honor and soul; and when one had to give up even one's life and pay the price, they did it without ever giving up their honor and soul.

Even in these misfortunes that have befallen us, through our own fault, but also through the fault of other nations, Europe and America, too, the only thing that remains for us as an actual consolation, and not only consolation, but real help—both to us and to those who are fighting in this war, and dying each day—is this: to truly be the people of God. To preserve ourselves from everything that is evil and sinful, for if we keep away from that, God will be with us, and we will survive as the people of God, regardless of the sacrifices; to preserve harmony, unity, to preserve love both for our brothers in faith and blood, but even the love toward our enemies. They do not see where they are going; they do not see that in their wrongdoing they are plunging into ruin and eternal torment; however, we know it and, mourning the unrepeatable man who through sin is plunging into ruin, we pray to his and our Lord to help him, so that this person, too, may open his eyes, strip away darkness from his eyes, to see where he is going, to repent and be saved as well.

Tomorrow, brothers and sisters, in the temple of St. Sava, in the new great temple, let us pray together at twelve noon, and offer a memorial service. Let us lift up our prayers to God and His Saints, that they may have mercy on us and grant us peace—both to us and our enemies—that this bloodshed may cease, and that as humans we may come to an agreement on the questions that have always existed among people and among nations.

May the Lord and St. George help the brothers of this holy temple and you, brothers and sisters, who celebrate him as your patron Saint; may they help all of us and our entire Orthodox nation. God bless you, and grant you every good thing!

ON THE HOLY APOSTLE AND EVANGELIST MARK

Sermon at the Divine Liturgy
on May 8/April 25, 1995, in Belgrade

The Lord died on the cross out of love for us, out of His endless love, but on the third day He rose again according to His endless divine power. We prayed to Him that He be merciful unto us and our nation, and all people of goodwill in these difficult and unfortunate times, where people are dying every day, for what has been five years already. We prayed to the Holy Evangelist Mark, too, who preached Him, the Son of God, and laid down his life for Him. We prayed that he might intercede before the Lord in the heavenly kingdom where he dwells, that the Lord may have mercy on us.

The Holy Apostle and Evangelist Mark is an apostle in the wider sense; he was not numbered among the twelve, but he had seen the Lord. Thus, in his Gospel, while describing the capture and trial of our Lord, he mentions a young man, at the time when the Lord was captured and all the Apostles had fled—a young man followed after Him. However, the enemies caught him, and since he was only draped with a cloth over his naked body, he left the cloth behind, and ran away naked; that moment, in the entire history of the capture and trial of our Lord, has no other significance for anyone else, but himself. Surely, the young man was he himself. He wrote the Gospel in Rome prompted by the Christians, and St. Peter was also there preaching; he mentions Mark as his beloved son, certainly not according to the body, but in spirit.

In St. Mark's Gospel, which he wrote, I said, especially as related to him by the Holy Apostle Peter, he cites a detail, which is not mentioned in the other Gospels. Namely, that the Lord told Peter, when he said he would not renounce Him, "Verily I say unto thee, That this day, even in this night, before the rooster crow twice, thou shalt deny me thrice" (Mark 14:30). Certainly, the Holy Apostle Peter, the one to whom these words were addressed, heard and remembered it better than the rest of the Apostles; however, for us it is important that he cites that detail "even before the rooster crows twice, you will deny me three times." Likewise, in the Gospel of Mark, it says that Peter denied Christ when a servant woman told him he was among those people who were the followers of Christ, and he denied it saying that he wasn't. St. Mark writes, "And he went out into the entryway; and the rooster crowed;" and another one said, "'Surely thou art one of them: for thou art a Galilaean, and thy speech agreeth thereto.' But he began to curse and to swear, saying, 'I know not this man of whom ye speak'" (Mark 14:70-71). A servant girl also said that he had been with them as well, and he denied it the third time. He does not keep it a secret that he should have gathered the strength, when the rooster crowed the first time, to remember the words of Christ, and to not to deny Him anymore.

This is a lesson for us and for everyone—that under no condition should we strive to falsely present ourselves as better than we are, but to always be with the truth, because the Truth is God. "I am the Truth," the Lord says (John 14:6). He is also Justice; He is Love as well. When we are with the truth, justice, and love, with all that is good, we are with God. May we never wish to justify ourselves, neither with a lie, nor with untruth, because one cannot justify oneself before God with these. However, to do this before the people and the world is pointless. The energy that others use to present themselves as better, we should use to truly be better ourselves. Only then will we raise ourselves up before God, and we will stand upright when we come before our holy ancestors.

Let us double and triple our prayers, brothers and sisters, to the God of peace that He may send peace to our country, and alleviate the suffering of those who struggle in Slavonia. May the Lord also receive in His heavenly kingdom those who died through no fault of their own, only because they believed that the international community, which was a guarantor of their position, would resolve everything in peace—and here we see what came about because of the criminals. We should always strive to be the way God wants us to be; then He will listen to our prayers and our pleas, and grant unto us what we need.

I congratulate the brotherhood of this holy temple, all the parishioners, and you, brothers and sisters, on the occasion of today's feast of the Holy Apostle and Evangelist Mark, I wish us all that his and our Lord may have mercy on us in these misfortunes, and help us. God bless you, and grant you every good thing!

ON THE HOLY APOSTLE AND EVANGELIST MARK—SECOND SERMON

Sermon at the Divine Liturgy on May 8/April 25, 1996, in St. Mark's church in Belgrade

Today we celebrate the feast of the Holy Apostle and Evangelist Mark, one of the four Holy Evangelists, who wrote his Gospel according to the preaching of the Holy Apostle Peter. Nonetheless, living at that time, St. Mark was also an eyewitness of the Lord Jesus; he knew Him, and listened to His teaching.

There is an episode in his Gospel, when they captured the Lord Jesus Christ, and then they caught a young man whose body was wrapped in a cloak only; then he left that cloak behind and ran away. This event, this episode, has no greater significance for our understanding of the suffering of our Lord Jesus, but it is important to the Apostle Mark the Evangelist, because he was that young man. Apart from that, he was the son of a widow in Jerusalem, and the nephew of the Holy Apostle Barnabas. With the Holy Apostles Peter and Barnabas, he went to preach the Gospel in Cyprus; thus, he took part in the spreading of the Gospel of Christ.

Our faith, brothers and sisters, is not merely a philosophical teaching and presentation of things. Our faith rests on the actual experience of the first witnesses of our Lord Jesus. The Holy Apostle Peter says, "For we have not followed cunningly devised fables, when we made known unto you the power and coming of our Lord Jesus Christ, but were eyewitnesses of his majesty" (2 Pet. 1:16). This same thing is spoken of by the Holy Evangelist John, that our faith is founded on the testimony of those who have seen and touched, just like the Holy Apostle Thomas, the resurrected Lord Jesus. "What our eyes have seen, what our hands have touched, this we announced to you as well" (1 John 1:1). This means that our faith is the faith that lasts until the present day, by which our ancestors lived, with the firm belief that the Lord is risen, and that He is alive in the heavenly kingdom; moreover, that we will come before Him as the Righteous Judge, to receive our pay from Him according to how we have deserved it in this world. This faith is expressed in words, but also in the way one lives. By this faith let us bear witness in this world of the evangelical teaching of our Lord Jesus, and thus sanctify our souls, and the soul and honor of our nation, so that when the time comes to stand before God, before His and our Holy Evangelist Mark, and our holy ancestors, that they would recognize us as their faithful servants.

I congratulate the brotherhood, the priests of this holy temple, and the parishes attached to this church, on the occasion of [the feast of] their temple's patron Saint, I wish you all the help and blessing of St. Mark, that we may truly be worthy of the Christian name we carry. God bless you, and grant you every good thing!

ON SAINT BASIL OF OSTROG

Sermon at the Divine Liturgy on May 12/April 29, 1997,
in the church of Sts. Constantine and Helen,
where the omophorion of St. Basil is kept

"And he came down with them, and stood in the plain, and the company of his disciples, and a great multitude of people out of all Judaea and Jerusalem, and from the sea coast of Tyre and Sidon, which came to hear him, and to be healed of their diseases; And they that were vexed with unclean spirits: and they were healed. And the whole multitude sought to touch him: for there went virtue out of him, and healed them all. And he lifted up his eyes on his disciples, and said, 'Blessed be ye poor: for yours is the kingdom of God. Blessed are ye that hunger now: for ye shall be filled. Blessed are ye that weep now: for ye shall laugh. Blessed are ye, when men shall hate you, and when they shall separate you from their company, and shall reproach you, and cast out your name as evil, for the Son of man's sake. Rejoice ye in that day, and leap for joy: for, behold, your reward is great in heaven: for in the like manner did their fathers unto the prophets.'"

Luke 6:17-23

In the name of the Father, and the Son, and the Holy Spirit! We have prayed to God on this holy day of the celebration of our Holy Father Basil of Ostrog, the Miracle-Worker, and on the day when we celebrate the resurrection of the Son of God. This faith in the Son of God Who died for our sake, but also resurrected by His divine power, has always given strength to all the Saints—holy martyrs, and holy men, women, and children—to endure all temptations in this world, even death, not fearing anyone or anything except God, knowing that even death for Christ means life. For He said, "Whosoever listens to my word and believes in Him who sent Me will not come under judgment, but has crossed over from death to life" (*cf. John 5:24*—T.N.).

Brothers and sisters, this [truth] was known by those of our forefathers, fathers, sisters, and children, who in the Second World War were thrown into the pits, and died in them; this [truth] was known by those in concentration camps, in Yasenovats and others; it is also known by those in this unfortunate, civil war—and every war is a misfortune, of course, because God does not want war, and for people to die; Cain always attacks, and Abel has to defend himself. These people knew that, and they were defending their freedom, their homes, and their faith, for it is this faith that gives us the strength, too, to endure on the path of God. We must never forget that the Orthodox faith means not only a teaching, but something we live, conduct ourselves, and act by each day.

St. Basil also lived in a difficult time of Turkish slavery, but he kept his love for God, and love for his neighbors, and for his flock, enduring various torments and sufferings; thus, God glorified him, because he had glorified God. For this reason, we celebrate him today as the one whom God has celebrated. Likewise, we celebrate him with a prayer that he help us in these times to endure as is meet and right, as Orthodox Serbs, as Orthodox Christians. For, I say, he knows the struggles and misfortunes of slavery, and the difficulties of war; he is great before God and able to help us. Nonetheless, I repeat to you, and to myself as well, brothers and sisters, God is always ahead of us, behind us, and on every side; He is always ready to help us; if we listen to Him, He will also listen to us. We must never forget this, nor take as our role models criminals, who think they can use crime to benefit their people, their family, or their faith. Others can think and act in this manner, but we—Orthodox Christians, Orthodox Serbs—must not do this. One should defend oneself from evil, and from criminals, but defend oneself in a manner becoming to Orthodox Serbs, with humanity and valor, which our people, through the mouth of Marko Miljanov, have expressed as their faith and their conviction.

May the Lord, His and our St. Basil and St. Sava, and all the Saints from our nation, help us to endure as it becomes the descendants of such ancestors. Not to follow after criminals and that which is evil! Do not envy an evil man!—it says so in Holy Scripture (Ps. 37:1; Prov. 24:19). For, we are to come before the judgment of God, where no one will be able to justify himself by crime, nor by untruth, nor by injustice, but only by truth, because God is the Truth, only by justice, because God is Justice, only by that which is holy and honorable, because all that is holy and honorable comes from God.

Our Holy Father Basil of Ostrog, to you we pray, look upon us, your distant spiritual descendants, sustain us in these unfortunate and difficult times to be and remain the people of God, both now and always! Amen. God bless you!

ON THE TRANSLATION OF THE RELICS OF ST. NICHOLAS OF MYRA IN LYCIA

Sermon at the Divine Liturgy on May 22/9, 1996, in the church of St. Nicholas in Zemun

We prayed to God, brothers and sisters, One in the Holy Trinity, Father, Son, and Holy Spirit, and we prayed to His, God's Saint and our Father, St. Nicholas the Wonderworker, the bishop of Myra in Lycia, the Holy Father who is celebrated in the entire Orthodox world today, and will continue to be celebrated until the end of the world. For holy are those men and women, our sisters and brothers, who strove to live in this world according to the will of God and according to His commandments; thus they sanctified their souls and their bodies. Likewise, God has glorified them, because they had glorified Him with their whole lives.

St. Nicholas was a son of rich parents. His uncle was the bishop of that city, and St. Nicholas became a monk at an early age. When his parents passed away, he distributed his entire estate to the poor, and he himself lived a monastic life, in poverty, striving to give his body what was due to it, and as much as it actually needed to survive, and to give to his soul no less than what it needed, feeding it with holy words, with his faith, and holy deeds according to that faith. He became bishop of Myra in Lycia in a miraculous way. When the time came to choose the new bishop, the new hierarch, as it always is among people, they were considering whom they would pick. Then the Lord appeared to one of them, a local priest of that time, and said, "The one who first enters the church tomorrow should be chosen to be the bishop." St. Nicholas always came to church early, rising early to God's service, to pray to God for all the people, and for all living and deceased. And when he came to the church, and when that priest asked him what his name was, he said, "Nicholas, humble Nicholas, father." And God had said that the priest who should be chosen would be called Nicholas.

Throughout his whole life, St. Nicholas was merciful. How much he helped the poor by giving in such a way that the left hand would not know what the right one was giving! He boldly stood up for those who, not fearing for their lives, were unjustly before God condemned by the powerful ones of this world. Although he never wrote any books, his life, and his deeds, are the best book that is read in the Church of God, and that is seen by and known to all those who have ears to hear, and who are willing, that is, who have eyes to see. St. Nicholas is in many aspects tied to our own history as well. He appeared in the Sheep's Field to St. Stephan of Dechani, after the latter had been blinded, and showed him his eyes on the palm of his hand; he told him not to despair, and that he would return them to him when the time came. And so it was. St. Nicholas gave him back his sight, and St. Stephan became the king after the death of his father Milutin.

Brothers and sisters, let us today and always consider the lesson in the lives of all the Saints who glorified God with their faith and their deeds, for which reason God glorified them, too, in this world, and in the other, eternal one. Let that be our life's path, and the purpose of our life. Our life here on earth will pass, but the life of the soul never passes. It will be either in blessedness and eternal joy, or in eternal torment, according to what we deserve.

We pray to the Lord, and to his and our Holy Father Nicholas, to help us who today represent the Serbian people and the Orthodox faith, so that we may live up to the tasks of the present time, the way our ancestors did, in good and evil, in freedom as well as in battles and slavery, in all circumstances, favorable and unfavorable. May we find ourselves together like this on the other side, in the heavenly kingdom, where St. Nicholas and all the Saints from our nation will be.

On the occasion of the patronal feast of this holy temple, I congratulate the priests and parishioners, and all of you, brothers and sisters, and all the people who celebrate the Holy Father Nicholas. I wish you every true good and blessing from the Lord and St. Nicholas. God bless you! Christ is Risen!

ON THE HOLY MARTYR CHRISTOPHER

Sermon at the Divine Liturgy on the
Sunday of the Holy Fathers, May 23/16, 1996,
in the ruins of the temple dedicated
to St. Christopher, in Barich

"...The words that I speak unto you I speak not of myself: but the Father that dwelleth in me, he doeth the works. Believe me that I am in the Father, and the Father in me: or else believe me for the very works' sake. Verily, verily, I say unto you, He that believeth on me, the works that I do shall he do also; and greater works than these shall he do; because I go unto my Father. And whatsoever ye shall ask in my name, that will I do, that the Father may be glorified in the Son. If ye shall ask any thing in my name, I will do it. If ye love me, keep my commandments. And I will pray the Father, and he shall give you another Comforter, that he may abide with you for ever; Even the Spirit of truth; whom the world cannot receive, because it seeth him not, neither knoweth him: but ye know him; for he dwelleth with you, and shall be in you. I will not leave you comfortless: I will come to you. Yet a little while, and the world seeth me no more; but ye see me: because I live, ye shall live also. At that day ye shall know that I am in my Father, and ye in me, and I in you. He that hath my commandments, and keepeth them, he it is that loveth me: and he that loveth me shall be loved of my Father, and I will love him, and will manifest myself to him. Judas saith unto him, not Iscariot, 'Lord, how is it that thou wilt manifest thyself unto us, and not unto the world?' Jesus answered and said unto him, 'If a man love me, he will keep my words: and He that loveth me not keepeth not my sayings: and the word which ye hear is not mine, but the Father's which sent me. These things have I spoken unto you, being yet present with you. But the Comforter, which is the

Holy Spirit, whom the Father will send in my name, he shall teach you all things, and bring all things to your remembrance, whatsoever I have said unto you. Peace I leave with you, my peace I give unto you: not as the world giveth, give I unto you. Let not your heart be troubled, neither let it be afraid.'"

John 14:10-27

In the name of the Father, and the Son, and the Holy Spirit! We have prayed, brothers and sisters, today, on this holy Sunday, the day of the resurrection of our Lord Jesus, which is the basis for the resurrectional aspect of Sunday liturgy throughout the year. Sunday is the day of the week that commemorates His resurrection; and the resurrection of the Son of God after His suffering and death on the cross is the greatest event in the act of our salvation. For the Holy Apostle Paul says, "And if Christ be not risen, then is our preaching in vain, and your faith is also in vain" (1 Cor. 15:14). Thus, the essence of our faith is in the life, suffering, teaching, and death of our Lord, by which He showed His endless divine power and might. He alone is the One Who through His divine power rose from the dead. There were people who by God's power and might resurrected others, but they could not resurrect themselves. He alone, the Almighty God, God and Man, God-Man, resurrected Himself, and thereby provided a guarantee that all of us, all those who have died until the present day, and until the end of the world, will rise from the dead when He comes into this world again—no more as a sufferer, but as the King and Judge, to give each one according to his or her deeds and merits.

We have prayed, brothers and sisters, in this holy place, the former Monastery of St. Christopher the Martyr to whom our ancestors have prayed throughout the centuries, in this and every other place. St. Christopher's Monastery is mentioned as early as the sixteenth century in the Turkish tax registers, and it is mentioned as an imperial *has* [*asset*—T.N.], that is, the income of this monastery that the abbot and his brotherhood had to pay went straight into the imperial treasury of the sultan. Most likely, the monastery was built even before the coming of the Turks, as early as in the time of the holy king Dragutin, and the income from it went into his royal treasury. In the Turkish times, it was destroyed like so many other churches and monasteries in this area. It was rebuilt, and torn down again, so that today all that is left of it are these ruins. However, St. Christopher, to whom this monastery is dedicated, the Holy Martyr, is alive before the living God, just as all the Saints are alive before the living God.

There are several descriptions of the life of the Holy Martyr Christopher, both in the East and the West. Most likely, he was martyred in the time of Emperor Decius in the third century after Christ, before the [*religious*—T.N.] freedom granted by the Emperor Constantine. He was a man of great strength and stature, a pagan at first; however, when he believed in Christ, he preached Him with all his soul and heart, and lost his life on account of this faith in Him, because he would not renounce Him. According to the Western hagiographies, he was from a pagan people; indeed, being so corpulent and strong, as a soldier he decided to serve only the mightiest, bravest people, so he hired himself out as a soldier to various sovereigns. However, when he saw that they also were scared and afraid, he went to the one who was not frightened. But this emperor, too, was terrified of demons. So Christopher decided to serve that demon, whom everyone dreaded, and he enlisted himself in his terrifying army. Riding one time with this army headed by the main demon, they came upon a crossroad with a cross on it, and the demon was terrified of the cross. Christopher decided to go to the one who terrified even the mightiest demon. So he asked, "Whose sign is that?" They explained to him that it was the sign of Christ. He went to a spiritual elder and told him he was ready and willing to serve this most powerful Emperor Christ; the elder, a monk, explained to him who Christ was, and Christopher vowed to serve Him. The monk told him to serve Christ with prayer, a holy life, and the reading of Holy Scripture. To this Christopher replied, "I am illiterate; I'm not used to that. I can serve Him only with my strength." "Well, then," the monk said, "Here is a river in which several people have drowned. You can carry these people across the river, because you are strong, and thus serve your neighbors in their need. Likewise, you will serve Christ Who gave us this teaching: to serve God out of love for God, and to serve our neighbors." Christopher voluntarily agreed. He made his abode next to the river, and carried people across who needed to get to the other side. One evening, as he lay down to rest, he heard a faint voice calling him by his name. He went out, looked, and did not see anyone. He lay down again. Again he heard the voice, rose once more, and went out. No one was outside. He lay down yet again, and heard it for the third time. He peacefully, without grunting, got up once more and went out, and he saw a child who was pleading to him to carry him across the river. He immediately took him upon his shoulders, and with a cane in his hand went to the river. The waves came, and the child became heavier and heavier; bent over completely, he barely made it across the river. When he stepped on dry ground, and put the child down, he said, "Child, you were heavier to me than anyone I have ever carried across. It seems to me you are heavier than earth itself." And the child replied, "Yes, I am the One Who created the earth and the world, Jesus Christ, the Son of God. I have blessed you, and while you were carrying me across, I baptized you in the river." And the child disappeared. Then St. Christopher began to preach the Son of God, the Creator of heaven and earth, and all things living and non-living in this world. He went to various towns and countries; in Lycia he was captured and taken before the emperor, and when he refused to renounce Christ, the Son of God, the emperor condemned him to death by the sword. And so he laid down his life for Christ, Whom he served both with his strength and his word, with his life and his faith.

A message from the lives of the Saints to all of us, brothers and sisters, is this: to serve our neighbors with all our soul, all our heart, and all our strength, out of love for them. For greatness before God is acquired by serving Him, the Almighty God, and all our neighbors. Hence, let this be our lesson that with our words, and especially our lives, we preach and witness the Orthodox faith in the Son of God, in Whom our ancestors believed, living a holy life and being able and willing to endure five centuries of slavery, yet never to renounce their faith, their soul, and the honor of their nation. In the Turkish times, they knew that if they converted, if they accepted the Turkish, Muslim faith, they would obtain all the rights of that empire, and they would prosper in authority and honors according to their abilities. And how many there are who did convert! But my ancestors and yours, brothers and sisters, knew well what they would gain, and what they would lose. And on their measuring scales, on their balances, they balanced it out and found that they would lose more than they would gain; thus, they were able to endure five hundred and more years as commonalty with no rights, yet never to renounce their honor and faith. This, then, should be our lesson and teaching, for those who are willing. For our Lord Jesus said more than once, "Whosoever wants to follow me, let him take up his cross and follow me… If you want to be perfect…" (Mark 8:34) and in other places. He leaves it up to our will to follow Him, to do what He wishes, what is for our salvation, and for the honor and salvation of our nation; to do what is for the good of the whole world, if we are willing. If we are not willing, we can also do the opposite—what is to our detriment, and that of our nation, and unto evil for the whole world. Nonetheless, we will come before Him, before the righteous Judge, to give an account for all that He has endowed us with: mind, knowledge, will, and freedom. We should keep this in mind at all times! This is the teaching and the lesson of St. Christopher, as well as of St. Sava, our spiritual father, and all the Saints, because that is the teaching of Jesus Christ, the Son of God.

Calling down upon all of you God's grace and the prayers of St. Christopher, I pray to the Lord and His Saint to have mercy upon us, and to sustain us to never renounce the holy and honorable name by which we are called Orthodox Christians, Orthodox Serbs. When we enter the heavenly kingdom, may we find ourselves there together with St. Christopher and all the Saints, including those from our nation. May this day and feast be happy, and God bless you!

ON THE HOLY APOSTLES PETER AND PAUL

Sermon at the Divine Liturgy on July 12/June 29, 1995, in the church of the Holy Apostles Peter and Paul, in Topchider, Belgrade

> "When Jesus came into the coasts of Caesarea Philippi, he asked his disciples, saying, 'Whom do men say that I the Son of man am?' And they said, 'Some say that thou art John the Baptist: some, Elias; and others, Jeremias, or one of the prophets.' He saith unto them, 'But whom say ye that I am?' And Simon Peter answered and said, 'Thou art the Christ, the Son of the living God.' And Jesus answered and said unto him, 'Blessed art thou, Simon Barjona: for flesh and blood hath not revealed it unto thee, but my Father which is in heaven. And I say also unto thee, That thou art Peter, and upon this rock I will build my church; and the gates of hell shall not prevail against it. And I will give unto thee the keys of the kingdom of heaven: and whatsoever thou shalt bind on earth shall be bound in heaven: and whatsoever thou shalt loose on earth shall be loosed in heaven.'"
>
> Matt. 16:13-19

In the name of the Father, and the Son, and the Holy Spirit! We have prayed in this holy temple where our ancestors prayed throughout many years, in good times and evil, in peace and in time of war; they prayed for freedom and the justice of God, always knowing and believing that justice holds up the country and cities and that, if need be that we suffer, we should suffer for the truth and justice of God, for what is human and humane, according to God's justice and God's will. Today as well, in these misfortunes in which our nation finds itself, only this faith can keep us on the path of God, for such are the circumstances and actions of our enemies that they pull even the strong ones to the path of crime, revenge, and injustice. However, looking up to our holy ancestors and keeping the Orthodox Christian faith in every way, we must remain human, the people of God, regardless of how the inhuman enemy would act! This does not mean, of course, not to defend ourselves from evil; still, not to return evil for evil, but to fight with evangelical strength and justice, and then God will be with us, and we will resist anyone and everyone. This—to uphold the justice of God among the unjust—was never easy, let alone in the present times. However, looking up to all the Saints from our nation, who knew how to speak and act, as well as to live, in an evangelical manner, we should also strive to remain on that path through the strength of our ancestors.

Today, brothers and sisters, we have an added joy of praying together to God, and of communing together—for we belong to the same Orthodox faith—with Metropolitan Nicodemus of Ierissos and Mount Athos, from our brother Greek church. I take this opportunity today to thank, through him, the Orthodox Greek people, the Greek church, and the Greek authorities for their brotherly help that they have extended to us from the beginning, and up to the present day as well. Even in peace, a man feels the need for brotherly words and actions, let alone when misfortunes and struggles arrive, as we say "to have a brother's compassion is an act of helping."

Let us pray today to the Holy Apostles to pray to the Lord for us sinners, too, that the Lord have mercy on us and gladden us with peace, so needed by us and all those who suffer, regardless of which side they are on, regardless of whether they know what they are doing or not, so that we may continue our lives in peace, and prepare ourselves for entering the Kingdom of Heaven, when the time comes to pass from this world into the other one. O Lord and St. Sava, and all the Saints from our nation, together with the first-enthroned of the Apostles, Peter and Paul, help us also today to live up to the demands of our time, and to be worthy descendants of our holy ancestors; likewise, that You, O Lord, may recognize us as Your own, and acknowledge us as Your own.

I congratulate the priests of this holy temple, all parishioners, and all of you, brothers and sisters, on the occasion of today's feast, the patronal feast day—*slava*—of this church, I wish you everything that is truly good, and prosperity from our Lord. God bless you!

ON THE HOLY APOSTLES BARTHOLOMEW AND BARNABAS

Sermon at the Divine Liturgy on June 24/11, 1995,
in the church of the Holy Apostles in Rakovitsa

"He that heareth you heareth me; and he that despiseth you despiseth me; and he that despiseth me despiseth him that sent me. And the seventy returned again with joy, saying, 'Lord, even the devils are subject unto us through thy name.' And he said unto them, 'I beheld Satan as lightning fall from heaven. Behold, I give unto you power to tread on serpents and scorpions, and over all the power of the enemy: and nothing shall by any means hurt you. Notwithstanding in this rejoice not, that the spirits are subject unto you; but rather rejoice, because your names are written in heaven.' In that hour Jesus rejoiced in spirit, and said, 'I thank thee, O Father, Lord of heaven and earth, that thou hast hid these things from the wise and prudent, and hast revealed them unto babes: even so, Father; for so it seemed good in thy sight.'"

Luke 10:16-21

In the name of the Father, and the Son, and the Holy Spirit! We have prayed in this temple dedicated to the Holy Apostles Bartholomew and Barnabas, and to St. Sava; we have served the holy Mystery of the Eucharist, the Liturgy. Most of you, along with the priests, have communed of the precious Body and Blood of the Son of God in this fasting period dedicated to the Holy Apostles. In Holy Scripture, in the Acts of the Apostles, we read that in Antioch, where prophets and preachers were, there were also among others Barnabas, and then Saul and the rest, when, it says, "...they were worshiping the Lord and fasting, the Holy Spirit said, 'Set apart for me Barnabas and Saul for the work to which I have called them'" (Acts 13:2). And after they fasted and prayed to God, it says, the Holy Spirit directed them to preach the Gospel, first in Cyprus, and then further out in the world.

The Holy Apostles, after the word of the Lord, fasted and thereby glorified God and sanctified their souls, preparing for the preaching of the Gospel and God's teaching. Inasmuch as, for us, brothers and sisters, the evangelical teaching, the Orthodox teaching, is not just a teaching that one can learn and recite by heart, but it is a teaching by which one lives. When their mouths were silent, their deeds preached, along with their holy and sanctified life. For this reason, the Church has established this fasting period after Pentecost, the resurrection of Christ, and the descent of the Holy Spirit, right before the feast of the Holy Apostles, so that we too would fast and thus prepare and be equipped, brothers and sisters, for a life according to God, and for the sermon, the confirmation of the Gospel, and our faith in the Son of God, crucified and resurrected, both with our life and deeds.

And now this edifice, this chapel, is an act of our faith as well, your faith, brothers and sisters, all of you who have helped both by your donations and your work to have this chapel built so wonderfully, to the glory of God, and for the benefit of all of us, all of you, brothers and sisters.

Therefore, we should always have in mind that the goal of our life is to attain, by our faith and our life according to faith, that everlasting life in the blessedness of the heavenly kingdom, in the nearness of God and in communion with all the Saints from our nation. That is the meaning and goal of our life, and that is also a way to help our neighbors as well, including our brothers and sisters who suffer in Bosnia and Herzegovina, in Croatia and everywhere. This is the greatest help that we can extend here and in every place.

I congratulate the brotherhood of this temple and this parish on the occasion of today's feast of the Holy Apostles Bartholomew and Barnabas; I congratulate also all the parishioners and all of you, brothers and sisters, who pray to God and strive to fulfill His will; thereby you show that you are worthy descendants of your holy ancestors who, brothers and sisters, wait for us, looking down from the heavens, listening to our words and watching our deeds, whether they are the way they are supposed to be and the way they kept them, often [*impaled*—T.N.] on the stake and [*hanging from*—T.N.] the rope, dying for their faith and for the honor of their nation. May the Lord and His Holy Apostles, and our Holy Father Sava, help us to live up to the demands of our time, always as humans; to always speak and act as we should, and as is befitting. God bless you and grant you every good thing!

ON THE FEAST OF THE BIRTH OF ST. JOHN THE BAPTIST—IVANDAN

Sermon at the Divine Liturgy
in the church of the Birth of St. John the Baptist,
on July 7/June 24, 1995,
at the Central Cemetery in Belgrade

> "But the angel said unto him, 'Fear not, Zacharias: for thy prayer is heard; and thy wife Elisabeth shall bear thee a son, and thou shalt call his name John. And thou shalt have joy and gladness; and many shall rejoice at his birth. For he shall be great in the sight of the Lord, and shall drink neither wine nor strong drink; and he shall be filled with the Holy Spirit, even from his mother's womb. And many of the children of Israel shall he turn to the Lord their God. And he shall go before him in the spirit and power of Elias, to turn the hearts of the fathers to the children, and the disobedient to the wisdom of the just; to make ready a people prepared for the Lord.'"
>
> Luke 1:13-17

In the name of the Father, and the Son, and the Holy Spirit! Having prayed today, brothers and sisters, to One God in the Holy Trinity, we prayed also to St. John the Baptist, the one for whom our Lord Jesus said that he was the greatest born of woman. St. John the Baptist is indeed the prophet and forerunner of the Lord; he stands between the Old and the New Testaments, yet he was made worthy of that honor and glory to be able to say, "Behold the Lamb of God, who taketh away the sins of the world!" (John 1:29); moreover, he revealed the One Whom prophets across the centuries had preached would come, as the One Who had already come. He is, as I said, on the border of the Old Testament and the New: he still does not belong to the New Testament Church, which had not been founded yet—it was finally established with the death and resurrection of the Lord, and the descent of the Holy Spirit on the Apostles. Still, he was the child of God's mercy, toward his parents and toward all mankind.

His parents were childless; the mother barren, as well as elderly, and the father already advanced in years. So the Lord sent his angel to announce to the father that he will have a son, who will be the long-awaited prophet, who will direct and prepare the people to welcome the Son of God. And when St. Elizabeth gave birth to a son, she said that the Lord took away her shame before people. Namely, the Jewish people believed in the prophecies of all the prophets that the Savior, the Lord's Anointed, the Messiah would come; they all wanted to live to see this realized in their own offspring, and to participate in this grace from God. Therefore, the Jewish people considered it a condemnation from God for some sins if a person was left without any offspring, with no children.

How many Saints lived in those times, and what times are these present ones we live in, and this world "which lies in evil"—what difference between the two! There is no need for me to reveal to you the secret that, among our people, there are fewer and fewer Serbs each day. Not only because the enemies are killing us, and because our people are dying fighting for justice, freedom, and truth; it is also because an absolute majority of our faithful as well, not to mention others who do not want children, do not want them because of their own comfort. It is not only the case of the present times, where one can barely make ends meet; this was the case even before the war—I know that well. Those who were the richest and most powerful were the ones with fewest children or none at all, because of comfort and the desire to enjoy themselves, without any obligations and responsibilities toward God and their nation.

Brothers and sisters, we will come before the face of God to give an answer before Him of how we used the capacities He gifted us with; He gave them to us with the expectation that we would fulfill His will, and only under that condition will He also fulfill what we request of Him. For then, when we fulfill His will, we will not want nor expect that which is evil, not even for our enemies.

May the Lord Jesus Christ, the Son of God, and St. John, His forerunner and baptizer, and the parents of St. John, Zacharias and Elizabeth, help us to understand God's commandments, and to find the strength within us to fulfill them, so that we could thus realize the meaning and goal of our life, to enter the heavenly kingdom, and be numbered with His people, godly and holy, the way our ancestors have also done. May this day and patronal feast be blessed for the brotherhood, the priests of this temple, and for all of you, brothers and sisters; likewise, may the Lord look upon all of us sinners, and grant peace to our country and our people, as well as to our enemies, so that in peace, as humans and the people of God, we may live and accomplish deeds that God expects from us, for which He had sent us in this our time. God bless you and grant you every good thing!

ON THE SYNAXIS OF THE HOLY ARCHANGEL GABRIEL

Sermon at the Divine Liturgy on July 26, 1995, in the church of the Holy Archangel Gabriel in Belgrade

In the name of the Father, and the Son, and the Holy Spirit! We have prayed, brothers and sisters, in this holy temple where our ancestors prayed before us. We also prayed to His and our Archangel Gabriel, that Holy Archangel whom God sent to serve the salvation of people, and to announce the coming of the Son of God, our Lord Jesus Christ. He appeared to the Prophet Moses by the bramble bush on Sinai, which burned, but was not consumed by the flames; when Moses, while grazing the flock of his father-in-law Jethro, came closer to see this miracle of the bush that burned, but was not consumed, he heard the voice from the bush, "Take off your sandals, for the place where you are standing is holy ground" (Exod. 3:5). And the Lord spoke to him from the bush saying, "I am the God of Abraham, the God of Isaac and the God of Jacob. I have seen the misery of your people in Egypt. Go now therefore to deliver them, and bring them out of that country" (Exod. 3:16-17). The Holy Archangel over time spoke to the Prophet Moses about all that needed to be done, which the latter wrote down in his five books of Holy Scripture of the Old Testament. The Holy Archangel appeared to the Prophet Daniel as well, who also preached on God's command about the revelation of the time the Lord Jesus would come. He appeared to St. Zacharias in the temple, notifying him that his wife Elizabeth would give birth to a son who would be the forerunner of the Son of God. He also appeared six months later to the Holy Theotokos, and announced to her that she would give birth to the Son of God. And when she asked, "How shall this be, seeing I know not a man?" he explained to her, because she did not express disbelief as Zacharias did, but only inquired about the manner in which this would happen, "The Holy Spirit shall come upon thee, and the power of the Highest shall overshadow thee: therefore also the holy one who shall be born of thee shall be called the Son of God" (Luke 1:35).

So our Lord Jesus came, the Savior of us all, brothers and sisters, and with His teaching, His entire life, the entire economy of salvation, as it says in Holy Scripture, and especially with His death on the cross and His resurrection, He brought salvation to all of us. Thereby, we are all objectively saved, but we have to adopt that salvation subjectively, every man for himself; in what way? With our faith and life according to that faith. We should strengthen the free will that we as created beings have received, so that it advances from the lower to the higher degree of freedom. God created us and gave us free will, but God did not create us incapable of sinning, but capable of not sinning. Hence, with the help of the grace of God, by our efforts and our life, we should continually strengthen this will, to pass over from those heights to the higher degree of free will; this is the will that God has as a free being by His nature, and the holy angels had from the moment they were established, and that holy people have when they reach that level of free will, which is the freedom—not to be able to sin. However, since they have freedom, people can act in the opposite manner of what God desires, and further lessen their own freedom, their being and existence, making it less and less, until at one point they cross the threshold and cross over into a complete lack of freedom, which means: to be unable not to sin. In such a state are all those angels who became demons, and all those people who sinned and have not repented by the end of their life. Therefore, we are called to grow in all virtues, to develop our intellectual abilities, and our capacities of feeling, heart, and willpower, but also this freedom, so that we would pass over from this lower freedom to the higher one, and be incapable of sinning, the way God intended.

Looking up to the Saints from our nation in this endeavor, let us pray to the Holy Archangels Gabriel and Michael, and to all the heavenly bodiless hosts, and all the Saints from our nation, to help us to truly be human, and the people of God, and thereby to realize the meaning of our life on earth, and of our existence. It is precisely what I have just said: the acquisition of the higher type of freedom—to be incapable of sinning, so that we may enter the heavenly kingdom, and in it to advance higher and higher, getting closer and closer to God, throughout all eternity, thus realizing the meaning of our life.

I congratulate you on the occasion of today's feast, my wish is that God and the Holy Archangel will help the brotherhood of this holy temple and this parish, all the parishioners, and the hosts of today's patronal feast celebration—*slava*—and you, too, brothers and sisters, all of us; likewise, to help our brothers in Bosnia and Herzegovina, and Croatia, who are fighting for freedom and God's justice, guarding their homes and their graves; fighting for freedom, I say—not repressing the freedom of another, but fighting for one's own, as they offer sacrifice unto God, their lives and their blood. O Holy Lord, merciful and Holy Archangel, help everyone, even us, to be and to remain human, and the people of God. Amen. God bless you!

ON ST. MARY MAGDALENE

Sermon at the Divine Liturgy on August 4/July 22, 1997, in the church of St. Mary Magdalene in Beli Potok

> "And it came to pass afterward, that he went throughout every city and village, preaching and proclaiming the glad tidings of the kingdom of God: and the twelve were with him, and certain women, which had been healed of evil spirits and infirmities, Mary called Magdalene, out of whom went seven devils, and Joanna the wife of Chuza Herod's steward, and Susanna, and many others, which ministered unto him of their own means."
>
> Luke 8:1-3

In the name of the Father, and the Son, and the Holy Spirit. We have prayed to God, brothers and sisters, and thus we began this day. Likewise, when we get up from our beds, let us pray to God; let us direct toward Him our first thoughts, our prayers, that He bless and help everyone, even us. This is what shows that we are Orthodox Christians, that we know the commandment of our Lord Jesus Christ, "The first," He says, "commandment: Love the Lord your God with all your heart, all your mind, and all your strength. This is," He says, "the first and greatest commandment." And the second one is like the first, "Love your neighbor as yourself" (Luke 10:27).

If we truly love God as our heavenly Father, then He Who is love will show love to us, to all those in our home, in our nation, and to all people of goodwill in this world. Likewise, if we also love our neighbors, learning to do this first and foremost in our families, and then further on, wider and wider, we should truly love our nation and every other nation in the world, and I say and repeat, all people of goodwill in the world. St. John the Evangelist says, "How can you say, how can we say, that we love God Whom we do not see, if we do not love our brother whom we see," and further he continues, "If we truly love God as our Father, we will love His children also, which are our neighbors" (cf. 1 John 4:20-21). Hence, out of love for God springs forth our love for neighbors, and vice versa. This is the greatest thing in the world. For this reason, our Lord Jesus asks us to also love our enemies: "For if you love those who love you, what reward have you? Do not even the tax collectors do the same? And if you greet your brethren only, what do you do more than others?" (Matt. 5:46-47). That is true Christian love. For the Lord Jesus Christ says, "That ye may be the children of your Father who is in heaven: for He makes his sun to rise on the evil and on the good, and sends rain on the just and on the unjust" (Matt. 5:45).

This, brothers and sisters, is the teaching of all the Saints, and St. Mary Magdalene as well, who was the first one to see the risen Lord; she saw Him on two occasions: first He appeared only to her, and the second time when she was with the other myrrh-bearing women, those who came according to the Jewish custom to anoint the body of the deceased. And when the risen Lord appeared, He greeted them with the words, "Rejoice!" And when He appeared to the Apostles, He told them, "Peace be unto you!" The Holy Fathers say that these two greetings have a deep meaning. Namely, in paradise our foremother Eve picked the forbidden fruit, and thereby broke God's commandment. When the Lord asked Adam first and then Eve, and spoke to them, instead of repenting and asking forgiveness from God, they blamed each other, and the devil, and everyone else, sensing that it was not only a justification of their own sin for which they alone were guilty; for we do the same when we justify our own sin and shift the blame to someone else. In this way, both they and we want to free ourselves from correction. For, if another is to blame, let him go ahead and correct himself; however, we should understand that we are in fact guilty, even if someone talks us into it and force us to do what is evil; if we consent, we are to blame. True, he is guilty for provoking me with an insult or whatever it was, but I am guilty for accepting to defend myself from the wrongdoers in an unworthy, inhuman, and unchristian manner.

This is, I repeat, the teaching of our Lord Jesus. Hence, He, the risen One, first greets Mary Magdalene and all the myrrh-bearers, and all women, with the news: "Rejoice!" In this way He mitigates that word of the Lord spoken in paradise, and He invites both women and everyone to the joy of the resurrection of Christ and life in Him. Conversely, the Lord greets the Holy Apostles, all the faithful, and all people of goodwill in the world with the words: "Peace be with you!" For men have been, and mostly remain, belligerent, and the orders for war, along with the misfortunes that war and conflict bring, originate with them. If we really listen to our Lord Jesus, and fulfill His commandments, we will let joy into our souls; we will let peace into our souls, too, peace with God; that peace will then radiate into the society where we move about, and into our family—it will be beneficial for our nation.

May the Lord Jesus and all his Saints help us, along with St. Mary Magdalene who first saw Him resurrected, and witnessed His resurrection in the world. On the occasion of today's feast, I congratulate the priests of this holy temple, and the surrounding parishioners of this parish, and you, brothers and sisters. I wish us all from the Lord that we look up to His Saints, to fulfill His commandments, that His blessings may enter our hearts together with Him; may peace descend upon this country of unrest, which lies in evil. God bless you and grant you every good thing!

ON THE FEAST OF THE BEHEADING OF ST. JOHN THE BAPTIST

Sermon at the Divine Liturgy
on September 11/August 29, 1995,
in the church of the Birth of St. John the Baptist,
at the Central Cemetery in Belgrade

"But when Herod heard thereof, he said, 'It is John, whom I beheaded: he is risen from the dead.' For Herod himself had sent forth and laid hold upon John, and bound him in prison for Herodias' sake, his brother Philip's wife: for he had married her. For John had said unto Herod, 'It is not lawful for thee to have thy brother's wife.' Therefore Herodias had a quarrel against him, and would have killed him; but she could not: For Herod feared John, knowing that he was a just man and an holy, and observed him; and when he heard him, he did many things, and heard him gladly. And when a convenient day was come, that Herod on his birthday made a supper to his lords, high captains, and chief estates of Galilee; And when the daughter of the said Herodias came in, and danced, and pleased Herod and them that sat with him, the king said unto the girl, 'Ask of me whatsoever thou wilt, and I will give it thee.' And he swore unto her, 'Whatsoever thou shalt ask of me, I will give it thee, unto the half of my kingdom.' And she went forth, and said unto her mother, 'What shall I ask?' And she said, 'The head of John the Baptist.' And she came in straightway with haste unto the king, and asked, saying, 'I will that thou give me by and by in a charger the head of John the Baptist.' And the king was exceeding sorry; yet for his oath's sake, and for their sakes which sat with him, he would not reject her. And immediately the king sent an executioner, and commanded his head to be brought: and he went and beheaded him in the prison, and brought his head in a charger, and gave it to the girl:

and the girl gave it to her mother. And when his disciples heard of it, they came and took up his corpse, and laid it in a tomb."

Mark 6:16-29

Today's Gospel reading about the death of St. John follows after the word of the Lord that man does not live on bread alone, but on every word that comes out of the mouth of the Lord. He suffered, as you heard, for the truth of the kingdom and God's commandments. This is always the most important thing for us—that we should never be afraid of anything or anyone; that is, not be afraid of those who can kill, according to the word of the Lord, but afterwards can do nothing more to us, but to be afraid of the one who, after he kills, has the power to throw us into hell. This is what our people, having received the Orthodox faith, knew and kept throughout the centuries. Our people have expressed this truth through the mouth of Mother Yevrosima from Serbian epic poems, when she counsels her son Marko not to be afraid of "anyone but one great God," "It is better for you to lose your head than to defile your soul with sin!" This teaching, brothers and sisters, from the life of St. John, and especially from the life, preaching, and death of the Lord Jesus, should always be before us; we should live by it and, should the time come, die for it, too.

King Herod, when he heard about our Lord Jesus—Who had started to preach, and all the people had begun to go to Him—having an unclean conscience, stood up and said, "It is John whom I have slain. He has risen from the dead" (Mark 6:16). It is the faith that the departed righteous ones are alive before God, in Abraham's bosom, as it says in the Old Testament; that is, they are written in God's book of the living, and alive before Him. Sinners are alive, too, but in eternal torments. Moreover, we should be edified, and it is always necessary to mention this to our people: not to allow drunkenness. For, here at this feast, when the emperor and the guests were drunk, then he was willing to made promises even about things that were not his. He was promising half of the empire, and by the mercy of the Romans, he was only the governor of Judaea. And what is most important, here, because he was already drunk, having become the slave of drunkenness, he was already a sinner. If a man does not abandon it, according to the words of Holy Scripture, he will not enter the heavenly kingdom; he should be excommunicated from the Church.

In these misfortunes that have befallen us, brothers and sisters, let us pray to God that we stay on His path regardless of what might happen in life, both to us and to our nation. Let us strive, as much as it is up to us, to be at peace with all people. Of course, peace does not depend on us exclusively. In particular cases it also depends on the other person. It also does not depend on our nation alone, but on the other nation as well. However, as much as it is up to us, let us strive to be at peace with all people.

May the Lord and St. John the Baptist, who laid down his life for the justice and truth of the heavenly kingdom, help us on this path; when it comes to the Kingdom of Heaven, to always be prepared to give up our life for it, and never for that which is of this world that is unworthy of man, which is criminal—let us always stay away from such a path. God bless you!

ON THE FEAST OF THE TRANSLATION OF THE RELICS OF ST. ALEXANDER NEVSKY

Sermon at the Divine Liturgy
on September 12/August 30, 1997,
in the church of St. Alexander Nevsky in Belgrade

> "And he came down with them, and stood in the plain, and the company of his disciples, and a great multitude of people out of all Judaea and Jerusalem, and from the sea coast of Tyre and Sidon, which came to hear him, and to be healed of their diseases; And they that were vexed with unclean spirits: and they were healed. And the whole multitude sought to touch him: for there went virtue out of him, and healed them all. And he lifted up his eyes on his disciples, and said, 'Blessed be ye poor: for yours is the kingdom of God. Blessed are ye that hunger now: for ye shall be filled. Blessed are ye that weep now: for ye shall laugh. Blessed are ye, when men shall hate you, and when they shall separate you from their company, and shall reproach you, and cast out your name as evil, for the Son of man's sake. Rejoice ye in that day, and leap for joy: for, behold, your reward is great in heaven: for in the like manner did their fathers unto the prophets.'"
>
> Luke 6:17-23

In the name of the Father, and the Son, and the Holy Spirit. From the life of the Holy Prince Alexander Nevsky, as well as all the Saints, let us be edified by the life they led, the faith they confessed, and what is most important, how they sanctified their bodies and brought them into the heavenly kingdom, and thereby fulfilled the meaning and goal of our life that God handed down to us; it is as the Lord Jesus says, "Where I am, there shall also my servant be" (John 12:26); since the Lord is in the kingdom, His servant should be there, too.

Always and above everything is this: that we should learn about faith and life according to faith. Such was the life of St. Alexander Nevsky, too. He lived at a time when Tatars ruled the Russian land. He confessed his faith in front of the Tatar khan, and he refused to bow down before idols; by this faith, he truly merited the heavenly kingdom. Hence, to such people God gave the power to conquer also those who attacked their freedom. For this reason he is called the Holy Prince of Neva, because he defeated all; it so happened that God helped the Russian people to liberate themselves from the Tatars at the time when we ourselves fell under the Turkish slavery.

The most important thing, then, is for each of us as organs in one body to strive to keep this organ healthy and performing the function for which it was equipped as best as possible, having in mind the common interest of the entire organism. I repeat it, saying it both to myself and to you, brothers and sisters: the organism, the whole, has no other interest but what is beneficial for each individual organ. We should be such an organ, and such should be our attitude toward the society, the nation we belong to, and the times we live in. Let each of us strive that the organism, the body of the nation, be healthy, by our faith, I say, and life according to faith, by our holy faith and holy life. Thus we will help our nation to be and remain the people of God.

During the times of these wars, the First World War, then twenty years later the Second World War, and in fewer than fifty years this present war, people have always died for freedom, for justice, for truth, for that which was in our nation most sincere, most worthy of sacrifice one would offer for one's people and one's faith. I am not saying that all of us who survived those times are exactly the best; in any case, those who were most ready for the sacrifice have died, and now we see how equipped we are to live up to our times, to represent the Serbian people, its freedom, its justice, its truth, its peace, and its community—in a word, its fullness. What others will do, and what they are doing, that depends on them, but what we will do depends on us. Will we act as human or inhuman, especially since we can see what other people are doing; we should condemn all that is untruthful, wrong, what is not in keeping with the justice of God, and what is unbecoming to the name of our nation. Well, since we condemn such acts, should we act in the same manner? Indeed, we will be all the more condemned, because "they know not what they do," (Luke 23:34) while we must know what we are doing according to the word of the Lord.

Let us pray to God in these difficult times, after the war, after the sanctions, and all those misfortunes that have befallen us. Pray to God and witness with your life the Son of God, Who came to enlighten and sanctify us, and to give us the heavenly kingdom, if we earn it. Praying to God and St. Alexander Nevsky, and all the Saints from our Serbian nation, I call down the blessings of God and all the Saints upon all of you. I wish a happy feast day to you, the priests of this holy temple, the parishioners, and all those who celebrate the Holy Prince. God bless you!

ON THE HOLY APOSTLE AND EVANGELIST JOHN THE THEOLOGIAN

Sermon at the Divine Liturgy on October 9/September 26, 1996, at the Faculty of Orthodox Theology of the University of Belgrade

> "Now there stood by the cross of Jesus his mother, and his mother's sister, Mary the wife of Cleopas, and Mary Magdalene. When Jesus therefore saw his mother, and the disciple standing by, whom he loved, he saith unto his mother, 'Woman, behold thy son!' Then saith he to the disciple, 'Behold thy mother!' And from that hour that disciple took her unto his own home... This is the disciple which testifieth of these things, and wrote these things: and we know that his testimony is true. And there are also many other things which Jesus did, the which, if they should be written every one, I suppose that even the world itself could not contain the books that should be written. Amen."
>
> John 19:25-27; 21:24-25

In the name of the Father, and the Son, and the Holy Spirit. We have prayed today, brothers and sisters, in this holy temple, and we have served the Divine Liturgy, the holy Mystery of the Eucharist of the Body and Blood of our Lord Jesus Christ, celebrating the Holy Apostle and Evangelist John to whom this temple and this institution, faculty, is dedicated.

The Holy Apostle John is called the "Apostle of Love," not because the others did not know or did not have love, but because he demonstrated, and certainly possessed, this virtue to a remarkable extent. Likewise, many Saints are named, for example, St. John the Merciful, not because others were not merciful, but because he possessed this virtue in an extraordinary degree. And St. John counsels us constantly, "God is love; and he that dwells in love dwells in God, and God in him" (1 John 4:16). Let us not forget, nonetheless, that God is justice as well, that He is the truth, and that He is every other virtue, too. Not to allow oneself, because God is Love, to cross over to the bad side, thinking that He, being Love, will forgive us everything and always, regardless of whether we are correcting ourselves, whether we live according to His commandments, whether we are fulfilling what He desires—what basically gives us the essence, value, and greatness both in this world and the other one. Hence, let us never forget that St. John the Evangelist said, "Whosoever commits sin transgresses also the law: for sin is the transgression of the law" (1 John 3:4), that is, he transgresses the law of God. Never forget that the law of God, and the commandments of God are everything that God expects from us, because He had given us the power and the strength to accomplish it—that this is good, and holy; it gives essence to our existence, and it establishes our being. St. Basil the Great gives us a lesson about it and the word for ages to come, "that the truth, justice, love, and every good contain essence, being, and existence, while on the other hand, untruth, injustice, hate, evil, and sin have no essence or being. The entire being of Satan is in the negation of truth, negation of justice, negation of love, and the negation of the commandments of God." Let us absorb this teaching before and above all. The more we keep God's commandments, and fulfil the evangelical precepts, the more we will be alive; we will have more being and essence, that is, we will be closer to God. God will dwell in us, and we in Him; thus should one strive.

Especially you, young adults today, in the society where you move about, witness the Son of God not only with your words, but also with your life. Do not ever forget, therefore, that one cannot be a Christian who speaks one thing, no matter how pious the words of the truth he utters, if he does not live by this truth, too. I place this upon your soul and upon your heart. I direct myself toward this teaching as well, and urge all those who have ears to hear. No one will benefit, not the Church, nor our nation, nor our family, nor we ourselves, if we do not absorb this teaching in such a way that we live by it. It is incomparably more valuable that two or three are gathered in the name of God who fulfill His teaching, than that there are millions of those who do everything the opposite way. The Holy Evangelist John says, "Love not the world, neither the things that are in the world... For all that is in the world, the lust of the flesh, and the lust of the eyes, and the pride of life... the world passes away, and the lust thereof: but he that doeth the will of God abides forever" (1 John 2:15-17). Let us learn, then, to acquire the blessedness of the heavenly kingdom that awaits us.

God wants everyone to be saved, but He does not force anyone, for He has given man freedom, and this freedom means that we are capable of not sinning. Strive in this regard to grow more and more, to reach the higher freedom that the angels possess owing to the grace of God, the Saints enjoy having achieved it, and God has according to His essence. Let us pass over into this higher freedom—to be incapable of sinning. The span is enormous. Where we will find ourselves depends on us. Whether or not other people will come to Christ and believe, do not forget, depends on us, according to the word of Christ, "Let your light so shine before men, that they may see your good works, and glorify your Father who is in heaven" (Matt. 5:16). This is, therefore, the program of our life as well, especially of us priests, and you, present students, who are being instructed in the teaching of Christ, and tomorrow will teach it to others, speak on it, and instruct your people.

May the Lord and St. John the Evangelist always be with us; and they will always be with us if we do not depart from them. Let us live up to the times in which we live, a time so difficult and miserable, and thereby bring the greatest benefit both to our nation, so afflicted, and to our families and ourselves—in the end, to all people of goodwill. God bless you and grant you every good thing. I wish a happy feast day to the esteemed dean and the professors, and all of you students who are in this institution, learning all that is holy, honorable, and well-pleasing to our merciful God. Amen.

ON THE HOLY APOSTLE THOMAS

Sermon at the Divine Liturgy on Sunday, October 19/6, 1997, in the Monastery of St. Stephan the Archdeacon, in Slanci

"Then the same day at evening, being the first day of the week, when the doors were shut where the disciples were assembled for fear of the Jews, came Jesus and stood in the midst, and saith unto them, 'Peace be unto you.' And when he had so said, he showed unto them his hands and his side. Then were the disciples glad, when they saw the Lord. Then said Jesus to them again, 'Peace be unto you: as my Father hath sent me, even so send I you.' And when he had said this, he breathed on them, and saith unto them, 'Receive ye the Holy Spirit: Whose soever sins ye remit, they are remitted unto them; and whose soever sins ye retain, they are retained.' But Thomas, one of the twelve, called Didymus, was not with them when Jesus came. The other disciples therefore said unto him, 'We have seen the Lord.' But he said unto them, 'Except I shall see in his hands the print of the nails, and put my finger into the print of the nails, and thrust my hand into his side, I will not believe.' And after eight days again his disciples were within, and Thomas with them: then came Jesus, the doors being shut, and stood in the midst, and said, 'Peace be unto you.' Then saith he to Thomas, 'Reach hither thy finger, and behold my hands; and reach hither thy hand, and thrust it into my side: and be not faithless, but believing.' And Thomas answered and said unto him, 'My Lord and my God.' Jesus saith unto him, 'Thomas, because thou hast seen me, thou hast believed: blessed are they that have not seen, and yet have believed.' And many other signs truly did Jesus in the presence of his disciples, which are not written in this book: But these are written, that ye might believe that Jesus is the Christ, the Son of God; and that believing ye might have life through his name."

John 20:19-31

From these words of the Holy Gospel, as well as from every word of God, let us be edified by faith in the Son of God, in His Gospel, and His teaching, and let us live in keeping with this faith, showing this faith in our life, not just for others to see; rather, let us live by it from our soul and according to our heart. This will be the best way to preach Christ and His Gospel before the people of this world, both the faithful and unfaithful, according to the word of Christ in another place, "Let your light so shine before men, that they may see your good works, and glorify your Father who is in heaven" (Matt. 5:16). When the Son of God appeared in this world, He showed through His appearance that He was a man, but in His countenance also shined through His divine face. Thus, after His one word, having come to John the Baptist, John sees in Him and witnesses, "...Behold the Lamb of God, which taketh away the sin of the world!... And I have seen, and testify that this is the Son of God" (John 1:29, 34). And here all His Apostles on one word from Him leave everything and follow after Him, and the Lord confirms their faith in Him with His acts and His miracles.

The word of St. Peter may be unclear to us, "[*Depart from me*—T.N.] Lord, for I am a sinful man." Here he feels his unworthiness to be before the Son of God, and expresses himself in that sense. It was different when the Lord, in another place, made the pigs jump into the sea and drown, because Jews were forbidden not only to keep pigs, but also to come into contact with them, for they would be rendered unclean, not only physically, but also ritually, in a devotional sense; so when the people perceived the [*material*—T.N.] damage done to them, they came and begged the Son of God to depart from them because of the damage, not because they had seen a miracle, nor because He had previously fed the people with bread.

Of course, our duty is to feel we are unworthy to stand before the Son of God, to be gifted with the Holy Communion, but we should strive to be as worthy as possible. His Holy Communion in us cleanses us from our sin, makes us stronger, and worthy of the Kingdom of God.

You know the event with St. Thomas after the resurrection of our Lord; you have heard it many times. Accordingly, our faith is not just the words of the people, but it has been confirmed, here, with eyes, but also with hands and other senses. The Holy Apostle John says, "That which we have heard, which we have seen with our eyes, which we have looked upon, and our hands have handled... declare we unto you..." (1

John 1:1-3). We should strive also to be made worthy to see the Son of God, that our hearts be made worthy to see the Son of God; strive to have our heart cleansed from sin, and then in this pure heart the Son of God and God will be reflected. Until then, I say, we should strive to cleanse our heart from sin, and to not to commit sins. "For this is the will of God: your sanctification" (1 Thess. 4:3). To be sure, it is hard for us, the way we are now, to keep God's commandments, for we have acquired bad habits; hence, they look easy to us, while God's commandments seem difficult; however, God's commandments are unassumingly easier than any sin, or a habit of sin.

Lord, help us to be worthy of the Orthodox name we bear, the name of Orthodox Serbs, to truly be your witnesses in this world which "lies in wickedness" (1 John 5:19). God bless you!

ON ST. DEMETRIUS

Sermon on November 8/October 26, 1996,
at the consecration of the cross and property for
the church of St. Demetrius of Thessaloniki in New Belgrade

In the name of the Father, and the Son, and the Holy Spirit. "This is the day the Lord has made; let us rejoice and be glad in it" (Ps. 118:24). In these days and years, brothers and sisters, there was little time for rest from misfortunes, difficulties, and struggles.

One such day in which we can rejoice is today, when we have consecrated this place and this precious cross, the place where with God's blessing we are to begin building a temple to the glory of God and St. Demetrius; likewise, a temple for the needs of all those who pray to God, and believe in Him, who live according to His commandments, and strive thereby to be saved, and to help their nation and all people of goodwill in the world. For honorable, good people are, in God's estimation, indeed of benefit to all, certainly most of all to their families and their nation.

We have consecrated this place and prayed to God, and we have pledged to dedicate this temple to His and our St. Demetrius; also, this temple is to be a sign of our gratitude to God, St. Demetrius, and to the brotherly Greek people who have helped us in the misfortunes of these war years; I think, they could not have done more for us. Without this help, we would have hardly been able to persevere in all these misfortunes that have befallen us, both through our own fault, but also through the fault of others.

St. Demetrius was born at the beginning of the fourth century, when Christians were still persecuted by the entire pagan Roman Empire. A child of pious parents, he also became a Christian, and was raised in a Christian spirit. His father was a military commander, and when St. Demetrius grew up, the Emperor Maximillian placed him in the place of his father, knowing about his courage, his value and abilities;

in particular, he ordered him to pay attention to the Christians, and to persecute them wherever he could. Contrary to that, St. Demetrius helped Christians, doing everything he could to strengthen them, and to fortify them in their faith. When the emperor found out, he ordered that he be thrown into the dungeon to be tortured. When St. Demetrius refused to renounce [*his faith*—T.N.], the emperor stripped him of his military honors, and ordered that he be executed; thus, soldiers killed St. Demetrius with a spear.

St. Demetrius knew, brothers and sisters, that there is something more important than life, and this whole world. This was known by our ancestors throughout the centuries, both in freedom and in slavery, in peace and in battles; they were taught by their mothers that it is better to lose one's life than to defile one's soul with sin. This precept was upheld in Kosovo by Prince Lazar and our ancestors, who came to defend their freedom and their land, to defend themselves and their faith, not to plunder what belongs to others, but to defend what is theirs.

To this St. Demetrius let us pray now and always, that he support us in all that is holy, honorable, and well-pleasing to the merciful God, the precepts our ancestors upheld, taught by St. Sava and other Saints from our nation, martyrs, and new martyrs.

Glory to God that over the course of so many years we managed to build only one small temple in Karaburma, and now, thanks to the efforts of the mayor and other authorities, we are allowed in multiple locations to raise temples for those who want and desire it. All the while, not imposing on others either our convictions, or our faith. Throughout the centuries we were never such a people, nor such a religion, to frighten and force someone into accepting our faith. Rather, even now and always, let us preserve what is ours; likewise, let us hope in the Lord and St. Demetrius that this temple, once it is built, will be to the glory of God, His and our St. Demetrius, and all the Saints, and that it will be of benefit to all the Orthodox, both to us and to our Greek brothers, and to all Orthodox who will be able to pray in it, to be edified in the word of God, and have their souls nourished by it. Just as the body needs food, so the soul needs nourishment, which is the word of God, God's teaching.

O Lord, be merciful to all, even unto us. Lord and St. Demetrius, help and bless us. Amen, God. Amen to my people.

ON THE HOLY UNMERCENARIES COSMAS AND DAMIAN

Sermon at the Divine Liturgy on November 14/1, 1995, in the church of St. George

> "And when he had called unto him his twelve disciples, he gave them power against unclean spirits, to cast them out, and to heal all manner of sickness and all manner of disease... These twelve Jesus sent forth, and commanded them, saying, 'Go not into the way of the Gentiles, and into any city of the Samaritans enter ye not: But go rather to the lost sheep of the house of Israel. And as ye go, preach, saying, "The kingdom of heaven is at hand." Heal the sick, cleanse the lepers, raise the dead, cast out devils: freely ye have received, freely give.'"
>
> Matt. 10:1, 5-8

We have prayed today, brothers and sisters, in this holy temple to the Holy Miracle-Workers Cosmas and Damian, and to their and our Creator and Savior. Each day the holy Church commemorates one of the Saints, those who with their life and faith pleased God, sanctified their souls, and acquired the Kingdom of Heaven, the unending life in the blessedness of the heavenly kingdom—in the vicinity of God and in communion with all the Saints. We celebrate, hence, those whom God has celebrated, because they glorified Him and confirmed Him in this life; thus they showed that it is possible to fulfill the evangelical teaching for the sake of one's salvation and the welfare of one's family, one's nation, and all mankind. For, in a holy man is realized the personhood of man in general. Moreover, such a man is well-pleasing to God and useful to people. The Holy Unmercenaries and Miracle-Workers Cosmas and Damian truly deserved this distinction by their life and their work, as well as their service to God, by serving God and their neighbors. They were from Asia, of pagan father and Christian mother, who knew to raise her children in the Orthodox faith. When the husband died, she was to those children both father and mother, and as I said, she raised them in the Christian faith. Later, when they grew up, they dedicated themselves to serving as physicians. However, as Christians they healed people both with medicines, the knowledge they had acquired, but also with their humane, Christian, and brotherly approach toward the sick, toward people who are in distress—those whose circumstances were truly most difficult, and who needed both a humane word, as well as human, brotherly help.

One should have in mind that we are all in this world temporarily; we are bodies, but also immortal souls. Therefore, all of us, physicians included, should take care not to forget the souls while treating the ailments of the body. One-sidedness is always unfortunate. To say, to claim, that man is body only—that is one-sidedness, only one side of our being. Likewise, one-sidedness would be to say that we are souls only, that we are not concerned with the body, and hence not to take care of it. All of us should not give the body more than it really needs. For, if we give it more, we have to take away from the soul. Accordingly, to the soul we should give no less than what belongs to it!

I also want to mention that we Orthodox Serbs, have a tradition of *slava*—a patron Saint of the family and of the temple, but especially in the sense of the family patron. Other Orthodox people celebrate their name day or birthday, and we, as you see, celebrate a patron (*slava*). In fact, *slava* is both a name day and a birthday, but not of an individual, rather of the family, of the entire clan. The spiritual birthday, when our ancestors became Christian, entered the Church of God and thus were born spiritually; and a name day, because on that day they were named Christian, and remained so to the present day.

May the Lord and His Saints help us in these difficult and unfortunate times to conduct ourselves as is meet and right, as the people of God, in all that is holy, honorable, and well-pleasing to the merciful God.

In this world struggles, sicknesses, and misfortunes are unavoidable. However, you know that we are all assistants, collaborators of God in the act of the preservation of our life, and our health both with regard to medical treatment, but also with regard to the act of our salvation. Let us do what we can as coworkers of God; anything more than what our time and circumstances demand of us will be done by Him, the Almighty God, as He has done to our ancestors throughout so many centuries, throughout our history which was never easy, yet it was honorable and righteous nonetheless. Our ancestors always had in mind the duty to be and remain human, and on no account inhuman.

May the Lord and the Holy Healers help the Serbian doctors, too, and all people of goodwill, and all of us, brothers and sisters. God bless you and grant you every good thing!

ON THE FEAST OF THE DEDICATION OF THE TEMPLE OF THE HOLY GREAT-MARTYR GEORGE IN LYDDA—DJURDJIC

Sermon at the Divine Liturgy on November 16/3, 1995, in the Ruzhitsa church in Belgrade

"These things I command you, that ye love one another. If the world hate you, ye know that it hated me before it hated you. If ye were of the world, the world would love his own: but because ye are not of the world, but I have chosen you out of the world, therefore the world hateth you. Remember the word that I said unto you, 'The servant is not greater than his lord. If they have persecuted me, they will also persecute you; if they have kept my saying, they will keep yours also. But all these things will they do unto you for my name's sake, because they know not him that sent me. If I had not come and spoken unto them, they had not had sin: but now they have no cloak for their sin. He that hateth me hateth my Father also. If I had not done among them the works which none other man did, they had not had sin: but now have they both seen and hated both me and my Father. But this cometh to pass, that the word might be fulfilled that is written in their law, "They hated me without a cause." But when the Comforter is come, whom I will send unto you from the Father, even the Spirit of truth, which proceedeth from the Father, he shall testify of me: And ye also shall bear witness, because ye have been with me from the beginning. These things have I spoken unto you, that ye should not be offended. They shall put you out of the synagogues: yea, the time cometh, that whosoever killeth you will think that he doeth God service.'"

John 15:17-27, 16:1-2

In the name of the Father, and the Son, and the Holy Spirit! We have completed the service of the holy Mystery of the Eucharist, the Mystery of the Body and Blood of our Lord. We have prayed to God here, and broken the ceremonial bread in commemoration of St. George the Great-Martyr. On this day we celebrate the restoration of the temple that was raised by the Emperor Constantine in the time of liberation, when Christianity was granted freedom of worship, in Lydda of Palestine, where the relics of the Great-Martyr George were translated according to his wish.

Always celebrating holy people who pleased God, especially the martyrs, the holy Church instructs us to persevere. To witness our faith with our actions and our words, the way God's holy Saints have done, whereby God glorified them both on earth and in heaven. Thus, we celebrate those whom God has celebrated, because they glorified Him with their lives. That is the program of our life as well. According to the words of St. Basil, "The goal of Christian life is to obtain that everlasting life in the Kingdom of Heaven, the blessedness of that kingdom that will have no end." We should subordinate everything to this goal! Just like that man from the Gospel parable of our Lord who found a treasure hidden in a field, a priceless treasure for which he was willing to sell everything in order to buy that seemingly empty field. However, what others did not know, he did; and it is this: it pays to sell everything, to do everything to obtain that field and the treasure hidden in it.

Hence, Christian, evangelical life is for us a treasure hidden in a field—others do not see that; they have not come upon that treasure; if they come upon it, and if they understand what it is about, they also will be saved and enter into blessedness. We, however, whose ancestors were Christian throughout the centuries, and knew about this treasure, living in such a manner that they may acquire it, we should uphold it both now and always. This will be the best help we can render unto ourselves, our families, our nation, and ultimately unto the whole world.

To those who today celebrate St. George as their family patron Saint—*slava*—as well as to our sponsor here: may the Lord grant you all true good; likewise, to all of us, may we be led into the heavenly kingdom, where St. George and all the other Saints of God are. God bless you, and a happy feast day!

ON THE HOLY APOSTLE AND EVANGELIST LUKE

Sermon at the Divine Liturgy on October 30/18, 1996, in St. Luke's chapel at St. Sava Hospital in Belgrade

> "And he said also unto his disciples, 'There was a certain rich man, which had a steward; and the same was accused unto him that he had wasted his goods. And he called him, and said unto him, "How is it that I hear this of thee? give an account of thy stewardship; for thou mayest be no longer steward." Then the steward said within himself, "What shall I do? for my lord taketh away from me the stewardship: I cannot dig; to beg I am ashamed. I am resolved what to do, that, when I am put out of the stewardship, they may receive me into their houses." So he called every one of his lord's debtors unto him, and said unto the first, "How much owest thou unto my lord?" And he said, "An hundred measures of oil." And he said unto him, "Take thy bill, and sit down quickly, and write fifty." Then said he to another, "And how much owest thou?" And he said, "An hundred measures of wheat." And he said unto him, "Take thy bill, and write fourscore." And the lord commended the unjust steward, because he had done wisely: for the children of this world are in their generation wiser than the children of light. And I say unto you, Make to yourselves friends of the mammon of unrighteousness; that, when ye fail, they may receive you into everlasting habitations.'"
>
> Luke 16:1-9

From this passage in the Holy Gospel written by the Holy Evangelist Luke, whom we commemorate today, we can and should learn a lot. It concerns, namely, a steward who is wasting his master's goods, and when the master decides that he should give an account of his stewardship, and that he cannot be the estate manager anymore, the former then says, "What will I do now? How will I make a living? I cannot dig, I am not used to it, and I am too ashamed to beg." And then he thought and had an idea; so he called all the debtors of his master and told them to write on their receipts less than they actually owed, so that when he was relieved of his duty as manager, they would support him.

That is the way of the world; however, at first glance, the following remains unclear to us in and of itself, of course, "And I say unto you," the Lord says, "use unrighteous wealth to gain friends for yourselves, so that when you fail, they may receive you into everlasting habitations." It seems as though the Lord wants from us, that is, He advises us to use such devices as stealing what belongs to others to make a living for ourselves. However, the meaning of these words is entirely different, according to the words of the Saints. With these words, the Lord wishes to say that all of us who have our own pay, and our own property, whether inherited, received as gift, or acquired in any other way, are only stewards of someone else's estate, that is, of God's property. We can spend for our needs only what is really needful. No luxuries, nor wastefulness, neither the attitude: "It is mine; I can do whatever I want with it." I can do what I want, but I will give an answer for it, because it is not mine; it is the property of the Master, God's property. So I should spend more than is really needful, which is, of course, not just food, clothing, books, and all that, but for a real need. You know yourselves what luxuries are, and what is whimsy; we should not waste on that which is a fashion, and what is of this world. The fact of the matter, therefore, is that we are, I repeat, the stewards of God's estate, like treasurers in this and every other institution. If a treasurer takes even one cent more than what belongs to him as his pay, he is stealing. It is likewise with us. How many are dying in the world; just look not only far from us in those countries in Africa and South America and farther, but also here in our country; how many are poor, not because they are idlers, or because they do not want to work, but because they cannot survive in this unfortunate war and post-war times and under these sanctions. Hence, if we spend more on ourselves on account of luxuries, to please the world, and out of vanity, to present ourselves as having the means, we take away from them, from those in poverty, because it is God's property, and we were told how we should handle it.

The Lord calls this surplus of ours—these luxuries—unrighteous mammon. I should add this, too: He says also that it is someone else's property. "And if ye have not been faithful in that which is another man's, who shall give you that which is your own? If therefore ye have not been faithful in the unrighteous mammon, who will commit to your trust the true riches?" [*cf. Luke 16:11-12*—T.N.] Hence, He says that we are obliged to prepare for ourselves our eternal home in the other world with this unjust wealth, which others spend on luxuries, which others spend on trends, thoughtlessly; this in spite of seeing how others, our brothers and sisters, live—through no fault of their own, I said, not because they are idlers. Therefore, we should help as much as we can, as much as it is possible. There are few of us here who are able to do so; still, as much as one can. Thus we will save for ourselves eternal wealth that is in the Kingdom of Heaven.

May the Lord and His and our Holy Apostle and Evangelist Luke help us to always know this boundary—where it is that the true need ends, and luxuries begin, which are unbefitting of a Christian.

When we come before Him, God will ask us, if we are faithful—but He will ask all the other unfaithful ones as well—what we have spent our estate on, the one He gave us to manage. We should always know what we are doing, so that we may be made worthy of the name we bear as Orthodox Serbs, who now represent both the Serbian people and the Orthodox faith. God bless you!

ON THE HOLY APOSTLE AND EVANGELIST LUKE AND ST. PETER OF CETINJE — SECOND SERMON

Sermon at the Divine Liturgy in the church of St. Luke in Krnyacha

> "But when he saw the multitudes, he was moved with compassion on them, because they fainted, and were scattered abroad, as sheep having no shepherd. Then saith he unto his disciples, 'The harvest truly is plenteous, but the laborers are few; Pray ye therefore the Lord of the harvest, that he will send forth laborers into his harvest.' And when he had called unto him his twelve disciples, he gave them power against unclean spirits, to cast them out, and to heal all manner of sickness and all manner of disease. Now the names of the twelve apostles are these; The first, Simon, who is called Peter, and Andrew his brother; James the son of Zebedee, and John his brother; Philip, and Bartholomew; Thomas, and Matthew the publican; James the son of Alphaeus, and Lebbaeus, whose surname was Thaddaeus; Simon the Canaanite, and Judas Iscariot, who also betrayed him. These twelve Jesus sent forth, and commanded them, saying, 'Go not into the way of the Gentiles, and into any city of the Samaritans enter ye not: But go rather to the lost sheep of the house of Israel. And as ye go, preach, saying, "The kingdom of heaven is at hand." Heal the sick, cleanse the lepers, raise the dead, cast out devils: freely ye have received, freely give.'"
>
> Matt. 9:36-38, 10:1-8

In the name of the Father, and the Son, and the Holy Spirit. We have prayed today, brothers and sisters, in this holy temple dedicated to the Holy Apostle and Evangelist Luke, one of the four Evangelists, holy men who recorded and wrote down the Gospel of Christ.

St. Luke was from Antioch. He studied Greek philosophy, and certainly was born Greek. We see this in the fact that the Greek in which he wrote the Gospel was one of the most beautiful and most scholarly. One can see that he was a learned man, and that he knew this language as his native tongue. The other Gospels were written in an easier and simpler Greek, because these Evangelists were Jews. He also acquired knowledge and skill as a physician. The Apostle Paul mentions him as his "beloved physician," the collaborator of the Apostle (Col. 4:14). After the descent of the Holy Spirit, he preached the Gospel, and found himself in Rome with the Apostle Paul when the latter was captured and imprisoned. After the death of St. Paul, he preached in Greece and in other countries, and around 60 AD wrote the third Gospel, which he dedicated to Theophilus, one of the Greek elders. He also wrote the Acts of the Holy Apostles, dedicating them to the same man; therein he delivers the history of the Church from the Ascension of Christ into heaven until the preaching of the Apostle Paul, and the period he was a part of, preaching the Gospel of Christ with him. St. Luke, as I said, was the disciple of the Holy Apostle Paul also when they crossed over from Asia Minor into Europe, to the city of Philippi. In the Acts of the Apostles he says in plural, "we," as he speaks of the Apostle Paul and his work, and then mentions himself—"we crossed over and arrived into Philippi, and the Apostle Paul began his preaching" (cf. Acts 16:12). As an elderly man of 84, St. Luke was killed by the pagans because of his preaching, as they did not believe in the Son of God and His teaching.

Today we also celebrate St. Peter of Cetinje, a great luminary of our Church from our nation, who in the eighteenth and the first half of the nineteenth century, led the Church of God in Cetinje as the Metropolitan of Cetinje and all of Montenegro, as well as the ruler of Montenegro. How many difficulties and struggles he endured to teach the people, and to fight against blood revenge and other evils that existed among the people, and still persist to this day among those who do not know Christ's teaching, do not want to know it, or know it only superficially. He commanded two battles against the Pasha of Skadar, in which the Montenegrins under his command won and preserved their freedom. However, the holy man did not go into battle to plunder others' property and to kill those people, but to defend the freedom of his people, and their right for a place under the sun. For this reason, God helped him and his people to attain their freedom, to be strengthened, and to win in battles. In the second battle at Krusi, before the very battle, St. Peter prayed to the Lord saying, "Lord, help me! If I am in the wrong, then let me be the first to die in this battle." And then he spoke to Kara Mahmud Pasha of Skadar, "If you are in the wrong, may God grant that you burn up in the living flames." The battle began. The brother of Kara Mahmud Pasha was in command, but the Montenegrins fended off their attack. Wishing to encourage his people, Kara Mahmud Pasha charged the enemy on his horse, but he tripped and fell. One Montenegrin cut off his head and the battle ended. When the battle was over, they brought the trophies and the head of Kara Mahmud Pasha to St. Peter of Cetinje on the battlefield. Although he did not know him, St. Peter said, "Eh, Kara Mahmud Pasha, what did you lack in Skadar on the river Boyana, that you had to come to us to fetch some dairy for yourself?" Then he addressed the Montenegrins, "Where is his body? Even if he is an enemy, he should be buried." They told him that the body was burned. Did the Montenegrins hear his curse and prayer at the beginning of the battle, or did he, being holy, foresee it happening?

I wish to say that a holy man, a righteous man, even when he is not guilty, presumes that he is. Conversely, a lawless non-man is never guilty; it is always someone else's fault. It is likewise, you know it yourselves, brothers and sisters, in this unfortunate civil war that befell us and lasted four years; criminals were always justifying themselves, and shifting the blame to us, saying that we Serbs were guilty for all this wartime misery, and for all the crimes that others had committed. This should always be a lesson and a moral unto us. Just as the message of St. Luke was: we can give our life for justice, for truth, for what is right and honorable; thereby we gain the everlasting life that is in God's hands. On no account, nor for any temporary, earthly, and worthless interests, should we lose our honor and our soul, the honor and soul of our nation.

O Lord, Holy Apostle and Evangelist Luke, and St. Peter of Cetinje, pray to God that we live up to the times in which we live; that we may, by looking up to all that is holy and honorable, build for ourselves an eternal home in the other world. God bless you and grant you every good thing!

I wish a happy feast of the temple patron to the priests of this holy temple, all parishioners, and all of you, brothers and sisters. Also, I wish a happy feast of their family patron—*slava*—to all our faithful who celebrate St. Luke as their domestic patron, the way our ancestors have done. God bless you!

ON THE SYNAXIS OF THE HOLY ARCHANGEL MICHAEL

Sermon at the Divine Liturgy
and the consecration of the frescoes in the cathedral church in Belgrade,
on November 21/18, 1996

> "He that heareth you heareth me; and he that despiseth you despiseth me; and he that despiseth me despiseth him that sent me. And the seventy returned again with joy, saying, 'Lord, even the devils are subject unto us through thy name.' And he said unto them, 'I beheld Satan as lightning fall from heaven. Behold, I give unto you power to tread on serpents and scorpions, and over all the power of the enemy: and nothing shall by any means hurt you. Notwithstanding in this rejoice not, that the spirits are subject unto you; but rather rejoice, because your names are written in heaven.' In that hour Jesus rejoiced in spirit, and said, 'I thank thee, O Father, Lord of heaven and earth, that thou hast hid these things from the wise and prudent, and hast revealed them unto babes: even so, Father; for so it seemed good in thy sight.'"
>
> Luke 10:16-21

In the name of the Father, and the Son, and the Holy Spirit! We prayed to God, brothers and sisters, on this day and every day, praying to Him, the Almighty God in the Holy Trinity that we may always be with Him; for we know He will never abandon us, if we do not abandon Him, not only by renouncing Him with our words, but also with our deeds that are contrary to Him, and unfortunate for us, our nation, and all mankind. We prayed that He be with us in all that is holy, honorable, and well-pleasing to Him, the merciful One, in all that sustained so many Orthodox nations, even us, in all the misfortunes that have befallen them throughout history.

We prayed, brothers and sisters, to His and our Holy Archangels Michael and Gabriel, and to other heavenly, angelic powers, in this temple dedicated to them by our ancestors, where they have prayed throughout centuries to God and the Saints; they prayed, I say and repeat, to remain the people of God, as is meet and right, regardless of the struggles in which they found themselves. They knew this at all times, in peace and in war, in slavery and in freedom, as well as in fights for liberation: that before us lies everlasting life in the Kingdom of Heaven, if we earn it by preparing ourselves, our whole person, and our soul for the heavenly kingdom with all that is holy and righteous.

Holy angels were created by God before the creation of humans, right at the very beginning of the creation of the entire world. For it says in Holy Scripture, "In the beginning God created the heaven and the earth" (Gen. 1:1). "In the beginning," that means in the beginning of time, because time did not exist up until then. God is in eternity, and eternity is an everlasting present. It is not time that begins and dissolves. Hence, the word "heaven" implies the creation of holy angels. They were created, as we were later on, with free will, but a lower type of free will that is to be "capable of not sinning," and, provided that they strived by strengthening that will, to be able to reach one day the higher freedom of being "incapable of sinning," which God has possessed always, and holy angels and holy people from the moment they reached it; thus, they live by it even today, and until the end of the world in the Kingdom of Heaven, and after the end of the world, in immortality. Nevertheless, I believe you know that a number of angels became prideful, wishing that they would be above everything; they fell away from God, and became evil demons. For, I say, there is the strengthening of one's will, and elevating oneself to the higher type of being "incapable of sinning." However, there is also falling in sin lower and lower, until one reaches a complete lack of freedom, being "incapable of not sinning," wherein those evil demons fell, and wherein people also fall through their sins, if they do not repent by the end of their life, and correct their life.

What, then, was it that kept the Holy Archangels Michael and Gabriel, and all the other holy angels, on the side of God, so that they would not fall into the same sin of pride, vanity, and misery? Even St. Basil the Great says that it was infinite love toward God. From Holy Scripture, from the words of the Holy Apostle Paul, we see that love was the first to weaken in those angels who became demons, until in the end they had lost it completely. Likewise, the Holy Apostle James says, "the angels also believe, and tremble," (James 2:19). Hence, they inevitably know of God; they cannot deny Him. Yet they deny Him by turning away from Him and walking in the opposite direction. And they "tremble," he says. While in another place, the Holy Apostle John says, "Perfect love casts out fear" (1 John 4:18). We as well, when we reach perfect love, will fear nothing; nonetheless, until then let us be afraid of sin, of that which separates us from God. Thus, love will keep us in the faith in God, and strengthen within us the will as freedom that God has gifted us with, so that we may arrive to the higher freedom of being "incapable of sinning," if we make an effort ourselves.

This is, therefore, what our ancestors have always known, what they have kept, enduring until the end, and living according to that faith every moment of every day, and until the end of their life. For this reason, they are in the heavenly kingdom, glorifying God together with the holy angels.

We know from Holy Scripture that the service of the holy angels is to glorify God and thereby themselves with their faith, and their love; likewise to fulfill the duties God assigns to them in the act of the salvation of humans. Service, then, is what elevates both us and them before God and before eternity. To be prepared to serve everyone in everything that is good, and for their and our salvation. How many times in the Holy Scripture was this service of holy angels expressed, before the birth of St. John the Baptist, and before the nativity of our Lord, when the Archangel Gabriel appeared, as well as when our Lord was born, and a multitude of heavenly angels appeared. We know from Holy Scripture that at the end of the world the Lord will send His angels with the voice of the trumpet to call and summon from all the ends of the earth all those previously departed. And these righteous ones will hear the voice of the Lord Jesus Christ, the Righteous Judge, "Come, ye blessed of my Father, inherit the kingdom prepared for you from the foundation of the world" (Matt. 25:34).

Both now and always, brothers and sisters, let us pray to God and to our ancestors to help us to be numbered with the righteous, because that is the meaning and goal of our birth, and the birth of all people (again, if they want it) and if they strive to reach it with the help of God.

This year we celebrate the patron Saints of this temple, the Holy Archangels, in this beautifully adorned holy temple, our cathedral church, thanks to the donations and help of good people, both individuals and businesses, as well as of the Serbian government, and the city parliament; I say and repeat, with the donations of individuals, but of course, with the resources of the cathedral church as well. I thank everyone for all the good they have done to the glory of God, and for the benefit of us all, that we may have a place to pray to God, and to be reminded of the beauty of the house of God, the Kingdom of Heaven that awaits us.

Lord, help and bless us, and you, Holy Archangels, be with us always. God bless you!

LITURGICAL HOMILIES AND ARCHPASTORAL LESSONS (1995-1998)

ON THE WORDS OF THE LORD: "ANYONE WHO WANTS TO BE FIRST MUST BE THE VERY LAST, AND THE SERVANT OF ALL."

Sermon at the Divine Liturgy on January 13/December 31, 1995,
in the patriarchal chapel
of St. Simeon the Myrrh-Gusher in Belgrade

"And he came to Capernaum: and being in the house he asked them, 'What was it that ye disputed among yourselves by the way?' But they held their peace: for by the way they had disputed among themselves, who should be the greatest. And he sat down, and called the twelve, and saith unto them, 'If any man desire to be first, the same shall be last of all, and servant of all.' And he took a child, and set him in the midst of them: and when he had taken him in his arms, he said unto them, 'Whosoever shall receive one of such children in my name, receiveth me: and whosoever shall receive me, receiveth not me, but him that sent me.' And John answered him, saying, 'Master, we saw one casting out devils in thy name, and he followeth not us: and we forbad him, because he followeth not us.' But Jesus said, 'Forbid him not: for there is no man which shall do a miracle in my name, that can lightly speak evil of me. For he that is not against us is on our part. For whosoever shall give you a cup of water to drink in my name, because ye belong to Christ, verily I say unto you, he shall not lose his reward.'"

Mark 9:33-41

When they arrived in Capernaum, the Lord heard his disciples quarreling along the way, so He asked them what they were talking about. They were silent, because they had been arguing about who among them is the greatest. The greatest according to Christ's criterion is the one who serves everyone. The one who wants to be the first should be the last.

Our pride and vanity lead us to think about primacy and greatness among people, and to fight to receive honors and praise here on earth and in society. However, the first before God is the one who is a servant to all, because the Lord Himself says of Himself that He did not come to be served, but to serve, and to give his life as a ransom for many (Mark 10:45).

Furthermore, the Lord says: whoever is not against you is with you. At the very beginning of the preaching of the Gospel the following applies—whoever is not immediately against it, he can be for the Gospel as well, and can be considered a disciple and follower. For, the Lord's sermon is the Gospel, the good news. Whoever does not reject it at the start is already on the good path, and is not against Christ and His disciples. However, later on as the preaching of the Gospel spread and was heard far and wide, the Lord does not say anymore: whoever is not against you is with you; rather: whoever is not with you is against you. He teaches His Apostles how to distinguish and separate their real followers and disciples. He tells them: whoever receives you, receives Me also. It will not be enough anymore not to be against, but it is necessary to be with Christ. As the Holy Apostle Paul says, "if we be dead with Christ, we believe that we shall also live with him..." (Rom. 6:8, 2 Tim. 2:11), and, "if so be that we suffer with him, that we may be also glorified together" (Rom. 8:17).

God bless you!

ON SIN AND FREEDOM

Sermon at the Divine Liturgy on January 24/11, 1995,
in the patriarchal chapel
of St. Simeon the Myrrh-Gusher in Belgrade

"At that time Jesus answered and said, 'I thank thee, O Father, Lord of heaven and earth, because thou hast hid these things from the wise and prudent, and hast revealed them unto babes. Even so, Father: for so it seemed good in thy sight. All things are delivered unto me of my Father: and no man knows the Son, but the Father; neither knows any man the Father, save the Son, and he to whomsoever the Son will reveal him. Come unto me, all ye that labor and are heavy laden, and I will give you rest. Take my yoke upon you, and learn of me; for I am meek and lowly in heart: and ye shall find rest unto your souls. For my yoke is easy, and my burden is light.'"

Matt. 11:25-30

"For my yoke is easy, and my burden is light," says the Savior, and to us sinful as we are His yoke, the yoke of the Lord, and God's commandments, seem heavy. They are heavy for us because we are already used to what is evil, to walk on the path of sin. I repeat yet again, is it not easier to be sober than a drunkard? Is it not easier to be a non-smoker than a smoker? Not only is it easier, but it is healthier, too, and cheaper! Moreover, every passion turns man into a slave, a slave to sin. As for the servant of God, he is free. However, all sinners one after the other will say: we are free; you are the slaves.

You had an opportunity to hear and read how some women attacked even the Nativity Encyclical of our bishops, and their plea and invitation to wives and husbands not to kill their child at conception, because it is from the moment of conception a complete person, a complete man, a human being who afterwards continues to develop. They sent a message to me, to my address, not to take away their right to decide about their own lives. I had no such intention whatsoever, neither did the Holy Synod, who issued the encyclical, mean to take away anyone's freedom—the gift that God had given us.

Man is a free being. He can live without sin; he is able not to sin. He can do this with the help of the grace of God. What he will do, and which side he will turn to—whether to go away from the Heavenly Father in the opposite direction, or to go to the Heavenly Father, toward His house and the Kingdom of Heaven—that is for him to decide. However, the freedom we were given includes responsibility as well. Without responsibility, there can be no freedom; it would be unworthy of God. There are Christian sects, as well as Muslims and other pagans, who believe in destiny. We do not believe in destiny: for example, that I or anyone else is destined to be a criminal, a drunkard, a good-for-nothing. If it were so—that I am destined and have to be that way, and because I am such, to end up in eternal torments—that would be inhuman, let alone undivine. There are Christian sects who think and believe that God has designated some people for paradise, and others for hell. That is completely unacceptable for us Orthodox Christians.

"...If anyone desires to come after Me," the Lord says, "let him take up his cross" (Matt. 16:24). "If you want to be perfect" (Matt. 19:21), — how many times does the Lord use this phrase "if you want"! It is up to our freedom, up to our free will, to do what God wants us to do, and not the opposite.

The Nativity Encyclical—those words had the purpose of pointing out to those who want to know what the will of God is, and what our duty is. Not only with regard to wives, but husbands as well, because they are just as guilty if it comes to an abortion. What the Lord has said, we have reiterated. As the Lord Jesus says, "Whosoever has ears to hear, let him hear" (Matt. 11:15). As for those who understood sin as an enjoyable thing, and do it because they seek pleasure, these words need not be addressed to them. According to the words of St. Paul, "give up on those with itching ears," (2 Timothy 4:3) that is, flee from a person who wants to hear what he is used to as pleasure, as an enjoyment. Whoever has ears to hear, let him hear! God bless you!

ON FOLLOWING CHRIST

Sermon given on February 6/January 24, 1995

> "Now it happened as they journeyed on the road, that someone said to Him, 'Lord, I will follow You wherever You go.' And Jesus said to him, 'Foxes have holes and birds of the air have nests, but the Son of Man has nowhere to lay His head.' Then He said to another, 'Follow Me.' But he said, 'Lord, let me first go and bury my father.' Jesus said to him, 'Let the dead bury their own dead, but you go and preach the kingdom of God.' And another also said, 'Lord, I will follow You, but let me first go and bid them farewell who are at my house.' But Jesus said to him, 'No one, having put his hand to the plow, and looking back, is fit for the kingdom of God.'"
>
> Luke 9:57-62

This is the confirmation of those words of the Lord, spoken on another occasion, "If anyone desires to come after Me, let him deny himself, and take up his cross, and follow Me" (Luke 9:23). The Lord does not promise us in this world either happiness, or that evangelical life in general will be easy. Instead, He says, "Foxes have holes and birds of the air have nests, but the Son of Man has nowhere to lay His head." He warns man of the difficulties that will befall him if he is of Christ, if he follows the path of Christ. People will attack us. Demons will attack us, too. From all sides we will have struggles, as the Apostle Paul says: troubles from friends and enemies. One should, therefore, prepare and strengthen oneself, take up the cross, and follow Him.

The refusal of a Christian to carry the cross is the renunciation of Christ. One cannot be a disciple of Christ without the readiness to face difficulties. It is important that we do not create difficulties for others; however, we should knowingly accept the difficulties that come from the world that "lies in evil;" accept them as our path, as our cross.

"Come," he says to another young man, "and follow me." And he says: "Lord, let me first go and bury my father." And Jesus said to him: "Let the dead bury their own dead, but you come with me and preach the Kingdom of God." The father of that young man was still alive, and the Lord says about him that he is "dead." For Him, dead are those who are still alive in this world, yet they have no faith in Him, and who live according to the spirit of this world, which lies in evil and will pass.

We should always have in mind what our ancestors knew and believed: that it is better to be dead for Christ, and dead in the eyes of this world, than to be dead in the eyes of Christ. We should have such devotion to Christ. This does not mean that we are seeking death. The rule of Christian martyrdom is: not to seek martyrdom. We are not invoking martyrdom, but when we are faced with the question whether to renounce Christ or to lose our life, then we should choose the path of Mother Yevrosima, who says to her son, "It is better for you to lose your head than to defile your soul with sin!" When he dies for Christ, the dead man is alive before God and alive in God, in the heavenly kingdom. Dead before Him is only a man who is a sinner, who does not repent, and who does not believe in Him.

"Let me first go and bid farewell to my family who are at my house, and then I will follow you" says yet another one. Christ cautions him that this could be dangerous for him. Maybe his family would obstruct and prevent him, so that he does not go after Christ. Whosoever puts his hand to the plow should not look back anymore! If we have resolved to follow what is good, let us not turn our head back! Let us move forward! And God is the One Who will help us to persevere and endure in this endeavor. God bless you! Amen.

ON THE TWO GREATEST COMMANDMENTS

Sermon at the Divine Liturgy on February 8/January 26, 1995, in the patriarchal chapel of St. Simeon the Myrrh-Gusher in Belgrade

"And one of the scribes came, and having heard them reasoning together, and perceiving that he had answered them well, asked him, 'Which is the first commandment of all?' And Jesus answered him, 'The first of all the commandments is, "Hear, O Israel; The Lord our God is one Lord: And thou shalt love the Lord thy God with all thy heart, and with all thy soul, and with all thy mind, and with all thy strength:" this is the first commandment. And the second is like, namely this, "Thou shalt love thy neighbor as thyself." There is none other commandment greater than these.' And the scribe said unto him, 'Well, Master, thou hast said the truth: for there is one God; and there is none other but he: And to love him with all the heart, and with all the understanding, and with all the soul, and with all the strength, and to love his neighbor as himself, is more than all whole burnt offerings and sacrifices.' And when Jesus saw that he answered discreetly, he said unto him, 'Thou art not far from the kingdom of God.' And no man after that dared ask him any question. And Jesus answered and said, while he taught in the temple, 'How say the scribes that Christ is the son of David? For David himself said by the Holy Ghost, "The Lord said to my Lord, Sit thou on my right hand, till I make thine enemies thy footstool." David therefore himself calls him Lord; and whence is he then his son?' And the common people heard him gladly."

Mark 12:28-37

In the Old Testament, God through His prophets gave commandments to the people who had grown and developed to a juvenile stage, but not to the fullness of maturity; first of all, the Ten Commandments of God, and then other ones as well.

In the New Testament that our Lord Jesus, the Son of God, brought to the people who were already mature, and fully capable of accepting His teaching if they wanted, He only gave two commandments: the commandment to love God and the commandment to love one's neighbor.

On these two commandments, says the Lord in the Gospel of Matthew, "hang all the Law and the Prophets" (Matt. 22:40). They contain all the commandments, and a person who is growing in love toward God, and love toward his neighbors, finds them easy. He will fulfill whatever the old commandments have prescribed and immeasurably more.

Jesus, seeing how wise an answer the young man had given, told him, "You are not far from the Kingdom of God." It is a great praise to hear from the mouth of the Son of God, "You are not far from the Kingdom of God." However, one should have in mind that not being far from the Kingdom of God still does not mean being in the Kingdom of God. Likewise we, Orthodox Christians, are baptized; we have received the holy Mysteries; we listen daily to Holy Scripture; we pray to God—still, let us strive with all our might to do whatever is needful, and to enter into the heavenly kingdom. Not to be satisfied with whatever we have accomplished, but to go further and further in spiritual feats until we reach love, which is the bond of perfection, and which has no need for any commandments anymore.

"And from then on no one dared ask him any more questions." Then the Lord asks, "Why do the teachers of the law say that the Messiah is the Son of David, since David himself, speaking by the Holy Spirit, declared: 'The Lord said to my Lord: sit at my right hand until I put your enemies under your feet.' (Ps. 110:1) When David himself calls him 'Lord.' How then can He be his Son?" From these words we know that our Lord Jesus is the Son of God according to His divine nature, and that He is the son, that is, the descendant of David according to His fleshly nature; for He is both God and man.

This is the teaching that the Gospel proclaims in which we Orthodox believe. God bless you!

ON THE WORDS OF THE LORD: "TO EVERYONE WHO HAS, MORE WILL BE GIVEN, BUT AS FOR THE ONE WHO HAS NOTHING, EVEN WHAT THEY HAVE WILL BE TAKEN AWAY"

Sermon at the Divine Liturgy on February 9/January 27, 1995, in the patriarchal chapel of St. Simeon the Myrrh-Gusher in Belgrade

"He said therefore, 'A certain nobleman went into a far country to receive for himself a kingdom, and to return. And he called his ten servants, and delivered them ten pounds, and said unto them, "Occupy till I come." But his citizens hated him, and sent a message after him, saying, "We will not have this man to reign over us." And it came to pass, that when he was returned, having received the kingdom, then he commanded these servants to be called unto him, to whom he had given the money, that he might know how much every man had gained by trading. Then came the first, saying, "Lord, thy pound hath gained ten pounds." And he said unto him, "Well, thou good servant: because thou hast been faithful in a very little, have thou authority over ten cities." And the second came, saying, "Lord, thy pound hath gained five pounds." And he said likewise to him, "Be thou also over five cities." And another came, saying, "Lord, behold, here is thy pound, which I have kept laid up in a napkin: For I feared thee, because thou art an austere man: thou takest up that thou layedst not down, and reapest that thou didst not sow." And he saith unto him, "Out of thine own mouth will I judge thee, thou wicked servant. Thou knewest that I was an austere man, taking up that I laid not down, and reaping that I did not sow: Wherefore then

> gavest not thou my money into the bank, that at my coming I might have required mine own with usury?" And he said unto them that stood by, "Take from him the pound, and give it to him that hath ten pounds." (And they said unto him, "Lord, he hath ten pounds.") For I say unto you, "That unto every one which hath shall be given; and from him that hath not, even that he hath shall be taken away from him." But those mine enemies, which would not that I should reign over them, bring hither, and slay them before me. And when he had thus spoken, he went before, ascending up to Jerusalem.'"
>
> (Luke 19:12-28)

"To everyone who has, more will be given, but as for the one who has nothing, even what they have will be taken away" (Luke 19:26). This is about those who are ready and willing to make an effort, so the Lord will add to them. As for those who do not have this readiness to do what they can as the coworkers of God, even what they have will be taken away from them. This is the meaning of these words. Not injustice: that to the one who has more will be given, that is, a rich man will have more added to him, while the poor will be deprived even of the little he has!

Let us strive as coworkers of God to do what we can, to have strength, and the Lord will give us His grace; as for the one who would not have it, and is waiting only for the Lord to act—well, even whatever grace others possess will be taken away from him. God bless you!

ON THE WORDS OF THE LORD: "ANYONE WHO WANTS TO BE FIRST MUST BE THE VERY LAST, AND THE SERVANT OF ALL."

Sermon at the Divine Liturgy on February 11/January 29, 1995, in the patriarchal chapel of St. Simeon the Myrrh-Gusher in Belgrade

"And he came to Capernaum: and being in the house he asked them, 'What was it that ye disputed among yourselves by the way?' But they held their peace: for by the way they had disputed among themselves, who should be the greatest. And he sat down, and called the twelve, and saith unto them, 'If any man desire to be first, the same shall be last of all, and servant of all.' And he took a child, and set him in the midst of them: and when he had taken him in his arms, he said unto them, 'Whosoever shall receive one of such children in my name, receiveth me: and whosoever shall receive me, receiveth not me, but him that sent me.' And John answered him, saying, 'Master, we saw one casting out devils in thy name, and he followeth not us: and we forbad him, because he followeth not us.' But Jesus said, 'Forbid him not: for there is no man which shall do a miracle in my name, that can lightly speak evil of me. For he that is not against us is on our part. For whosoever shall give you a cup of water to drink in my name, because ye belong to Christ, verily I say unto you, he shall not lose his reward.'"

Mark 9:33-41

Greatness before God is acquired through the greatness of service, and that is within the reach of us all. Will people see us, our good deeds, and internal virtues? Still, serving our neighbors, if it is not seen by them, will certainly be seen by God. It is within our power, then, whether we will be acknowledged before God or not.

As for the children whom God places as an example to us, they trust their elders, and they are benevolent; true, they can get angry, but they also recover fast.

Regarding the word of Christ, "Whoever is not against you is with you;" the Lord uttered it at the beginning of His preaching, when He had not yet done all that He did for our salvation; in His estimation, this was enough at the time. Afterward, for those who are already acquainted with the teaching of Christ, this principle is already too small, and the following word of Christ holds, "Whoever is not with Me is against Me" (Matt. 12:30).

Furthermore, this as well: even the smallest good deed in serving our neighbors will not go to waste. Even if one gives a cup of water to someone who is thirsty, doing so in the name of Christ, his reward will not go to waste. God bless you!

ON THE WORDS OF THE LORD: "DO NOT GO AMONG THE GENTILES OR ENTER ANY TOWN OF THE SAMARITANS"

Sermon at the Divine Liturgy on February 13/January 31, 1995,
in the patriarchal chapel
of St. Simeon the Myrrh-Gusher in Belgrade

"...Go not into the way of the Gentiles,
and into any city of the Samaritans enter ye not."
Matt. 10:5

That the Lord told the Apostles not to preach His teaching to the Gentiles and the Samaritans, does not mean that the Lord was excluding them from His preaching. For we know that He said in the end, after His resurrection, "Go ye into all the world and preach the gospel to every creature" (Mark 16:15). However, now, in the beginning, they should preach to the Jewish people to whom the Lord indicated through the prophets that the Savior would come; this was so that they would not reject the teaching of Christ, if they who were ready to receive Him were not the foremost ones to hear the preaching. Then afterwards, the Lord ordered that the Apostles go and preach to all the nations.

It is our duty as well to preach to all the teaching of Christ, but not impose it. First and foremost, of course, in our nearest environment, to our family, and then further on, never forcing it upon others.

ON THE WORDS OF THE LORD: "WOE TO YOU, BETHSAIDA!"

Sermon at the Divine Liturgy on February 16/3, 1995,
in the patriarchal chapel
of St. Simeon the Myrrh-Gusher in Belgrade

> "Even the very dust of your city, which cleaveth on us, we do wipe off against you: notwithstanding be ye sure of this, that the kingdom of God is come nigh unto you. But I say unto you, that it shall be more tolerable in that day for Sodom, than for that city. Woe unto thee, Chorazin! woe unto thee, Bethsaida! for if the mighty works had been done in Tyre and Sidon, which have been done in you, they had a great while ago repented, sitting in sackcloth and ashes. But it shall be more tolerable for Tyre and Sidon at the judgment, than for you. And thou, Capernaum, which art exalted to heaven, shalt be thrust down to hell."
>
> Luke 10:11-15

Why did the Lord not send ministers to them as well, so that they, too, may repent? At that time, there was still quite a bit of paganism in those towns. They had not yet arrived at the fullness of time; that time had not arrived yet for the Lord to come and reap His wheat.

It will be woe to us, too, who have been given so much—whoever is given more, more will be asked of him—if we do not do as much as those, who are not of our faith, who do not know God, are doing. For, to repeat the word of the Lord, "Whoever is given more, more will be asked of him" (Luke 12:48). It will be more bearable on the day of judgment for the towns of Sodom and Gomorra, and Tyre and Sidon, than Chorazin, Bethsaida, and Capernaum. It will be more bearable for them, because it will be taken into account that they had not heard the teaching that was preached in other towns.

Let us always have in mind that the Lord will also judge us differently than those who have not heard His sermon, whose ancestors were not Christian, whose ancestors were not baptized; rather, it will be different for us to whom all was given.

Make an effort, then, brothers and sisters, with the help of God's grace, that we may be worthy of the name we carry, the name of Orthodox Christians, the name of our people, who thus far have been the people of God; let us also be that as well. God bless you.

ON THE WORDS OF THE LORD: "THEREFORE KEEP WATCH, FOR YOU DO NOT KNOW WHEN THE MASTER OF THE HOUSE IS COMING"

Sermon at the Divine Liturgy on February 17/4, 1995,
in the patriarchal chapel
of St. Simeon the Myrrh-Gusher in Belgrade

> "Heaven and earth shall pass away: but my words shall not pass away. But of that day and that hour knows no man, no, not the angels which are in heaven, neither the Son, but the Father. Take ye heed, watch and pray: for ye know not when the time is. For the Son of Man is as a man taking a far journey, who left his house, and gave authority to his servants, and to every man his work, and commanded the porter to watch. Watch ye therefore: for ye know not when the master of the house cometh, at even, or at midnight, or at the cockcrowing, or in the morning: Lest coming suddenly he find you sleeping. And what I say unto you I say unto all, 'Watch.' After two days was the feast of the Passover, and of unleavened bread: and the chief priests and the scribes sought how they might take him by craft, and put him to death. But they said, 'Not on the feast day, lest there be an uproar of the people.'"
>
> Mark 13:31-37, 14:1-2

"About that day or that hour" of the second coming of the Son of man to earth, no more as a sufferer, but as the judge, "no one knows," it says, "not even the angels in heaven, nor the Son, but only the Father." Surely, the Son of God knows, but not according to his human nature as man. For this reason, the Son of God did not reveal to us when this hour will be, so that we would not forget ourselves; rather, to always be ready to come before Him, and receive His judgment from Him: whether we are for eternal life in joy and blessedness, or for eternal torments.

"Therefore keep watch because you do not know when the master of the house will come back," when the Son of God will come. May He always finds us willing and ready, walking on the path that He has ordained. The Pharisees and the scribes, hating Him, wanted to kill Him; however, not on the feast day of Pascha, when so many people gathered, so that the people would not riot. Nonetheless, He did suffer and die right at the time of the feast of Pascha, when the paschal lamb was eaten; He willingly took up suffering, to the misfortune of His enemies.

Let us always be prepared to come before Him. God bless you!

ON THE WORDS OF THE LORD: "THEREFORE BE WISE AS SERPENTS AND HARMLESS AS DOVES"

Sermon at the Divine Liturgy on February 21/8, 1995,
in the patriarchal chapel
of St. Simeon the Myrrh-Gusher in Belgrade

> "Behold, I send you forth as sheep in the midst of wolves: be ye therefore wise as serpents, and harmless as doves. But beware of men: for they will deliver you up to the councils, and they will scourge you in their synagogues; and ye shall be brought before governors and kings for my sake, for a testimony against them and the Gentiles. But when they deliver you up, take no thought how or what ye shall speak: for it shall be given you in that same hour what ye shall speak. For it is not ye that speak, but the Spirit of your Father which speaks in you. And the brother shall deliver up the brother to death, and the father the child: and the children shall rise up against their parents, and cause them to be put to death. And ye shall be hated of all men for my name's sake: but he that endures to the end shall be saved."
>
> Matt. 10:16-22

It is hard for a sheep to survive among the wolves, but it is not impossible, because the Lord tells us in which way we can survive as His sheep even among the wolves. And that is: to be wise as snakes, and harmless as doves. Wisdom will keep us from becoming prey, so that the wolves do not tear us apart, that is, so that our enemies do not neutralize us. And harmlessness and goodness will preserve us from becoming wolves ourselves.

Even today, and throughout the centuries, how many times a thought came to many that the only way to survive among the wolves is to become a wolf oneself—among the Turks only as a Turk! And how many are those who because of this decided to undergo *Turkification*, to accept the Muslim faith, and they were *Turkified*! On the other hand, our other ancestors, brothers, remained the sheep of Christ in the name of His love.

One should, therefore, have wisdom; to develop the God-given wisdom more and more, and simultaneously, to develop goodness, too. For, wisdom without goodness turns into wickedness, and harmlessness without wisdom turns into witlessness. Neither one more than the other, but to be "wise as snakes, and harmless as doves."

"If they have persecuted me, they will also persecute you," says the Lord (John 15:20). We have to come to terms with this, and prepare ourselves even in such cases to remain the way we ought to be, the way our ancestors were: the people of God, God's nation. And then, when the end of our life comes, we will enter the blessedness of the heavenly kingdom. That is precisely the meaning and goal of our life. God bless you!

ON THE HOUR OF CRUCIFIXION

Sermon at the Divine Liturgy on February 24/11, 1995,
in the patriarchal chapel
of St. Simeon the Myrrh-Gusher in Belgrade

"And they bring him unto the place Golgotha, which is, being interpreted, 'the place of a skull.' And they gave him to drink wine mingled with myrrh: but he received it not. And when they had crucified him, they parted his garments, casting lots upon them, what every man should take. And it was the third hour, and they crucified him… And when the sixth hour was come, there was darkness over the whole land until the ninth hour. And at the ninth hour Jesus cried with a loud voice, saying, 'Eloi, Eloi, lama sabachthani?' which is, being interpreted, 'My God, my God, why hast thou forsaken me?' And some of them that stood by, when they heard it, said, 'Behold, he calls Elias.' And one ran and filled a sponge full of vinegar, and put it on a reed, and gave him to drink, saying, 'Let alone; let us see whether Elias will come to take him down.' And Jesus cried with a loud voice, and gave up the ghost. And the veil of the temple was rent in twain from the top to the bottom. And when the centurion, which stood over against him, saw that he so cried out, and gave up the ghost, he said, 'Truly this man was the Son of God.' There were also women looking on afar off: among whom was Mary Magdalene, and Mary the mother of James the less and of Joses, and Salome; (Who also, when he was in Galilee, followed him, and ministered unto him;) and many other women which came up with him unto Jerusalem."

Mark 15:22-25, 33-41

"And it was the third hour, and they crucified him;" this was recorded according to the Jewish calculation of time, and according to ours it is nine o'clock in the morning; with the Jews, the day begins at six in the evening; the day lasts twelve hours, and the night twelve hours. When the sixth hour had come, there was darkness over the whole land, which was at noon. And at the ninth hour He died, which is three in the afternoon.

I should mention this as well: "Eloi, Eloi, lama sabachthani?" which is translated, "My God, My God, why have You forsaken Me?"—this does not mean that God had forsaken Him, that He had left the Son on the cross; rather, that He, adopting our sinful nature, was praying for us, because we had been forsaken by God on account of our sins. God bless you!

ON THE SUFFERING OF CHRIST

Sermon at the Divine Liturgy on February 28/15, 1995,
in the patriarchal chapel
of St. Simeon the Myrrh-Gusher in Belgrade

> "And he came out, and went, as he was wont, to the Mount of Olives; and his disciples also followed him. And when he was at the place, he said unto them, 'Pray that ye enter not into temptation.' And he was withdrawn from them about a stone's cast, and kneeled down, and prayed, saying, 'Father, if thou be willing, remove this cup from me: nevertheless not my will, but thine, be done.' And there appeared an angel unto him from heaven, strengthening him. And being in an agony he prayed more earnestly: and his sweat was as it were great drops of blood falling down to the ground... And as soon as it was day, the elders of the people and the chief priests and the scribes came together, and led him into their council, saying, 'Art thou the Christ? tell us.' And he said unto them, 'If I tell you, ye will not believe: And if I also ask you, ye will not answer me, nor let me go. Hereafter shall the Son of man sit on the right hand of the power of God.' Then said they all, 'Art thou then the Son of God?' And he said unto them, 'Ye say that I am.' And they said, 'What need we any further witness? for we ourselves have heard of his own mouth.'"
>
> Luke 22:39-44, 66-71

This is about the suffering of Christ. "And [He] prayed, saying, 'Father, if You are willing, take this cup away from Me; nevertheless not My will, but Yours, be done.'" The Lord had our human nature as well. The soul does not want to be separated from the body, because we were created to not die. Still, through the sin of the forebears of man, man became mortal. Death is, therefore, unnatural for man, and when man dies, the soul does not want to separate from the body. Hence, the fear humans have. And He, having the same human nature, taking sins upon Himself, prayed, "If You are willing, take this cup away from Me."

I will mention this as well about the meaning of Christ's words, when they ask Him if He is the Son of God, "You say that I am." This is according to the Jewish manner of expression, and it means: it is as you say. For, here we immediately see the conclusion of the high priest, "What further testimony do we need? For we have heard it ourselves from His own mouth." It is wrong to think, as some heretics do, that Christ says here: You say that I am, but I am not saying that, neither am I the Son of God, but you say that I am He. Rather, here this means: it is just as you have said. For, I repeat, the high priests thus conclude, "What further testimony do we need; you have heard it yourselves from His own mouth that He is the Son of God." God bless you!

ON THE POWER OF FAITH

Sermon given in Krnjacha on April 2/March 20, 1995

> "Then one of the crowd answered and said, 'Teacher, I brought You my son, who has a mute spirit. And wherever it seizes him, it throws him down; he foams at the mouth, gnashes his teeth, and becomes rigid. And I spoke to Your disciples, that they should cast it out, but they could not.' He answered him and said, 'O faithless generation, how long shall I be with you? How long shall I bear with you? Bring him to Me.' Then they brought him to Him. And when he saw Him, immediately the spirit convulsed him, and he fell on the ground and wallowed, foaming at the mouth. So He asked his father, 'How long has this been happening to him?' And he said, 'From childhood. And often he has thrown him both into the fire and into the water to destroy him. But if You can do anything, have compassion on us and help us.' Jesus said to him, 'If you can believe, all things are possible to him who believes.' Immediately the father of the child cried out and said with tears, 'Lord, I believe; help my unbelief!'"
>
> Mark 9:17-24

From the words of the Lord we see, brothers and sisters, how important faith is in our life. This faith that God is Almighty, that He is merciful, and that He will help us; if we also make an effort to witness our faith with our life, He will help us, for if we are not such, and He does for us what we want, often—I'm not saying always—this would be to our detriment, and especially to the detriment of our neighbors.

The word of the Lord that He speaks unto us here, "All things are possible to him who believes," and that this spirit is not cast out except by fasting and prayer, does not mean as some interpret, that the Lord healed in such a way that He raised their faith, and then that faith of theirs, by their power, performed a miracle—namely, that He was doing that not by His own, but by human power. Rather, from other instances where the Lord healed we see otherwise. When that woman with the issue of blood touched the side of His robes, the issue of her illness ceased and she was healed. And the Lord, sensing that the power left Him, turned around and said, "Who touched me?" (Luke 8:45).

Hence, our faith is, in fact, only the power that connects us to the almighty power of God. The Lord, therefore, does not heal by suggestion, but by His power, and it is up to us, then, only to connect ourselves by our faith and our life according faith to that [*power supply which is*—T.N.] the almighty power of God.

This is demonstrated by all the Saints, in their lives and in their acts. Likewise, on this fourth Sunday of Great Lent, the holy Church celebrates St. John Climacus, that great Father and shepherd, monk at Mount Sinai, who was called "of the Ladder" after the book he wrote, *The Ladder of Divine Ascent*, a book that presents the ladder that we climb in order to reach the heavenly kingdom, and earn life eternal.

Here he speaks of various sins that prevent people from entering the Kingdom of Heaven. And he suggests, advises, to free ourselves from these sins, and instead of them to plant their opposite virtues. It is particularly important for us to acquire humility. St. John Chrysostom says that the Lord, wishing to build the edifice of evangelical virtues, placed as its foundation—humility, because it is blessed to be poor in spirit. This is the blessedness of those who see how much God does for them daily, as He does for other people, and how little we respond to Him with gratefulness for these gifts of His. So then, such people are always humble before God. Contrary to that Pharisee who bragged before God, and listed how he did more than God had asked, as if God was now indebted to Him, and not as if he was indebted to God for the mercy he received from Him. Whereas that publican did not dare even to lift up his eyes to heaven, but in humility he lowered himself; thus the Lord concludes, "The one who exalts himself will be humbled, but the one who humbles himself will be exalted" (Matt. 23:12). St. John also explains this saying, "Vanity, pride, is like a *tribulus*. However you throw it down, one spike always sticks up." This vanity always exists in us. We want to present ourselves before the world well: how nicely dressed we are, how elegant, how smart we are, and so on. In any case, there is no need for me to explain it further, neither to myself nor to you; we all know our own selves, and what vanity is.

Fighting against vanity, we will realize how much strength one needs for this fight throughout the whole life; however, we should make every effort in this endeavor, and God will help us to attain humility before God, and to be exalted before the world, in order to enter the Kingdom of Heaven.

ON THE POWER OF FAITH
SECOND SERMON

Sermon at the Divine Liturgy on July 9/June 26, 1995, in Vavedenye Monastery in Belgrade

> "Now when Jesus had entered Capernaum, a centurion came to Him, pleading with Him, saying, 'Lord, my servant is lying at home paralyzed, dreadfully tormented.' And Jesus said to him, 'I will come and heal him.' The centurion answered and said, 'Lord, I am not worthy that You should come under my roof. But only speak a word, and my servant will be healed. For I also am a man under authority, having soldiers under me. And I say to this one, "Go," and he goes; and to another, "Come," and he comes; and to my servant, "Do this," and he does it.' When Jesus heard it, He marveled, and said to those who followed, 'Assuredly, I say to you, I have not found such great faith, not even in Israel! And I say to you that many will come from east and west, and sit down with Abraham, Isaac, and Jacob in the kingdom of heaven. But the sons of the kingdom will be cast out into outer darkness. There will be weeping and gnashing of teeth.' Then Jesus said to the centurion, 'Go your way; and as you have believed, so let it be done for you.' And his servant was healed that same hour."
>
> Matt. 8:5-13

We have gathered, brothers and sisters, on the fourth Sunday after Pentecost, to pray for the peace and salvation of all people of goodwill, even our enemies, that the Lord, Who is Peace, and Who said, "My peace I give you!" would give unto us as well much needed peace.

However, the Lord will hear our prayers and listen to us, and He will do what we ask of Him, on the condition that we fulfill His will; then He will also fulfill our petitions, for our Lord Jesus said, "If you remain in me and my words remain in you, ask whatever you wish, and it will be done for you" (John 15:7). This, then, whether the Lord will hear us, and listen to us, depends on our faith and our life according to faith.

From the Gospel reading we heard today, we see what faith means. For, that centurion was a pagan, an idol-worshipper at that, but he showed great faith in Jesus beseeching Him to heal his servant who was ill at home, on his deathbed; and the Lord said He would come and heal him. "I am not worthy, Lord, that you should enter under my roof," the centurion replied, "but only say the word and my servant will be healed. For I also am a man with soldiers under my authority. And I say to this one, 'Go,' and he goes; and to another, 'Come,' and he comes; and to my servant, 'Do this,' and he does it." And the Lord marveled as the faith of this pagan man, and He said, "Go your way; your servant is healthy." And, indeed, his servant was healed at that very moment.

The Lord heals with His almighty power. Many people do not understand that, and they think that those miracles that Christ performed were suggestion or autosuggestion. However, from these and other examples—like that of a woman who was ill, and only touched the side of His robe, and was healed—we see that it is the almighty power of God that heals. Our faith, though, is simply our own connection to this almighty power of God, just like at our home or here we press a button and turn something on, whether a light bulb, or some other appliance, making it part of the electric circuit; this pressing down on the switch to turn on the electric circuit, this is like our faith that plugs us into the [*power supply that is the*—T.N.] almighty power of God. Whoever believes, "who has ears to hear, let him hear!" (Matt. 11:15).

Today we had a particular joy, brothers and sisters, to have prayed together and communed with two Metropolitans of the church of Constantinople, Metropolitan John Zizioulas and Metropolitan Meliton. It is the church wherefrom we received Christianity, and wherefrom the brothers Cyril and Methodius were sent into the Slavic lands to enlighten those people also with the evangelical teaching. Rejoicing, therefore, in this union that connects all of us Orthodox through Holy Communion with the Lord Jesus and all the faithful in the world, we congratulate these brothers here who were baptized and entered the Church of God, who have become members, cells, limbs of the Body of Christ. We impress on their mind and in their heart, as well as our own, to confirm their faith by their life, and thereby for us all to be witnesses of the Son of God in this world that "lies in evil." And may the Lord have mercy on us, and gladden us with peace. God bless you and grant you every good thing!

ON THE SCRIBES AND THE PHARISEES

Sermon at the Divine Liturgy on August 21/18, 1995,
in the patriarchal chapel
of St. Simeon the Myrrh-Gusher in Belgrade

"But woe unto you, scribes and Pharisees, hypocrites! for ye shut up the kingdom of heaven against men: for ye neither go in yourselves, neither suffer ye them that are entering to go in. Woe unto you, scribes and Pharisees, hypocrites! for ye devour widows' houses, and for a pretense make long prayer: therefore ye shall receive the greater damnation. Woe unto you, scribes and Pharisees, hypocrites! for ye compass sea and land to make one proselyte, and when he is made, ye make him twofold more the child of hell than yourselves. Woe unto you, ye blind guides, which say, 'Whosoever shall swear by the temple, it is nothing; but whosoever shall swear by the gold of the temple, he is a debtor!' Ye fools and blind: for whether is greater, the gold, or the temple that sanctifieth the gold? And, 'Whosoever shall swear by the altar, it is nothing; but whosoever sweareth by the gift that is upon it, he is guilty.' Ye fools and blind: for whether is greater, the gift, or the altar that sanctifieth the gift? Whoso therefore shall swear by the altar, sweareth by it, and by all things thereon. And whoso shall swear by the temple, sweareth by it, and by him that dwelleth therein. And he that shall swear by heaven, sweareth by the throne of God, and by him that sitteth thereon."

Matt. 23:13-22

When we think about this word of our Lord, where He condemns the scribes and the Pharisees for making long prayers for a pretense, the point of the matter is not that we should not make long prayers to God; however, it means that we should not offer false prayers ever, nor anywhere; rather, we should pray sincerely, that is, to prove the sincerity of our prayer by our life.

Let us ponder these words, "Woe to you, scribes and Pharisees, hypocrites! For you shut up the kingdom of heaven against men; for you neither go in yourselves, nor do you allow those who are entering to go in." How many people and nations are there in this world today who do not believe in God! Many have read the Holy Scripture of the Old and New Testaments, but they remained pagan. They often say, with best intentions in mind, that when they see our life, the life of today's Christians, and how far it is from the Gospel and from our Lord's teaching, that it is hard for them to believe. For we become a wall that does not allow those who would want to enter the heavenly kingdom to do so.

This, among other things should be a constant warning to us, that with our lives we must not be an impediment to other people, who look upon our life and make conclusions accordingly about the truthfulness of the Kingdom of Heaven; therefore, to witness the faith in our Lord Jesus by our Orthodox life. The Lord counsels that by saving our souls, by living according to the evangelical teaching, we also help others to approach the heavenly kingdom. God bless you!

ON THE NEW SERBIAN CASUALTIES WHO DIED AT THE HANDS OF NATO

On Friday, September 1/August 19, 1995, at 6 p.m., His Holiness Patriarch of Serbia Paul served a prayer service (*moleben*) to the new Serbian martyrs in the church of St. Mark. The tragic events of those days—the horrific bombings by NATO airplanes of innocent Serbs in Sarajevo, Gorazde, and in the Serbian Bosnia and Herzegovina—were the reason for serving a *moleben* in Belgrade again. In a church full of the faithful, priests from virtually every Belgrade parish served.

In the name of the Father, and the Son, and the Holy Spirit! "If anyone desires to come after Me, let him deny himself, and take up his cross and follow Me" (Luke 9:23). Those who were the greatest in our nation accepted these words of His, and expressed in their own words: we are bound to carry the cross. They understood, brothers and sisters, that the Son of God Who addressed these words to us was the first one to take His own cross up to Golgotha; He was crucified on it, and on it He died. He knows the weight of the cross. He knows the agony of crucifixion, and the bitterness of death. However, He is also the Almighty God, Who with His divine power resurrected as well, and Who promised, brothers and sisters, that all those who suffer and die by the hand of evil-doers on His path will be resurrected in the day when He comes again into this world, no more as a sufferer, but as the King of kings, and Lord of lords. May this faith, brothers and sisters, sustain us today as well, and our entire nation in these struggles and misfortunes, in suffering and death, which enemies inflict upon us daily! Let this faith uphold us, so that we do not falter, nor fall into despair! We should remember the words of Christ, "...there is nothing concealed that will not be revealed, nor hidden that will not be made known" (Luke 12:2).

Brothers and sisters, we should never be afraid of anything except the One God! Just as our people throughout the centuries repeated the words, "for Marko fears no one but One Great God." Fear only sin, and that which is unjust, which is a crime, that which kills the soul of an individual as well as the soul of a nation—therefore, we should only be afraid of sin. Do not be afraid of suffering on the path of God!

You know that the Holy Apostle Paul was captured and taken to Rome to the court of Emperor Nero. He was a prisoner in the imperial dungeon. Having been condemned and slain by the sword, he died. Nero's empire passed, and he passed with it, and mankind remembers him only for his evil, for his crimes. Yet the kingdom into which the Holy Apostle Paul entered, that kingdom, and he along with it, never passes. The evildoers, the Neros shall pass; justice and truth abide forever. May we be on the side of justice and the truth, and all that is holy and honorable, and we will survive forever!

May the Lord help, and St. Sava, the Holy Prince Lazar, and the Holy New-Martyrs, that we endure on the path of God until the end! And when we come before our holy ancestors, I repeat this to myself and to you, brothers and sisters, may we not be ashamed before them, nor they be ashamed of us and our deeds, both today and when we come before them. May we also rejoice throughout eternity in the Kingdom of Heaven with all the Saints. This is the most important thing both for us, for those who are bombing us, and for those who are dying for the truth and justice, for peace and freedom for all, even for us. God bless you and grant you every good thing!

ON BLASPHEMY AGAINST THE HOLY SPIRIT

Sermon at the Divine Liturgy on September 6/August 24, 1995, in the patriarchal chapel of St. Simeon the Myrrh-Gusher in Belgrade

"Verily I say unto you, All sins shall be forgiven unto the sons of men, and blasphemies wherewith soever they shall blaspheme: But he that shall blaspheme against the Holy Ghost hath never forgiveness, but is in danger of eternal damnation. Because they said, 'He hath an unclean spirit.' There came then his brethren and his mother, and, standing without, sent unto him, calling him. And the multitude sat about him, and they said unto him, 'Behold, thy mother and thy brethren without seek for thee.' And he answered them, saying, 'Who is my mother, or my brethren?' And he looked round about on them which sat about him, and said, 'Behold my mother and my brethren! For whosoever shall do the will of God, the same is my brother, and my sister, and mother.'"

Mark 3:28-35

I have spoken many times regarding the blasphemy against the Holy Spirit. Blasphemy against the Holy Spirit is consciously, maliciously speaking falsehood against the Son of God, because the Holy Spirit is the Spirit of Truth. Hence, the man who speaks against the truth consciously, out of malice, cannot repent either, because he does not want to repent. Since he does not want to repent, there can be no forgiveness. If a man, having considered all facts and all circumstances, subsequently reaches a wrong conclusion based solely on insufficient facts—this is not a blasphemy against the Holy Spirit; this is not against the truth. In this case, he was simply unable to perceive the entire truth, and he came to the wrong conclusion merely relying on partial, incomplete facts. It is not blasphemy to deceive oneself and others out of ignorance. It is an entirely different matter when someone does it out of malice, like the Pharisees did when He healed a deaf and dumb man; they said the Lord does it with the help of Beelzebub, the prince of demons. If a kingdom is divided against itself, this kingdom will be ruined, because it destroys itself; one part of it goes against the other. Likewise, demons who received reason from God, certainly will not rise one against the other. Hence, the Pharisees were aware it was not true; He could not cast out a demon with the help of a demon. But, as I stated, they said this against Him out of malice.

Then Christ spoke this word, "Every sin will be forgiven, but this sin cannot be forgiven." If it is a blasphemy against God, we cannot repent. Since we cannot see God, many say: Let me see God and I will believe. However, they will not *believe* then—when a person sees God, then he will *know*; and now we see as if in a mirror. Similarly, whoever blasphemes against Jesus Christ, the Son of God, can be forgiven. One can clearly see that He is a man. Yet, to conclude thereafter that He is also God! How many are those who have not seen this! Even the Apostle Paul did not believe that He was God, until he saw Him. Have we understood now? The blasphemy against the Holy Spirit is a conscious, malicious speaking of falsehood, because the Holy Spirit is the Spirit of Truth. And whoever speaks against someone in malice, that person will not repent; hence, this cannot be forgiven.

Who are the brothers and sisters of Christ? I spoke about this many times as well. These are Joseph's children from his first marriage. His wife died, and then he betrothed himself to the Holy Theotokos according to the Law of Moses. We also know from Holy Scripture that, before they came together, she conceived of the Holy Spirit. And Joseph, seeing that she was pregnant, and thinking it was a sin, had in mind to release her secretly, although one is stoned for such offense, according to the Law. Then an angel of God appeared unto him, and told him that she conceived of the Holy Spirit, and that the One Who would be born of her would be holy and would be called the Son of God. Hence, from his first, his actual marriage, Joseph had four sons: James, Joseph, Simon, and Judas (Matt. 13:55-56), and several daughters are mentioned: "And his sisters, are they not all with us?" Thus, there were at least two sisters. We should know to inform ourselves and others as well that the Holy Theotokos certainly did not have relations with her husband; on the contrary, she was a virgin before the birth of our Lord, likewise in giving birth, and she remained a virgin after giving birth. This we should know to advise ourselves and others, because we have Christian sects and Protestants, who think that the brothers and sisters of Christ are the children that the Mother of God gave birth to afterwards, with Joseph. You should know our teaching, our faith. For it is clear—when even pagan priestesses were obliged to live in celibacy, and if one of them sinned, she would be stoned—how could it be that she who gave birth to the Son of God would not remain virgin until the end of time!

This should suffice. Yet to mention also: it seems as if, in a way, Christ is renouncing His mother, brothers, and sisters. This is not the case at all. That is not the gist of His words when He says, "Who is my mother, or my brethren?" Rather, here He shows to all of us that we can all have such familiarity with Him, if we fulfill the will of God: "For whoever does the will of God is my brother and my sister and mother." Therefore, we can also be so close to Him as His mother, brothers, and sisters, on condition that we fulfill the will of God. Fulfilling the will of God in order to achieve this familiarity—that is our task. Those who have ears to hear, let them hear. God bless you!

ON THE WORDS OF THE LORD: "YOU ARE THE LIGHT OF THE WORLD"

Sermon at the Divine Liturgy on September 7/August 25, 1995,
in the patriarchal chapel
of St. Simeon the Myrrh-Gusher in Belgrade

"You are the light of the world. A city that is set on a hill cannot be hidden. Nor do they light a lamp and put it under a basket, but on a lampstand, and it gives light to all who are in the house. Let your light so shine before men, that they may see your good works and glorify your Father in heaven. Do not think that I came to destroy the Law or the Prophets. I did not come to destroy but to fulfill. For assuredly, I say to you, till heaven and earth pass away, one jot or one tittle will by no means pass from the law till all is fulfilled. Whoever therefore breaks one of the least of these commandments, and teaches men so, shall be called least in the kingdom of heaven; but whoever does and teaches them, he shall be called great in the kingdom of heaven."

Matt. 5:14-19

The Lord's commandment also refers to all of us today, to those who "have ears to hear" what the Lord is saying (Matt. 11:15). In the dark, the spiritual darkness of this world, we should be lamps that give light so that they "may see your good works and glorify your Father in heaven," with our words in their proper time, and with our lives at every moment to witness to the truth of the Gospel, the truth of the Son of God. For He tells us about the Law of God that He has given, that not one iota, not one letter of it, will be abolished, and that He came to fulfill it with His own life. Likewise we should also offer up our life as a sacrifice to God! For sacrifices were established in the time of the Old Testament. Already the sons of Adam and Eve, Cain and Abel, offered a sacrifice to God; Cain from farming, for he was a farmer, and Abel from livestock, for he was a stockbreeder. God gave the written laws wherein it says what could be offered up as sacrifice to God. People offered whatever they invested their efforts in. Everyone offered their labor. One could not offer wild fruit, or wild animals that people hunted for their food; rather, the fruit and the wheat, and generally all those things in which people have invested their labor. Similarly, one offered domestic animals, wherein man also invested effort to raise them. Of birds one could offer only pigeons and doves, because at that time, and even today, pigeons are sometimes kept as domestic animals.

I caution you also, that we should offer up our effort toward the bloodless sacrifice as well. It happens that we write a list with many names of our relatives, acquaintances, and friends, and we bring it to church for the priest to read. The entire effort of the person is in that he merely wrote down the names, and in such great number. I beseech you to keep in mind that we offer of our own labors at least a dollar or a half-dollar, and not to rely only on the effort of the priest! I myself will take none of that money. The one who cannot offer a half-dollar or something else, should read the names he wrote silently in his mind, and the Lord will take a note of that. We have to offer up our own efforts, not to shift our duty to another, and only give what we deem we should.

I wish to say this as well. In these critical times, of crisis and misfortune, and of tense nerves, there are many people who fall under the influence of unclean spirits because of their vanity and pride. The devil praises them how they are more exalted in spirit than the rest, and therefore the Mother of God appears to them, as well as the Archangels Michael and Gabriel; that they are God's special elect, and that, as those who have authority, they should subsequently teach others what they should do, how they should fast, when and how to pray—while they themselves are not taught sufficiently. Beware of vanity, and of pride! Of this St. Gregory the Theologian says, "Why do you pretend to be the head, when you are a finger or a nail on the foot!" Humble yourselves, and when something appears, or some thoughts that are often implanted by the one who wishes us ruin, one should say, "Lord, preserve me from this, because I am not yet mature enough to know how to tell the spirits apart." One girl, a student of mathematics, came to ask me if I would receive the "holy godbearer from Medjugorje." — "And how did you get in touch with the 'godbearer of Medjugorje?' Were you born there?" I asked her. No, the girl was from Nish. "Well, she is present here, and she appears to me." — "And what does she say to you?" — "She is asking whether you would receive her?" — "That 'godbearer' who appears to you and who asks whether I will receive her better not come! And the One I venerate, and the entire Orthodox Church, she knows whether she should come to me, and I will bow down to her when she comes." Then I told her, "My child, you have gone far in your vanity and pride. You will have a hard time coming back." Here is only one example of how widespread this is. Understand that humility is the foundation of our spiritual life! St. John Chrysostom says that when the Lord had in mind to build the edifice of evangelical virtues, and to instruct us in the way we should build the edifice of evangelical virtues and good deeds, He placed humility as its foundation. "Blessed are the poor in spirit..." (Matt. 5:3) that is, the humble ones, the meek, who always know how much good God does for them, and how little they respond to it; they always draw back, and always feel their own sinfulness and their unworthiness. Only a vain man promotes himself. One man even said he was God!

Therefore, I implore you; humility is that which is love toward God, is what kept the Archangels Michael and Gabriel close to God; love toward God preserved them not to fall into the sin of pride which pushed into hell Satanael, who used to be an angel; it turned him into Satan. What will pride, then, do to us!

May the Lord help us to be liberated from the desire to look great and important before the world; rather, may we put that effort into truly becoming great before God. This is accomplished by humility, by serving one's neighbor, by serving God and people. God bless you!

ON MARTHA AND MARY

Sermon at the Divine Liturgy on September 13/August 31, 1995,
in the patriarchal chapel
of St. Simeon the Myrrh-Gusher in Belgrade

> "Now it came to pass, as they went, that he entered into a certain village: and a certain woman named Martha received him into her house. And she had a sister called Mary, which also sat at Jesus' feet, and heard his word. But Martha was cumbered about much serving, and came to him, and said, 'Lord, dost thou not care that my sister hath left me to serve alone? bid her therefore that she help me.' And Jesus answered and said unto her, 'Martha, Martha, thou art careful and troubled about many things: But one thing is needful: and Mary hath chosen that good part, which shall not be taken away from her.' And it came to pass, as he spoke these things, a certain woman of the company lifted up her voice, and said unto him, 'Blessed is the womb that bore You, and the breasts which nursed You!' But he said, 'Yea rather, blessed are they that hear the word of God, and keep it.'"
>
> Luke 10:38-42, 11:27-28

Let us be edified by these words that our Lord addressed to Martha! Certainly, our Lord is not against welcoming Him and hosting Him in the flesh, serving Him bodily. However, in all this, one should not forget the spiritual need, for many times He said that the soul of man does not live on bread alone, but on every word that comes out of the mouth of God. We have bodies; we need bodily food; but we are also souls, and the soul requires nourishment as well, and that is the word, the teaching of God. Hence the Lord says not to trouble ourselves too much about the body, but to show concern for the soul, more so than for the body.

And as He spoke these things, a woman suddenly lifted up her voice and cried out, "Blessed is the womb that bore You, and the breasts which nursed You!" And He said, "Yea rather, blessed are they that hear the word of God, and keep it." Here we see that we can also acquire this familiarity that His mother has toward Him, if we listen to the word of God, keep and fulfill it. Not to give oneself too much importance, as if we were God's special elect. Listen to this word of God, the word of the Gospel, and right away strive to fulfill it. Likewise, what is certainly most important for us: to beware of vanity, of pride that whispers to us how we are God's special elect, miracle workers who heal; and of vanity in general: how well we speak, how we dress ourselves nicely, how people laud us—because then faith will depart from us. "How can you believe," says John the Evangelist, "who receive honor from one another, and do not seek the honor that comes from the only God?" (John 5:44). Therefore, faith departs from the one who does not seek the glory of God and humility, but creates an idol of himself. Take care to remember this! God bless you!

ON THE WORDS OF THE LORD: "FOR MY YOKE IS EASY AND MY BURDEN IS LIGHT"

Sermon at the Divine Liturgy on September 14/1, 1995, in the patriarchal chapel of St. Simeon the Myrrh-Gusher in Belgrade

> "All things have been delivered to me by my Father, and no one knows the Son except the Father. Nor does anyone know the Father except the Son, and the one to whom the Son wills to reveal Him. Come to me, all you who labor and are heavy laden, and I will give you rest. Take my yoke upon you and learn from me, for I am gentle and lowly in heart, and you will find rest for your souls. For My yoke is easy and my burden is light."
>
> Matt. 11:27-30

"My yoke is easy and my burden is light." This teaching of our Lord, the evangelical teaching, should be fulfilled and lived; it should ripen in us and bear the fruit of good deeds, for to us, the way we are, the path of God seems difficult. It is because we have already gotten used to sin, because we have acquired bad, sinful habits, that the path of God is hard for us. How many times have I repeated to myself and to all who will listen: is it not easier to be sober, than a drunkard? Is it not easier not to smoke, than to waste money and ruin your lungs with smoke; also, of course, that is a sort of drug—why become a slave of such an enemy? Is it not easier to suffer if someone slightly insults you, than to return evil for evil, and even double?

Nevertheless I say, let us make an effort to take the yoke of the Lord upon ourselves, to be prepared to face difficulties in this world, and by following Him to be freed by Him; For He took up His cross to Golgotha, and He knows the weight of a cross. Still, He is mighty to lighten it for us when He deems it necessary, so that we would not falter under the weight of the cross—only if we as coworkers of His do what we can. Then, with His power He will certainly always do His part to lighten the load for us as much as is needed. God bless you!

ON DISCERNING THE SPIRITS

Sermon at the Divine Liturgy on September 18/5, 1995,
in the patriarchal chapel
of St. Simeon the Myrrh-Gusher in Belgrade

"There was in the days of Herod, the king of Judaea, a certain priest named Zacharias, of the course of Abijah: and his wife was of the daughters of Aaron, and her name was Elisabeth. And they were both righteous before God, walking in all the commandments and ordinances of the Lord blameless. And they had no child, because that Elisabeth was barren, and they both were now well stricken in years. And it came to pass, that while he executed the priest's office before God in the order of his course, according to the custom of the priest's office, his lot was to burn incense when he went into the temple of the Lord. And the whole multitude of the people were praying without at the time of incense. And there appeared unto him an angel of the Lord standing on the right side of the altar of incense. And when Zacharias saw him, he was troubled, and fear fell upon him. But the angel said unto him, 'Fear not, Zacharias: for thy prayer is heard; and thy wife Elisabeth shall bear thee a son, and thou shalt call his name John...' And Zacharias said unto the angel, 'Whereby shall I know this? for I am an old man, and my wife well stricken in years.' And the angel answering said unto him, 'I am Gabriel, that stand in the presence of God; and am sent to speak unto thee, and to shew thee these glad tidings. And, behold, thou shalt be dumb, and not able to speak, until the day that these things shall be performed, because thou believest not my words, which shall be fulfilled in their season.' And the people waited for Zacharias, and marveled that he tarried so long in the temple. And when he came out, he could not speak unto them: and they perceived that he had seen a vision in the temple: for he beckoned unto them, and remained speechless. And it came to pass, that, as soon as the days of his ministration were accomplished, he departed to his own house."

Luke 1:5-13, 18-23

In the Old Testament temple, as well as in the pagan temples, people did not enter inside the temple, but they stood around the temple and brought their offerings there. They brought them to the priests who then offered them up as a sacrifice on the altar. The Jerusalem temple, the Old Testament one, was separated into two parts. There was the sanctuary where priests entered daily to light the sevenfold candlestick and to burn incense. Only one priest at a time would enter at the time of prayer, and bring in a censer full of burning coals and incense, and place it on the altar of incense, which was in the temple. They would go in on the Sabbath as well, when they would leave on the table of showbread twelve loaves of bread in the name of the twelve tribes of Israel. The other part of the temple was "the holiest of holies," wherein no one entered, except priests, and only once a year at that, on the Day of Atonement. The priest would sprinkle the top of the ark, which held the two tablets of Moses with the Ten Commandments he received on Mount Sinai, and the golden pot with manna. Only on that one day did the priest enter the holiest of holies.

It was decided in a special way who would do the censing. When it was his turn, Zacharias entered with the censer full of burning coals and incense; then the Angel Gabriel appeared to him on the right side of the altar, and brought him the good news that his wife would give birth to a son. Zacharias asked how this would happen, how he would know this, and because of his disbelief, on that day he became mute. Beware, brothers and sisters, in these our times, of our imaginings, the thoughts we have, and the ability to debate those questions that interest us; let us not understand that as a special annunciation from God, for there is also the adversary who implants thoughts in us, who wants us to face the same ruin that he brought upon himself. I always repeat: when such thoughts come to us, let us say, "Lord, help! You know that I am not mature enough to be able to tell the spirits apart; therefore deliver me from this vision." Keep watch over yourselves, because in this time of crisis there are many who use this imagination of theirs, and they interpret the action of the devil as an appearance of holy powers, holy angels, and of even God Himself.

Let us bring in a little bit of humility into our soul, and an awareness of our own spiritual level. We are not yet able to discern the spirits. Beware of various sects, and these Hindu sects and teachings about the migration of souls, which is utterly unacceptable from the standpoint of the Gospel. A man is bound to die, and then, the judgment. In the Gospel we see that God sent His holy angels and Saints to appear to people, but those were special cases. For example, just as an angel appeared to Zacharias here, and later to Joseph, so that the latter would know about the manner in which the Most Holy Mother of God had conceived. Humility! Let us not think that we are God's special elect. Each one of us, in our own position, can be great. Even the most simple man and woman can be greater before God than some priest, patriarch, or bishop, if they make an effort. However, let us take care to remember the words of St. Gregory the Theologian, "Why do you pretend to be the head, when you are a finger?"

May the Lord help us to value His words at all times, to live according to His word, and thus to witness to the Son of God, and to help ourselves the most, but also all others who along with us wish to be saved. Thereby we also help our long-suffering nation in these horrific agonies and travails. God bless you!

ON THE UNITY OF LIFE AND THEOLOGY

Sermon given at the beginning of October, in 1995,
on the occasion of the beginning of the first academic year
in the new building of the Faculty of Orthodox Theology

At the beginning of our work in this new building of the Faculty, we prayed to the Lord to help the teachers and you students, and all of us as well, so that studying the evangelical teaching at all times, we may introduce it into our own lives straightaway. Always have in mind the word of St. Gregory the Theologian that "Christian theory without praxis is equally imperfect as praxis without theory." Let us always have this in mind. A person cannot in any way be useful to his church and his people if he does not make an effort to fulfill the will of God and to save his soul. The same St. Gregory the Theologian says, "It is impossible for a person to bring someone else to God, if he himself did not come to God. It is impossible for him to set ablaze the little candle of light in the soul of another, while inside himself there is darkness, rather than light." Therefore, always have in mind this necessity: to teach according to God, and to live according to that teaching. "If you know these things, blessed are you if you do them," says the Lord (John 13:17).

St. Justin the Martyr and Philosopher was a learned man, however, he was a pagan, and he heard his fellow citizens, his compatriots, accuse Christians of slaughtering their children and drinking their blood; they understood the suppers of love, *agape*, to be some kind of orgy. "When I saw, "Justin says, "how Christians boldly go to death for their beliefs, I concluded that what the enemies said was not true. What evildoer would want to stop his voluptuous lawless life? He would try by all manner of means to extend it. However, because of their beliefs, they were prepared to sacrifice themselves, to die." Believing in Christ the Lord and in the heavenly kingdom, they were thus prepared to confirm their faith by their actions.

It is needful both today and always to help oneself and others. The one who is not first and foremost striving to save his own life, to enter the Kingdom of Heaven, cannot be of any use, neither to his church, nor to his people, nor mankind. For, the one who is truly saving his life, who strives to live according to God, inevitably helps all who have eyes to see and ears to hear, so that they, too, are edified by it, and drawn to the Kingdom of Heaven, if they desire it.

There, dear brothers and sisters in Christ, with such actions let us witness the Lord Jesus in this difficult time, and in this world that lies in evil. Not to present ourselves better than we are, pharisaically. Rather, to employ this energy, which others use for these other purposes, to truly be better, closer to God and to our holy ancestors, and thereby to be able to help both our nation, and all people of goodwill; and most of all, to help ourselves. May we find ourselves in the Kingdom of Heaven on the side where the Lord will recognize and acknowledge us as His own.

To the Dean and esteemed professors, to the teachers and all of you, I wish help and blessings from the Lord. God bless you!

ON THE REVELATION OF JOHN

Sermon given on return from Patmos,
on October 1/September 18, 1995,
in the church of St. Sava in Belgrade

"...Whosoever will come after me, let him deny himself, and take up his cross, and follow me. For whosoever will save his life shall lose it; but whosoever shall lose his life for my sake and the gospel's, the same shall save it. For what shall it profit a man, if he shall gain the whole world, and lose his own soul? Or what shall a man give in exchange for his soul? Whosoever therefore shall be ashamed of me and of my words in this adulterous and sinful generation; of him also shall the Son of man be ashamed, when he cometh in the glory of his Father with the holy angels. And he said unto them, 'Verily I say unto you, that there be some of them that stand here, which shall not taste of death, till they have seen the kingdom of God come with power.'"

Mark 8:34-38, 9:1

This year, brothers and sisters, the holy Church celebrates 1900 years since the writing of the last book of the New Testament, Revelation, that is, the Apocalypse of our Lord Jesus Christ, which was written by the Holy Evangelist John. He wrote it on the island of Patmos where he was exiled, as he himself says. Thus, he found himself on the island because of his faith in God and for witnessing to Jesus Christ. In this work he wrote, the history of the Church from its beginning until its end is expounded in prophetic visions and mysterious images, which as they occur, will become clearer and more evident. He explicated what difficulties, persecutions, and travails the Church of God and her faithful in this world would endure. He also stated how the Antichrist would come who would take his seat in God's Church and represent himself as God. St. John presented all this to us so we would know how to prepare and brace ourselves for those days regardless of when they would come—now or later. However, to be ready for any struggle, difficulty, and persecution in this world which are inevitable.

You know the circumstances in which we have found ourselves, from whence we return; our condition during the First and Second World Wars, and this present one as well—extraordinary circumstances under a government that was atheistically and materialistically inclined. You know how many troubles we all had.

Let us prepare for struggles, so that we do not falter and lose our souls for the sake of our bodies, from fear of death. This is the message of St. John the Evangelist as well. For, at the end of the world, the holy Church of God will be glorified, because the head of the Church is the Lord Jesus, and He is God Almighty. This, too, gives us the strength to endure on the path of God, as is befitting, not giving up nor getting off the track; the way all the Saints were, who endured every manner of persecution, every torture, even death. They did it with the faith that those on God's path, who suffer death for His justice and truth, are alive before the living God; these are alive before Him, and the dead are only sinners who do not repent, and who continue their life of spiritual and physical ruin.

Let this, brothers and sisters, be the message of the Holy Gospel of our Lord Jesus, and His book of the New Testament, the Apocalypse of St. John: in these trials and tribulations that befall us, let us double and triple our prayers to God for peace in this world, for peace both unto us and unto our enemies, because we all need peace, even though they know not what they do. Let us always strive to know what we are doing, that is, according to the wisdom of the Gospel, the teaching of God, to always do unto others what we wish for ourselves, to beware of every sin. Likewise, to not fear those who can kill the body, and after that can do no more, but to fear the one who after he kills the body has authority to throw us into hell, into eternal torments; this means to fear God and therefore to fear sin, which distances us from God, and results in our being in eternal torments in our immortal body.

May the Lord help all of us, brothers and sisters, to worthily bear the name of Orthodox Christians, and thereby to witness with our holy life quietly with our deeds, with our life to all others in this world. This will be the best help, I say, to our suffering nation, to all mankind, and to our enemies; still the greatest blessing will be unto us ourselves, because we will realize the meaning of our life, and that is: to enter the heavenly kingdom where there is no sickness, nor sorrow, nor sighing. May the Lord bless you and grant you every good thing.

ON FAITH AND LIFE ACCORDING TO FAITH

Sermon at the Divine Liturgy on October 8/September 25, 1995, in the Monastery of the Entry of the Mother of God into the Temple, in Belgrade

> "Then Jesus went out from there and departed to the region of Tyre and Sidon. And behold, a woman of Canaan came from that region and cried out to Him, saying, 'Have mercy on me, O Lord, Son of David! My daughter is severely demon-possessed.' But He answered her not a word. And His disciples came and urged Him, saying, 'Send her away, for she cries out after us.' But He answered and said, 'I was not sent except to the lost sheep of the house of Israel.' Then she came and worshiped Him, saying, 'Lord, help me!' But He answered and said, 'It is not good to take the children's bread and throw it to the little dogs.' And she said, 'Yes, Lord, yet even the little dogs eat the crumbs which fall from their masters' table.' Then Jesus answered and said to her, 'O woman, great is your faith! Let it be to you as you desire.' And her daughter was healed from that very hour."
>
> Matt. 15:21-28

In the name of the Father, and the Son, and the Holy Spirit! We have prayed, brothers and sisters, in this holy temple today, and we have served the Divine Liturgy, the Mystery of the Body and Blood of our Lord Jesus Christ. We have heard the words of the Holy Gospel that are unto us spiritual food at all times, for we are bodies that need food, but we are also souls, which need nourishment as well; and the food for the soul is the word of God, the teaching of God. We also heard of the miracle that the Lord performed by healing the daughter of the Canaanite woman because of her great faith. "O woman, great is your faith! Let it be to you as you desire. And her daughter was healed from that very hour."

In these misfortunes that have befallen our people, brothers and sisters, the way we will be able to help—ourselves and our entire nation, even our enemies, and the whole world—is by being so faithful that the Lord Himself tells us our faith is great. Not only great in words, though, but a faith that manifests itself in our lives, that is shown in our actions. It is the Orthodox faith. For, the Lord Jesus says, "If you know these things, blessed are you if you do them" if you keep them (John 12:17). We are not, thus, blessed if we know only; we are not blessed if we do only. Rather, when we know, and do them. It is an entirely different matter to know, and another to do. Certainly, how can we do something, if we do not know what is good and God-pleasing? However, we can know perfectly and tell others about it, but ourselves we live in a completely opposite manner.

Lord, be merciful to us, even unto our enemies who know not what they do. You Who are the God of Peace, bring peace to our country, and grant us the peace we all need so much! Lord, help us to be worthy of our Orthodox Christian name that we bear, worthy of our holy ancestors who knew in all circumstances and difficulties of life to be and remain Your people.

We pray to them, our holy ancestors headed by St. Sava, to sustain us to be in this world witnesses of the name of God, faith in Lord Jesus, and life according to that faith. Thus, may the Lord have mercy on us and send peace to our country. God bless you and grant you every good thing! Amen.

ON THE WORDS OF THE LORD: "AND YOU WILL BE HATED BY ALL FOR MY NAME'S SAKE"

Sermon at the Divine Liturgy on November 9/October 27, 1995, in the patriarchal chapel of St. Simeon the Myrrh-Gusher in Belgrade

"But before all these, they shall lay their hands on you, and persecute you, delivering you up to the synagogues, and into prisons, being brought before kings and rulers for my name's sake. And it shall turn to you for a testimony. Settle it therefore in your hearts, not to meditate before what ye shall answer: For I will give you a mouth and wisdom, which all your adversaries shall not be able to gainsay nor resist. And ye shall be betrayed both by parents, and brethren, and kinsfolks, and friends; and some of you shall they cause to be put to death. And ye shall be hated of all men for my name's sake. But there shall not a hair of your head perish. In your patience possess ye your souls. And when ye shall see Jerusalem compassed with armies, then know that the desolation thereof is nigh. Then let them which are in Judaea flee to the mountains; and let them which are in the midst of it depart out; and let not them that are in the countries enter thereinto. For these be the days of vengeance, that all things which are written may be fulfilled. But woe unto them that are with child, and to them that give suck, in those days! For there shall be great distress in the land, and wrath upon this people. And they shall fall by the edge of the sword, and shall be led away captive into all nations: and Jerusalem shall be trodden down of the Gentiles, until the times of the Gentiles be fulfilled. And there shall be signs in the sun, and in the moon, and in the stars; and upon the earth distress of nations, with perplexity; the sea and the waves

> roaring; Men's hearts failing them for fear, and for looking after those things which are coming on the earth: for the powers of heaven shall be shaken. And then shall they see the Son of man coming in a cloud with power and great glory."
>
> Luke 21:12-27

"But it will turn out for you," it says, "as an occasion for testimony." We bear testimony in this world of the Son of God and His teaching both by words and by our life. This will be the best sermon of ours to all people of goodwill "...that they may see your good deeds, and glorify your Father who is in heaven" (Matt. 5:16).

Beware of verbosity; especially of imposing your faith unto others by your words, the way those sectarians do. Witness by your life that our Lord is alive, and that it is possible to live by His teaching, which is done by bringing it into our lives. For us humans, the way we are—already used to sin—the teaching of God, and His commandments, seem difficult. Yet, they are in fact immeasurably easier than sin. However, when one is used to sin, then the commandment of God is hard, and sin is easy, because man has acquired a sinful habit. Thus, with our faith and our life according to faith, we should witness the Son of God and His teaching in this world.

"And you will be hated by all for my name's sake." One has to be clear about this. For, a man who lives according to God seems ludicrous in the eyes of this world, which lies in evil. You yourself know how many sins are all around, on all sides. And how, then, in the eyes of people of course, it is ludicrous to be an evangelical man, God's man, and son and daughter of God, living by His teaching.

However, when the Son of God appears again, He will come in His glory with the angels of God; then "all the tribes of the earth [since the world began] will mourn" (Matt. 24:30). On that day, may we rejoice at the coming of the Son of God, and His acknowledgment of our faith, and our life according to faith. God bless you!

ON THE WORDS OF THE LORD: "FOR MY YOKE IS EASY AND MY BURDEN IS LIGHT"

Sermon at the Divine Liturgy on November 11/ October 29, 1995,
in the patriarchal chapel
of St. Simeon the Myrrh-Gusher in Belgrade

> "All things have been delivered to me by my Father, and no one knows the Son except the Father. Nor does anyone know the Father except the Son, and the one to whom the Son wills to reveal Him. Come to me, all you who labor and are heavy laden, and I will give you rest. Take my yoke upon you and learn from me, for I am gentle and lowly in heart, and you will find rest for your souls. For My yoke is easy and my burden is light."
>
> Matt. 11:27-30

"Take my yoke upon you and learn from me, for I am gentle and lowly in heart, and you will find rest for your souls." It is never excessive to keep reminding ourselves and all others of the need to acquire humility—this basic Christian virtue. St. John Chrysostom says that when God had in mind to build an edifice of evangelical virtues, he placed humility as its foundation. "Blessed are the poor in spirit, for theirs is the kingdom of heaven" (Matt. 5:3). Poor in spirit are those who are aware of how little good they offer in response to the good that God constantly gives them; they always feel indebted to God; unlike that Pharisee who considered God his own debtor. *I give a tenth of everything. You ordered that I give only a tenth of my earthly income, of my earthly crops, and cattle. I give of everything. I fast two times a week, and you ordered to do it once a year* (Cf. Luke 18:12). We need humility that straightens us up before God, so that God can hear us.

Of course, humility is not lassitude. It is an active disposition of man, by which he fights pride, the pride that is always present, and that—I repeat this to myself and all—brought an angel down.

Let us never be afraid that anyone could degrade us. Anyone can humiliate, but no one can degrade us but ourselves with our own deeds, and our own actions. Be afraid of this!

May the Lord help us so that with humility, and the other virtues we raise upon that foundation, we may truly find rest for our souls; likewise, may we always have before our eyes that His yoke is easy when we carry it, and His burden is light. God bless you!

ON THE WORDS OF THE LORD: "BUT RATHER REJOICE, BECAUSE YOUR NAMES ARE WRITTEN IN HEAVEN"

Sermon at the Divine Liturgy on December 16/3, 1995,
in the patriarchal chapel
of St. Simeon the Myrrh-Gusher in Belgrade

> "He that heareth you heareth me; and he that despiseth you despiseth me; and he that despiseth me despiseth him that sent me. And the seventy returned again with joy, saying, 'Lord, even the devils are subject unto us through thy name.' And he said unto them, 'I beheld Satan as lightning fall from heaven. Behold, I give unto you power to tread on serpents and scorpions, and over all the power of the enemy: and nothing shall by any means hurt you. Notwithstanding in this rejoice not, that the spirits are subject unto you; but rather rejoice, because your names are written in heaven.' In that hour Jesus rejoiced in spirit, and said, 'I thank thee, O Father, Lord of heaven and earth, that thou hast hid these things from the wise and prudent, and hast revealed them unto babes: even so, Father; for so it seemed good in thy sight.'"
>
> Luke 10:16-21

"Nevertheless, do not rejoice in this, that the spirits are subject to you, but rather rejoice because your names are written in heaven." This is the most significant and most essential thing, that our names are written in God's book of the living.

And living before God are those who listen to His word and fulfill it. Dead before Him are those who do not listen to Him and His word, and do not fulfill His will, who do not act according to His teaching; who proclaim with their mouth that they are Christian, but with their actions they show that they are not, "By their deeds you will recognize them... *Therefore by their fruits you will know them*" (Matt. 7:20).

Moreover, the one who is written in the book of the living, he is beneficial to his family, and his nation, even his enemies, and the whole world. The one who truly fulfills the will of God, who strives to fulfill the beatitudes, and to be blessed, to become that even while still in this world, truly cannot be anything but beneficial to others. He cannot be selfish, with no concern for others, and for serving them; regardless of the fact that others do not see this, do not recognize it, or condemn it. "They persecuted me; they will persecute you also" (John 15:20). The Lord performed many good deeds, and you know that others said, "Why are you listening to him? There is a demon in him" (John 10:20). I speak of the enemies of the Son of God.

Therefore, one should strive and know that the meaning and goal of our life is to acquire, to earn, while in this world, that other everlasting one. May the Lord help all of you, and all of us, to be alive before Him with our faith and our holy life. God bless you!

ON THE COMMUNION OF THE HOLY MYSTERIES

Sermon given at the Divine Liturgy on December 17/4, 1995, in the church of St. Sava in Belgrade

You have communed today, brothers and sisters, of the Body and Blood of our Lord and Savior Jesus Christ, and He said, "Unless you eat the flesh of the Son of Man and drink His blood, you have no life in you. Whoever eats my flesh and drinks my blood has eternal life, and I will raise him up at the last day" (John 6:53-54). It is clear from these words what the significance is of this greatest Mystery of our faith, the Holy Eucharist, the Body and Blood of our Lord.

We will not have eternal life unless we approach the greatest Mystery. On the other hand, the Holy Apostle Paul admonishes us saying that every man should examine himself, and thus approach the Body and Blood of our Lord: "For he who eats and drinks in an unworthy manner eats and drinks judgment to himself, not discerning the Lord's body. For this reason many are weak and sick among you, and many sleep. For if we would judge ourselves, we would not be judged" (1 Cor. 11:29-31).

Hence, on the one hand, if we do not commune, we will have no life. On the other hand, if we approach communion unworthily, we will have no life. Certainly, none of the living people and Saints considered themselves worthy of this greatest faith of ours, but we have to strive, with the help of the grace of God, to be as worthy, as pure as we can, to show in this manner our faith in the Lord by our pure life, according to the evangelical teaching. Therefore, whenever we commit a sin it is necessary to confess it, so that we do not approach this greatest holy Mystery unconfessed, with an impure heart and soul.

Man should examine himself and his life on a daily basis, how he spent that day; he should survey his deeds, extracting from his soul what is evil, those weeds that have grown within it at the instigation of the evil one, and from bad examples, along with previous bad habits. In their place, we should plant a virtue opposite to that sin, so that, when the Nativity of the Son of God comes, we can offer our pure and holy souls to Him as a gift, like purified gold. If we are not able to offer, like the wise men, gold, frankincense, and myrrh, we can and should offer what is even more valuable: our pure and holy souls.

May the Lord help all of you, brothers and sisters, all of us, in this way to assist our family, the people we come in contact with, as well as our nation in these difficult times that have befallen us. And most of all, to help ourselves, and make ourselves the citizens of the everlasting Kingdom of Heaven; to gladden also our holy ancestors who expect us to be the way they had been in the troubles that befell them. God bless you and grant you every good thing!

ON SPEAKING THE TRUTH

Sermon given on December 28/15, 1995,
in the patriarchal chapel
of St. Simeon the Myrrh-Gusher in Belgrade

> "And it came to pass, that on one of those days, as he taught the people in the temple, and preached the gospel, the chief priests and the scribes came upon him with the elders, And spoke unto him, saying, 'Tell us, by what authority doest thou these things? or who is he that gave thee this authority?' And he answered and said unto them, 'I will also ask you one thing; and answer me: The baptism of John, was it from heaven, or of men?' And they reasoned with themselves, saying, 'If we shall say, "From heaven;" he will say, "Why then believed ye him not?" But and if we say, "Of men;" all the people will stone us: for they be persuaded that John was a prophet.' And they answered, that they could not tell whence it was. And Jesus said unto them, 'Neither tell I you by what authority I do these things.'"
>
> Luke 20:1-8

When the scribes and the Pharisees asked Him by what authority He taught the people, or who gave Him this authority, the Lord conditioned His answer by their answer to His question, "The baptism of John, was it from heaven, or of men?" They thought: if we say from heaven, He will ask us why we didn't believe John. For John was the one who pointed to Christ and said, "Behold! The Lamb of God who takes away the sin of the world" (John 1:29). These words of John contain the answer to the question that they were asking now. To believe John means to believe in Christ as the Son of God, and that He is teaching by His divine authority. Yet, the scribes and the priests refused to accept precisely this very fact. However, they also did not dare say that John's baptism was "of men." They were afraid of the people who would stone them, because they were convinced that John was truly a prophet. Hence, they said, "We do not know." They lied, and the Lord knew they did not tell the truth. For this reason, He does not reply: I do not know either (where His authority came from), but He says, "Neither will I tell you." He deliberately concealed the truth, not wanting to tell them.

The father of all lies is the devil, and he himself is falsehood, whereas in God is the truth, and God is the Truth. In Him there is no lie. We should strive to tell the truth, not to lie. For, if we lie and do not speak the truth, we are not with God then, but with the devil, for there is no lie in God. We should get ourselves accustomed to good, to always say what really is. One should fight against sin. Gradually and slowly, one grows in virtue. No one is strong right away, and at the very beginning does not have the strength to speak the truth openly; rather, he says nothing, but still does not say a lie. Had the priests and the scribes not answered Christ's question with, "We do not know," but instead said: we do not want to say, they would have kept the truth hidden, but would not have said a lie.

We have to strive to gradually free ourselves from sin. If it would happen, for example, that someone is running from the enemy, and this person hides, and we know where he is hiding, then those who are chasing him come and ask us: where is he?—in that case, in order to save an innocent man, we can say: we do not know. However, when we are stronger in virtue and in speaking the truth only, we will say: we cannot tell you where he is. That means that we know where the innocent is hiding, but we do not want to, we cannot, tell—we will conceal this truth even if it means that we ourselves might suffer.

The one who does not lie, who tells the truth, is on the side of God; he is with God, and belongs to God. For, every truth is from God, nothing but the truth, and nothing but the good!

ON THE WORDS OF THE LORD: "RENDER THEREFORE TO CAESAR WHAT IS CAESAR'S, AND TO GOD WHAT IS GOD'S."

Sermon at the Divine Liturgy on December 28/15, 1995,
in the patriarchal chapel of St. Simeon the Myrrh-Gusher in Belgrade

> "And the chief priests and the scribes the same hour sought to lay hands on him; and they feared the people: for they perceived that he had spoken this parable against them. And they watched him, and sent forth spies, which should feign themselves just men, that they might take hold of his words, that so they might deliver him unto the power and authority of the governor. And they asked him, saying, 'Master, we know that thou sayest and teachest rightly, neither acceptest thou the person of any, but teachest the way of God truly: Is it lawful for us to give tribute unto Caesar, or no?' But he perceived their craftiness, and said unto them, 'Why tempt ye me? Show me a penny. Whose image and superscription hath it?' They answered and said, 'Caesar's.' And he said unto them, 'Render therefore unto Caesar the things which be Caesar's, and unto God the things which be God's.' And they could not take hold of his words before the people: and they marveled at his answer, and held their peace."
>
> Luke 20:19-26

One should give to the body what it needs—food and other material things, but also unto the soul what is its nourishment—and that is spiritual food, the word of God. The scribes sent their spies to catch the Lord in His word, so they could thereby condemn Him. In order to make Him say something for which they could condemn Him, they pretended that they were seemingly interested in His teaching, so they begin the interrogation with condescension and ingratiation. We know you teach rightly and do not show partiality. They test Him and ask whether it is lawful to pay taxes to Caesar. And the Lord, seeing through them, asks for them to show him the denarius. So, when they have established that it has Caesar's image on it, He then tells them to give unto Caesar what is Caesar's, and to God what is God's. They thought, if He says, "Give only to Caesar," then He would be guilty, because He would blaspheme against God and not consider God. If, however, He says that they should only give to God, and nothing to Caesar, that is, to the authorities, he would be guilty again before the law and the authorities. He would be guilty before Rome, and could be condemned for instigating people to riot against the Emperor. However, the Lord gives them an answer they did not expect, and for which they cannot condemn Him: "render unto Caesar what is Caesar's, and unto God what is God's."

This is what God wants from us. Not just one, but one and the other—both to the emperor what is his, and to God what is God's. Therefore, let us live by the law, but to render unto God what He expects from us.

ON CHRISTIAN ZEAL

Sermon given in 1995, in the patriarchal chapel of St. Simeon the Myrrh-Gusher in Belgrade

"And the Jews' Passover was at hand, and Jesus went up to Jerusalem. And found in the temple those that sold oxen and sheep and doves, and the changers of money sitting: And when he had made a scourge of small cords, he drove them all out of the temple, and the sheep, and the oxen; and poured out the changers' money, and overthrew the tables; And said unto them that sold doves, 'Take these things hence; make not my Father's house an house of merchandise.' And his disciples remembered that it was written, 'The zeal of thine house hath eaten me up.'"

John 2:13-17

Our Savior drove the merchants out of the temple, as the Apostle John says, out of zeal, for after that event, His disciples remembered that it was written (about Him), "Zeal for your house consumes me." Here the Lord shows us an example of zeal. Nonetheless, if we want to know what our zeal should be like in all circumstances, we should remind ourselves of the words of the Apostle Paul about those members of the Jewish people who did not accept Christ, "...For I bear them witness that they have a zeal for God, but not according to knowledge" (Rom. 10:2). True zeal is the one that is rational, evangelical, like the one that the Savior has shown. Such is the zeal we should have ourselves, a rational zeal. If we have that, we will avoid all fanaticism and all excess. May the Lord help us to have the same kind of zeal for virtue and every good deed that the He has shown for His Father's house!

ON THE SIGN OF JONAH THE PROPHET

Sermon at the Divine Liturgy on January 1/December 19, 1996,
in the patriarchal chapel
of St. Simeon the Myrrh-Gusher in Belgrade

"And the Pharisees came forth, and began to question with him, seeking of him a sign from heaven, tempting him. And he sighed deeply in his spirit, and saith, 'Why doth this generation seek after a sign? verily I say unto you, There shall no sign be given unto this generation.' And he left them, and entering into the ship again departed to the other side. Now the disciples had forgotten to take bread, neither had they in the ship with them more than one loaf. And he charged them, saying, 'Take heed, beware of the leaven of the Pharisees, and of the leaven of Herod.' And they reasoned among themselves, saying, 'It is because we have no bread.' And when Jesus knew it, he saith unto them, 'Why reason ye, because ye have no bread? perceive ye not yet, neither understand? have ye your heart yet hardened? Having eyes, see ye not? and having ears, hear ye not? and do ye not remember? When I brake the five loaves among five thousand, how many baskets full of fragments took ye up?' They say unto him, 'Twelve.' 'And when the seven among four thousand, how many baskets full of fragments took ye up?' And they said, 'Seven.' And he said unto them, 'How is it that ye do not understand?'"

Mark 8:11-21

In another place in the Gospel, the Lord says that no other sign would be given to this generation except the sign of Jonah the Prophet. And the sign of Jonah the Prophet was in that he was thrown into the sea, was swallowed by a giant fish, and spent three days in the belly of the fish; then, upon the order from God, that fish expelled him to the land, and he remained alive. Likewise, our Lord Jesus was to be three days in the bowels of the earth, and on the third day He would rise. However, they did not understand this.

Let this be a sign for us that our Lord Jesus, the God-man, out of His endless love for mankind died for all people, for all of us, and on the third day He rose according to His divine power. He suffered and died on the cross according to His human nature, and resurrected according to His endless divine nature. He died for all, but in the Divine Liturgy it is mentioned as well that this Blood of His is spilled for many. Namely, not everyone will be saved, because they will not accept His salvation. Those who by their faith, and their life according to faith, accept His salvation, they will be saved, and those are many.

May the Lord bless us also to be numbered with them by our faith, our life according to faith, and by God's blessing. God bless you!

ON THE WORDS OF THE LORD: "BLESSED ARE YE POOR, FOR YOURS IS THE KINGDOM OF HEAVEN"

Sermon at the Divine Liturgy on January 24/11, 1996,
in the patriarchal chapel of St. Simeon the Myrrh-Gusher in Belgrade

> "And he came down with them, and stood in the plain, and the company of his disciples, and a great multitude of people out of all Judaea and Jerusalem, and from the sea coast of Tyre and Sidon, which came to hear him, and to be healed of their diseases; and they that were vexed with unclean spirits: and they were healed. And the whole multitude sought to touch him: for there went virtue out of him, and healed them all. And he lifted up his eyes on his disciples, and said, 'Blessed be ye poor: for yours is the kingdom of God. Blessed are ye that hunger now: for ye shall be filled. Blessed are ye that weep now: for ye shall laugh. Blessed are ye, when men shall hate you, and when they shall separate you from their company, and shall reproach you, and cast out your name as evil, for the Son of man's sake. Rejoice ye in that day, and leap for joy: for, behold, your reward is great in heaven: for in the like manner did their fathers unto the prophets.'"
>
> Luke 6:17-23

"Blessed are the poor in spirit..." And the poor in spirit are those who are humble, those who at all times sense how much God does for us, and how little we give in return for these goods that He provides us with; thus, they always feel indebted to God.

From the story of the publican and the Pharisee, you know how the Pharisee exalted himself, and instead of feeling that he is indebted to God, it is as if he makes God into his own debtor by his words: I fast two times a week and God had ordered through Moses to fast one time a year; I give a tenth of everything, while You ordered to give a tenth of the fruits of wheat, cattle, and other for upkeep of the temple and the priests—yet I give a tenth of everything.

Furthermore, that word from James 4:6, "Verily I tell you that the Lord opposes the proud, but gives grace to the humble." Namely, Christ commanded: "Do not store up for yourselves treasures on earth, "... provide yourselves money bags which do not grow old, a treasure in the heavens that does not fail, where no thief approaches nor moth destroys" (Luke 12:33). How much time and strength we have to invest in acquiring wealth, and how much both strength and other things in order to keep it. Of course, this does not mean that rich people cannot be saved as well, those who use their riches the way the Lord expects them to; however, it is difficult for the rich to enter the Kingdom of Heaven.

Hence, the takeaway here is not that we should all be beggars, not to have anything, but to strive to have the basic things we need for life. "When you have food and clothing," the Apostle says, "be content with this" (1 Timothy 6:8). Also, when we have a roof over our head, of course. However, we all want wealth for those conveniences that wealth affords, so that we can buy even the things that we do not need, luxurious things, and those that lead to our ruin.

May the Lord help us to understand His word, to use the means we have, our salary, or generally all the means we have acquired or earned, only for those things we truly need! If it is more than that, we violate God's commandment in that way, and we harm our souls. God bless you!

ON THE WIDOW'S TWO MITES

Sermon at the Divine Liturgy on January 25/12, 1996,
in the patriarchal chapel
of St. Simeon the Myrrh-Gusher in Belgrade

> "And he said unto them in his teaching, 'Beware of the scribes, which love to go in long clothing, and love salutations in the marketplaces, and the chief seats in the synagogues, and the uppermost rooms at feasts: Which devour widows' houses, and for a pretense make long prayers: these shall receive greater damnation.' And Jesus sat over against the treasury, and beheld how the people cast money into the treasury: and many that were rich cast in much. And there came a certain poor widow, and she threw in two mites, which make a farthing. And he called unto him his disciples, and said unto them, 'Verily I say unto you, That this poor widow hath cast more in, than all they which have cast into the treasury: For all they did cast in of their abundance; but she of her want did cast in all that she had, even all her living.'"
>
> Mark 12:38-44

From our Lord's rebukes of the scribes and the Pharisees, who, as He says, like to go around in long robes, and to have people greet them on the streets, who want the best seats in the synagogues, and first places at feasts, we see that the issue here is not the long robes; rather, Pharisees made their robes even longer to show themselves how pious they are, how they have long tassels, long thread fringe on the hems of those robes—the fringes of remembrance, because according to Mosaic Law, it was ordered that these tatters be a reminder to them of the Law of God. So, it is not about the robes and their length, but about the spirit that prompted Pharisees and scribes to act in this manner.

Likewise, the Lord condemns those who, out of vanity, love the first places at feasts, and says, "When you are invited by anyone to a wedding feast, do not sit down in the best place, lest one more honorable than you be invited by him; and he who invited you and him come and say to you, 'Give place to this man,' and then you begin with shame to take the lowest place. But when you are invited, go and sit down in the lowest place, so that when he who invited you comes he may say to you, 'Friend, go up higher.' Then you will have glory in the presence of those who sit at the table with you" (Luke 14:8-10). St. Basil the Great cautions us, because vanity can be manifested in this extreme as well: "Do not," he says, "fight for the last places." For, this comes down to the same thing, that is, out of vanity to show how you respect the word of Christ. Hence, take care that one can act both ways out of vanity, and never allow yourself to be vain and prideful; rather, act calmly and humbly, the way the Lord commands!

Furthermore, the same can be said about the giving of money for the maintenance of the Jerusalem Temple, because the rich gave much. However, that poor widow, according to the word of the Lord, gave the most—she gave all she had. One Saint says: "One should not look at how much is given, but how much is left." Certainly, the point is not that you should give to the temple and the poor so much that you yourself have nothing afterwards, so that you and your household starve. For, I repeat to myself and to you, let us not spend too much, but also not give too much to this world. Because, if we give it more than it needs, we have to take away from the soul, for we have to take away from the commandments of God. Therefore, "give unto Caesar what is Caesar's, and unto God what is God's" (Mark 12:17).

Let us give the body as much as it needs in food, clothing, and other, but not luxury. I cannot imagine, not only the Lord, but even the Apostle Paul and other Saints, as slovenly; but I also cannot imagine that they dressed themselves luxuriously, and put on themselves what is not needed, that they piled gold upon themselves.

Do you understand what this is about? To not give the body more than it really needs. For, if we give it too much, we take away from the soul. Likewise, to not give the soul any less than what is due to it, of course, to not give more to it than it really needs. Act with an awareness that the body has its needs and that the soul has its own. And to know how much each is due, and to give as much to the authorities, to this world; to give unto Caesar what is Caesar's, and to give unto God what is God's. God bless you!

ON THE SECOND COMING AND WATCHFULNESS

Sermon at the Divine Liturgy on February 8/January 26, 1996, in the patriarchal chapel of St. Simeon the Myrrh-Gusher in Belgrade

> "Heaven and earth shall pass away: but my words shall not pass away. But of that day and that hour knoweth no man, no, not the angels which are in heaven, neither the Son, but the Father. Take ye heed, watch and pray: for ye know not when the time is. For the Son of Man is as a man taking a far journey, who left his house, and gave authority to his servants, and to every man his work, and commanded the porter to watch. Watch ye therefore: for ye know not when the master of the house cometh, at even, or at midnight, or at the cockcrowing, or in the morning: Lest coming suddenly he find you sleeping. And what I say unto you I say unto all, 'Watch.'"
>
> Mark 13:31-37

According to Holy Scripture, and here, according to the word of the Lord, as well as according to the science of this world, we know that this world will come to an end one day. The Lord cautions us not to deceive ourselves with the thought that this end will not come for thousands of years. It can come today, or tomorrow, because, "of that day," He says, "and of that hour knows no man; not even the angels in heaven, nor the Son, but only the Father." Not even the Son knows, that is, He as man. According to His divine nature, everything that belongs to the Father "is Mine," He says. As God He certainly knows, but He does not inform us when this will happen, because this would not be beneficial for us. We would delude and deceive ourselves: there is still time, and then we will prepare ourselves, when that time comes. This way, let us keep His word; let us hear and heed it.

"Take heed, watch and pray; for you do not know when that time will come." It can come suddenly and "in whatsoever ways I find you, in them will I judge you." Let us always have this before our eyes, to live each moment, each minute, according to the Gospel, because there are only two choices at all times: either life according to the Gospel, or the opposite of it. Either we will walk the strait and narrow path that leads to life, or the wide one, the path of sin, on which many are already walking.

May the Lord help us to always be watchful, always ready to come before Him, and to give an account of how we have used the gifts that He has given us. God bless you!

ON THE GOD-MAN CHRIST

Sermon at the Divine Liturgy on February 20/7, 1996,
in the patriarchal chapel
of St. Simeon the Myrrh-Gusher in Belgrade

"And he came out, and went, as he was wont, to the Mount of Olives; and his disciples also followed him. And when he was at the place, he said unto them, 'Pray that ye enter not into temptation.' And he was withdrawn from them about a stone's cast, and kneeled down, and prayed, Saying, 'Father, if thou be willing, remove this cup from me: nevertheless not my will, but thine, be done.' And there appeared an angel unto him from heaven, strengthening him. And being in an agony he prayed more earnestly: and his sweat was as it were great drops of blood falling down to the ground... and [they] led him into their council, saying, 'Art thou the Christ? tell us.' And he said unto them, 'If I tell you, ye will not believe: And if I also ask you, ye will not answer me, nor let me go. Hereafter shall the Son of man sit on the right hand of the power of God.' Then said they all, 'Art thou then the Son of God?' And he said unto them, 'Ye say that I am.' And they said, 'What need we any further witness? for we ourselves have heard of his own mouth.'"

Luke 22:39-44, 66-71

We hear the words of the Lord when He prays, "Father, if it is Your will, take this cup away from Me." He speaks this as a man, of the same nature as the one we have, because man does not want death; he is afraid of death because of sin. For, death came because of sin, and it is contrary to the nature of man, created by God to be immortal. And he, taking upon Himself our sins and our body, that same body that we ourselves have, therefore, is afraid of death, because all humans are afraid of death. This only shows that He had the same nature, the true human nature as all of us; that He was not only God, but God and man.

Let us mention this as well. When they ask Him, "Are you the Son of God?" and He says, "You say that I am," do not think that He means, "I did not say that, but you say that." This was a manner of taking an oath with the Jewish people: the judge reads the oath, and the one who is supposed to take it says, "You say," that is, "it is as you say." That is also the case here; He confirmed that He was the Son of God by this oath: "You say." This means: "It is as you say." God bless you!

ON THE CONVERSATION WITH NICODEMUS

Sermon at the Divine Liturgy on April 18/5, 1996, in the patriarchal chapel of St. Simeon the Myrrh-Gusher in Belgrade

"There was a man of the Pharisees, named Nicodemus, a ruler of the Jews: The same came to Jesus by night, and said unto him, 'Rabbi, we know that thou art a teacher come from God: for no man can do these miracles that thou doest, except God be with him.' Jesus answered and said unto him, 'Verily, verily, I say unto thee, Except a man be born again, he cannot see the kingdom of God.' Nicodemus saith unto him, 'How can a man be born when he is old? can he enter the second time into his mother's womb, and be born?' Jesus answered, 'Verily, verily, I say unto thee, Except a man be born of water and of the Spirit, he cannot enter into the kingdom of God. That which is born of the flesh is flesh; and that which is born of the Spirit is spirit. Marvel not that I said unto thee, Ye must be born again. The wind bloweth where it listeth, and thou hearest the sound thereof, but canst not tell whence it cometh, and whither it goeth: so is every one that is born of the Spirit.' Nicodemus answered and said unto him, 'How can these things be?' Jesus answered and said unto him, 'Art thou a master of Israel, and knowest not these things? Verily, verily, I say unto thee, We speak that we do know, and testify that we have seen; and ye receive not our witness. If I have told you earthly things, and ye believe not, how shall ye believe, if I tell you of heavenly things?'"

John 3:1-12

Whoever is not born from above cannot be saved. The matter discussed here is the baptism, the New Testament one, which is the door for entering the Church of Christ, the ship that saves from the storms on the sea of this life. One thus becomes a shoot on the vine that is Christ, from Whom one receives food to be able to bear the fruit worthy of a man and a Christian. In another place, the Lord also says, "Whoever believes and is baptized will be saved" (Mark16:16). Therefore, faith and baptism; faith in Him, I repeat always to myself and to you: living faith that manifests itself in deeds and in life. For, a faith that is only in the mind, on the tongue, which would not usher a person into life—such a faith would be dead.

May the Lord help us to acquire this faith, the living faith, which is always shown in the works of God, in the God-determined acts, by means of which we will be witnesses of the Son of God, His teaching, and the heavenly kingdom in this world that lies in evil. May the Lord grant us this faith, and bless you all!

ON THE WEDDING IN CANA

Sermon at the Divine Liturgy on April 22/9, 1996,
in the patriarchal chapel
of St. Simeon the Myrrh-Gusher in Belgrade

> "And the third day there was a marriage in Cana of Galilee; and the mother of Jesus was there: And both Jesus was called, and his disciples, to the marriage. And when they wanted wine, the mother of Jesus saith unto him, 'They have no wine.' Jesus saith unto her, 'Woman, what have I to do with thee? mine hour is not yet come.' His mother saith unto the servants, 'Whatsoever he saith unto you, do it.' And there were set there six waterpots of stone, after the manner of the purifying of the Jews, containing two or three firkins apiece. Jesus saith unto them, 'Fill the waterpots with water.' And they filled them up to the brim. And he saith unto them, 'Draw out now, and bear unto the governor of the feast.' And they bare it. When the ruler of the feast had tasted the water that was made wine, and knew not whence it was: (but the servants which drew the water knew;) the governor of the feast called the bridegroom, and saith unto him, 'Every man at the beginning doth set forth good wine; and when men have well drunk, then that which is worse: but thou hast kept the good wine until now.' This beginning of miracles did Jesus in Cana of Galilee, and manifested forth his glory; and his disciples believed on him."
>
> John 2:1-11

This miracle of our Lord Jesus Christ by which He begins to help people does not mean that He turned water into wine with the goal to get people drunk; rather, we can understand that, when wine runs out at a wedding, there is poverty. In such circumstances, what would happen with the guests—what kind of trouble would ensue? They would say, "If you had no means, why did you invite that many people to the wedding?" And the Lord, in order to help the people, turned water into wine. At the same time, this is a symbolic representation of His blessing of marriage, which had been established in paradise, and which, despite the sin of Adam and Eve, was neither harmed nor destroyed, but remained valid. The Lord Jesus, as we know, numbers this Mystery among the holy Mysteries of the New Testament Church.

Moreover, symbolically, this miracle means that His teaching will be as strong as the wine compared to the water.

And why does He say, "Woman, what have I to do with thee?" while addressing His mother? To our ears, it sounds somehow harsh for a son to thus treat his mother. In the Hebrew language, this expression "woman" does not have such a harsh connotation; rather, it is a sign of utter respect and love. That much we should know. God bless you!

ON THE GLORY FROM PEOPLE AND THE GLORY FROM GOD

Sermon at the Divine Liturgy on April 26/13, 1996,
in the patriarchal chapel
of St. Simeon the Myrrh-Gusher in Belgrade

"I can of mine own self do nothing: as I hear, I judge: and my judgment is just; because I seek not mine own will, but the will of the Father which hath sent me. If I bear witness of myself, my witness is not true. There is another that bears witness of me; and I know that the witness which he witnesses of me is true. Ye sent unto John, and he bare witness unto the truth. But I receive not testimony from man: but these things I say, that ye might be saved. He was a burning and a shining light: and ye were willing for a season to rejoice in his light. But I have greater witness than that of John: for the works which the Father hath given me to finish, the same works that I do, bear witness of me, that the Father hath sent me. And the Father himself, which hath sent me, hath borne witness of me. Ye have neither heard his voice at any time, nor seen his shape. And ye have not his word abiding in you: for whom he hath sent, him ye believe not. Search the scriptures; for in them ye think ye have eternal life: and they are they which testify of me. And ye will not come to me, that ye might have life. I receive not honor from men. But I know you, that ye have not the love of God in you. I am come in my Father's name, and ye receive me not: if another shall come in his own name, him ye will receive. How can ye believe, which receive honor one of another, and seek not the honor that cometh from God only? Do not think that I will accuse you to the Father: there is one that accuses you, even Moses, in whom ye trust. For had ye believed Moses, ye would have believed me; for he wrote of me. But if ye believe not his writings, how shall ye believe my words?"

John 5:30-47, 6:1-4

Let us pay attention to these words of our Lord: "How can you believe, who receive honor from one another, and do not seek the honor that comes from the only God?" How can we believe, and how can we progress spiritually, if there is pride and vanity within us; for, vanity means to receive glory from people, to present ourselves before people as better than we are, while forgetting the most important thing: to truly be better than we are, by our efforts and with the help of the grace of God; to truly be better and better each day. Let this be before our eyes at all times. Not to ask for glory from other people by any means, because people, as you yourself know, even when they have the best intentions in mind, let alone having their own standards of measure and interests, cannot grasp everything in its entirety; and for this reason they will praise us.

This moment of vanity and pride, and the desire to represent ourselves before others as better than we are, was also present in the story of Ananias and Sapphira, as we heard today from the Epistle reading. In those times of the early Church, which was persecuted by the unfaithful, first the Jews, and then the Roman Empire, the only ones who could remain Christian were those who had an unshakeable faith in the Lord Jesus, who believed that He is God, the God-man—that He is the Almighty God and Man—that He died for us and resurrected, and that He awaits us in His kingdom. "Where I am, there will my servant also be," (John 12:26) He said. Only such faith could inspire a man to become a Christian. Everything else in this world spoke to the contrary. For, he would be persecuted as a Christian; he could have been sentenced to death; his family would have been condemned, too, and would suffer. And in this early Church, you heard that those who had suffered as Christians, along with their families, were left with nothing, and thereby they inspired love in those who supported them. No one said of his own property that it belonged to him, because everything was shared. There is no reason not to call this a sort of communism; communism is a Latin word, and it means this precisely: communal property, collective, not individual. This does not mean, of course, that we are for the Communists in the sense in which they preach materialism, but that we do not have anything against such a society wherein property would be shared, that is, communal, in such a sense. Today, we as Christians know that people will lose their souls regardless of the political inclination, if they have a materialistic attitude, if they do not believe that God exists, if they do not believe that the soul is immortal. They will lose it, whether they are for the king, or the republic, or any other thing.

And so, in the early times, everything was shared, and no one said he was the owner of his own property. And Barnabas, which translated from Hebrew means "the son of consolation," had a field and sold it; then he brought it to the Apostles' feet, so that they could distribute it to those who need it. Conversely, a man Ananias with his wife Sapphira sold a field, and he gave one portion of the money to the Apostles, while hiding the other. He could have given the money or not; he could have given it all or a portion of it. However, he presented the matter as if that was all he got for it, and that he had turned it all in, whereas he did not. Then the Apostle Peter, before whom this happened, said, "Why did you lie to the Holy Spirit? When you gave as much, you could have given nothing, but why do you say that you have given all of it?" Then Ananias fell dead at his feet. The wife Sapphira came to him and the Apostle asked her, "Is this the price you got for the land?" that is, the price they told them they got for it. "The feet of the men who buried your husband are at the door [and they will carry you out also]" (Acts 5:9).

Do you understand this misfortune of vanity and pride, and the desire to show ourselves before people as better than we are? We would want to do the same before God, too, but that is impossible to do. Let us not want to appear better than we are in front of people! Do not present yourselves as better than you are! For, this is the origin of slander against another, of gossiping and humiliation—how this person is nothing, which means that we are something great; this is like pushing one's neighbor down with one's feet, so that the distance between us and him would be such that others would see how much better we are than him; a lie, of course.

Therefore, strive, brothers and sisters, to bring humility into your souls. Humility is not lassitude. An enormous strength is needed to humble ourselves before God; in this way, in fact, we exalt ourselves; we truly become better. Never forget that pride was what turned an angel into a devil. What will it do to us, then? For, "God opposes the proud, but gives grace to the humble" (Prov. 3:34). Let us be with Him, the Almighty God, the Lord Jesus Christ, Who was humble unto death on the cross—He, the God-man. May He help us to straighten ourselves up before the people, and before Him. When we come before Him, may He recognize and acknowledge us as His, primarily in humility, upon which all the other virtues are built. God bless you!

ON THE WORDS OF THE LORD: "NO ONE CAN COME TO ME UNLESS THE FATHER WHO SENT ME DRAWS HIM"

Sermon at the Divine Liturgy on May 2/April 19, 1996,
in the patriarchal chapel of St. Simeon the Myrrh-Gusher in Belgrade

> "And this is the will of him that sent me, that everyone which seeth the Son, and believeth on him, may have everlasting life: and I will raise him up at the last day. The Jews then murmured at him, because he said, 'I am the bread which came down from heaven.' And they said, 'Is not this Jesus, the son of Joseph, whose father and mother we know? how is it then that he saith, "I came down from heaven?"' Jesus therefore answered and said unto them, 'Murmur not among yourselves. No man can come to me, except the Father which hath sent me draw him: and I will raise him up at the last day. It is written in the prophets, and they shall be all taught of God. Every man therefore that hath heard, and hath learned of the Father, cometh unto me. Not that any man hath seen the Father, save he which is of God, he hath seen the Father. Verily, verily, I say unto you, He that believeth on me hath everlasting life.'"
>
> John 6:40-47

Let us mention the word of the Lord that anyone whom the Father draws will believe in the Lord Jesus. This does not mean that God sanctifies some by force and saves them, but that, as we have said yesterday, the inspiration for salvation comes to us created beings from God; it is invested in us for our salvation. Only by our sins do we push away the grace of God, God's help that He gives to those who listen to Him.

Additionally, a word on this: "Is not this Jesus, the son of Joseph, whose father and mother we know?" "And aren't his brothers James, Joseph, Simon and Judas?" Four. "And his sisters, are they not all with us?" Brothers and sisters of the Lord are the sons and daughters of Joseph from his first marriage; after his wife died, the Holy Theotokos was betrothed to him. Hence, these are not the children of the Holy Virgin, after the birth of the Lord, but they are Joseph's children; he was before the Law and before people indeed the husband of the Holy Theotokos, and in that sense also the father of the Lord Jesus, likewise, before the Law and the people. Essentially, you know that the Lord Jesus was conceived of the Holy Spirit, and that He was born of the Holy Virgin. God bless you!

ON THE GREATEST VIRTUE

Sermon at the Divine Liturgy on May 4/April 21, 1996,
in the patriarchal chapel of St. Simeon the Myrrh-Gusher in Belgrade

> "These things I command you, that ye love one another. If the world hate you, ye know that it hated me before it hated you. If ye were of the world, the world would love his own: but because ye are not of the world, but I have chosen you out of the world, therefore the world hateth you. Remember the word that I said unto you, The servant is not greater than his lord. If they have persecuted me, they will also persecute you; if they have kept my saying, they will keep yours also. But all these things will they do unto you for my name's sake, because they know not him that sent me. If I had not come and spoken unto them, they had not had sin: but now they have no cloak for their sin. He that hateth me hateth my Father also. If I had not done among them the works which none other man did, they had not had sin: but now have they both seen and hated both me and my Father. But this cometh to pass, that the word might be fulfilled that is written in their law, 'They hated me without a cause.' But when the Comforter is come, whom I will send unto you from the Father, even the Spirit of truth, which proceedeth from the Father, he shall testify of me: And ye also shall bear witness, because ye have been with me from the beginning. These things have I spoken unto you, that ye should not be offended. They shall put you out of the synagogues: yea, the time cometh, that whosoever killeth you will think that he doeth God service."
>
> John 15:17-27, 16:1-2

Love is the greatest virtue, but the love that is the greatest, which is the "bond of perfection," (Col. 3:14) cannot be attained all at once, until one has acquired all other virtues first, beginning with humility, humbleness.

The Apostle Paul also cautions us that, "…now these three remain: faith, hope, and love. But the greatest of these is love" (1 Cor. 13:13). Namely, when we have cleansed our hearts, then we will be able to see God even here in this world; and we will see Him also in the other one, if we make ourselves worthy to look upon His face, if we are not sent to eternal darkness on account of our sins.

Then our faith will turn into knowledge, into seeing. And hope—hope will turn into fulfillment. Our hope is that we will enter into the Kingdom of Heaven, and be numbered with all those Saints; that we will be looking at the face of God. Our hope, then, will turn into fulfillment. And love—it has nothing else to turn into. It will be both now and then our bond with God, love that unites us with God; it unites all our capacities within us, including those rational ones; it unites us with all people of goodwill, and then we have peace. This is why love is the greatest virtue.

Let us strive, then, while walking toward the heavenly kingdom, and fulfilling God's commandments, to prepare ourselves each day on this path for the attainment of this greatest virtue—of entering the Kingdom of Heaven, and of love that will unite us with God, and with all the Saints. God bless you!

ON LIVING BY CHRIST

Sermon at the Divine Liturgy
on May 9/April 26, 1996,
in the patriarchal chapel
of St. Simeon the Myrrh-Gusher in Belgrade

> "Then Jesus spoke to them again, saying, 'I am the light of the world. He who follows Me shall not walk in darkness, but have the light of life.' The Pharisees therefore said to Him, 'You bear witness of Yourself; Your witness is not true.' Jesus answered and said to them, 'Even if I bear witness of Myself, My witness is true, for I know where I came from and where I am going; but you do not know where I come from and where I am going. You judge according to the flesh; I judge no one. And yet if I do judge, My judgment is true; for I am not alone, but I am with the Father who sent Me. It is also written in your law that the testimony of two men is true. I am One who bears witness of Myself, and the Father who sent Me bears witness of Me.' Then they said to Him, 'Where is Your Father?' Jesus answered, 'You know neither Me nor My Father. If you had known Me, you would have known My Father also.' These words Jesus spoke in the treasury, as He taught in the temple; and no one laid hands on Him, for His hour had not yet come."
>
> John 8:12-20

Brothers and sisters, for us believers, the Lord is Everything. He is the Bread of Life; He is the Living Water; He is the Light; He is the Good Shepherd; therefore, everything for our life. Believing in Him, we live by Him; we realize the meaning and goal of our life, and we are enabled to enter into the everlasting blessedness of the heavenly kingdom.

Hence, always have in mind that we live by Christ. The Holy Apostle Paul says, "It is no longer I who live, but Christ lives in me" (Gal.

2:20). By this life eternal, living in Christ and with Christ, we will, I say and repeat, realize the meaning and goal of our life, and that is, according to the holy words of the Gospel, the blessedness of the everlasting Kingdom of Heaven. I wish to you and to myself that we may enter this blessedness of the heavenly kingdom already in this world.

ON THE TWO FREEDOMS AND TWO BONDAGES

Sermon at the Divine Liturgy on May 11/April 28, 1996,
in the patriarchal chapel
of St. Simeon the Myrrh-Gusher in Belgrade

> "Then said Jesus to those Jews which believed on him, 'If ye continue in my word, then are ye my disciples indeed; And ye shall know the truth, and the truth shall make you free.' They answered him, 'We be Abraham's seed, and were never in bondage to any man: how sayest thou, "Ye shall be made free?"' Jesus answered them, 'Verily, verily, I say unto you, Whosoever committeth sin is the servant of sin. And the servant abideth not in the house for ever: but the Son abideth ever. If the Son therefore shall make you free, ye shall be free indeed. I know that ye are Abraham's seed; but ye seek to kill me, because my word hath no place in you. I speak that which I have seen with my Father: and ye do that which ye have seen with your father.' They answered and said unto him, 'Abraham is our father.' Jesus saith unto them, 'If ye were Abraham's children, ye would do the works of Abraham. But now ye seek to kill me, a man that hath told you the truth, which I have heard of God: this did not Abraham. Ye do the deeds of your father.' Then said they to him, 'We be not born of fornication; we have one Father, even God.'"
>
> John 8:31-41

There are two freedoms, brothers and sisters, and two bondages. One is this worldly freedom, of this world, and the other one is the freedom from sin. One is, thus, the bondage of this world from evildoers, and from the oppressors of this world in general, and the other one is the bondage of sin.

Certainly, we are also bodies; we are earthly, and we need freedom in this world. How much does our nation, and other justice-loving and truth-loving nations need freedom! But we are also souls, and we need freedom from sin. That first freedom, just like life, will pass, and it passes. But freedom from sin, the freedom of a righteous man, never passes—and it unites us with all the Saints in the heavenly kingdom.

Take care, then, not to be slaves of sin. You know from your own and from others' experience what kind of bondage this is. In the least, to put it that way, the passions that we acquire lead us to slavery. Take, for example, a smoker, a drunkard, not to mention other sins, fornication and crimes. What kind of slavery is that, and how great!

Therefore, let us strive to introduce the teaching of Christ and His truth into our lives, and to gradually endeavor, with the help of God's grace, to be free from sin; in this way, the Lord will deliver us from the devil and from death. Whereas He says to the Jews while speaking with them, "My word has no place in you." Let us do everything; let us empty our soul and our heart from sin, so that truth can fit into it. For, when a glass has water, until we have emptied that glass, we cannot pour anything else into it, even if we had the best drink. It is likewise with our souls. "You cannot serve God and mammon!" said the Lord (Matt. 6:24). "Behold, I stand at the door and knock," He says, at the door (of our heart). "If anyone hears My voice and opens the door, I will come in to him and dine with him, and he with Me" (Rev. 3:20).

Let us strive so that the word of God, the truth of God, always has a place in our heart; then we, too, will have a place in the heavenly kingdom, in the blessedness of that kingdom. God bless you!

ON THE BEATITUDES

Sermon at the Divine Liturgy on June 8/May 26, 1996,
in the patriarchal chapel
of St. Simeon the Myrrh-Gusher in Belgrade

"And there followed him great multitudes of people from Galilee, and from Decapolis, and from Jerusalem, and from Judaea, and from beyond Jordan. And seeing the multitudes, he went up into a mountain: and when he was set, his disciples came unto him: And he opened his mouth, and taught them, saying, 'Blessed are the poor in spirit: for theirs is the kingdom of heaven. Blessed are they that mourn: for they shall be comforted. Blessed are the meek: for they shall inherit the earth. Blessed are they which do hunger and thirst after righteousness: for they shall be filled. Blessed are the merciful: for they shall obtain mercy. Blessed are the pure in heart: for they shall see God. Blessed are the peacemakers: for they shall be called the children of God. Blessed are they which are persecuted for righteousness' sake: for theirs is the kingdom of heaven. Blessed are ye, when men shall revile you, and persecute you, and shall say all manner of evil against you falsely, for my sake. Rejoice, and be exceeding glad: for great is your reward in heaven: for so persecuted they the prophets which were before you. Ye are the salt of the earth: but if the salt have lost his savor, wherewith shall it be salted? It is thenceforth good for nothing, but to be cast out, and to be trodden under foot of men.'"

Matt. 4:25, 5:1-13

Our Savior's sermon on the beatitudes should always inspire us to such a manner of life so as to acquire the heavenly kingdom and the blessedness of that kingdom. And this blessedness is acquired here already; it begins even here and now; the Saints already begin here with the blessedness and enter the Kingdom of Heaven, into life eternal.

"Blessed are the poor in spirit, for theirs is the kingdom of heaven." Who are the poor in spirit? The enemies of faith, especially of Christianity, say and interpret this to mean that blessed are the fools. Of course, not fools for God in the eyes of the world, but literally, that only a fool can be a Christian. St. John Chrysostom says for the beatitude about those poor in spirit that it is the "beatitude of the humble." More than once I told you, and it is beneficial both for you and for myself to stress this word that "the Lord," says Chrysostom, "when He had in mind to build the edifice of Christian virtues, placed humility as its foundation." This is the feeling of how little we respond with good to the good that God does for us; how little we respond with faith, the living faith that is manifested in actions; and the feeling of how indebted we are to God. Always be reminded of Christ's parable about the publican and the Pharisee, how that Pharisee in his prayer made God into his debtor, because he did more than God was asking! And how the publican did not dare lift up his eyes to heaven and said, "God, be merciful to me, a sinner." And the Lord in the end says, "...this man, rather than the other, went home justified before God" (Luke 18:14). "Because God opposes the proud, but gives grace to the humble" (Prov. 3:34); those were the words of Christ.

Humility is not lassitude. Humility is a virtue, which is acquired with difficulty, with struggle, by conquering one's inner pride and high opinion of oneself. "Because God opposes the proud, but gives grace to the humble," He cannot approach a prideful man, because he has built a wall around himself, just like the devil had built a wall of pride, and fell away and became a demon.

How many times individuals come to me with "messages" from God, because they are "special elects" of God. I tell them, "You are God's special elects. I am not. I am merely one of the many priests in the Church of God, nothing else. I strive to obtain humility, but I have not attained it. I am still struggling, and God sees it and will help me." It is a tragedy! They do not sense to what degree they are entrapped by the one who, through pride, turned himself from an angel into a devil. How many times I say, "Do you have a mirror? Look at yourself in the mirror and see where you are."

And these neuroses! People are under nervous strain. They are not content to be a finger on the hand; they want to be the head. Man then becomes self-important, and then, of course, loses it and says how he is one of the special elect who speaks with the angels, with God. One even came and said that he "was God"! Therefore, look at yourself, man!

I beseech you, brothers and sisters, understand the gist of this, that without humility, without this feeling that we are nothing, we will not be able to enter the kingdom. Do not regard yourselves as special chosen ones of God. God is with all of us, if we are with Him. It will be enough for you to fulfill what the Lord says, "Let your light so shine before men, that they may see your good works, and glorify your Father who is in heaven" (Matt. 5:16), and by remaining silent, you will proclaim the teaching of Christ.

There are two misfortunes in this world: from the unbelieving people, the enemies of Christ, and from those who exalt themselves through vanity. This is heresy. Hence, the Church has enemies: first, these outside enemies who persecute her, who are always belligerent; they use their energy against God and against faith. Here, in a place last year, the Society of Pensioners and Elderly took as their patronal feast the Holy Healers Cosmas and Damian; in the hall where they gathered, they placed the censer, and cut the ceremonial bread. Then, later that day, the icon and the censer were found in the toilet! The godless men who did this said, "We do not agree with this. There are this many of us, so remove it!"

Such examples should teach us what we must not do! We have our beliefs, our faith, and life according to that faith. We should always act as humans, on the principle, "do unto others what you would have them do to you" (Matt. 7:12). How others will act, the unbelievers, it is clear to us. One should feel more sorry for them than for oneself. They can do nothing to us, neither to God, nor the icon, nor the Holy Healers. They ruin themselves as those people for which the Lord prayed from the cross, "Father, forgive them for they know not what they do" (Luke 23:34). Amen.

ON THE WORDS OF THE LORD: "I DID NOT COME TO BRING PEACE, BUT A SWORD"

Sermon at the Divine Liturgy on June 21/8, 1996,
in the patriarchal chapel of St. Simeon the Myrrh-Gusher in Belgrade

> "Whosoever therefore shall confess me before men, him will I confess also before my Father which is in heaven. But whosoever shall deny me before men, him will I also deny before my Father which is in heaven. Think not that I am come to send peace on earth: I came not to send peace, but a sword. For I am come to set a man at variance against his father, and the daughter against her mother, and the daughter in law against her mother in law. And a man's foes shall be they of his own household. He that loveth father or mother more than me is not worthy of me: and he that loveth son or daughter more than me is not worthy of me. And he that taketh not his cross, and followeth after me, is not worthy of me. He that findeth his life shall lose it: and he that loseth his life for my sake shall find it. He that receiveth you receiveth me, and he that receiveth me receiveth him that sent me. He that receiveth a prophet in the name of a prophet shall receive a prophet's reward; and he that receiveth a righteous man in the name of a righteous man shall receive a righteous man's reward. And whosoever shall give to drink unto one of these little ones a cup of cold water only in the name of a disciple, verily I say unto you, he shall in no wise lose his reward."
>
> Matt. 10:32-42

From these words of our Lord, "I did not come to bring peace, but a sword," we should understand what the issue is, for He Who is the Prince of Peace, Who is our peace, and Who said, "Peace I leave you;

my peace I give you" (John 14:27), now says here that He did not come to bring peace. How can this be? From further texts we see what this is about. "I came," He says, "to set a man against his father, a daughter against her mother, and a daughter-in-law against her mother-in-law; and a man's enemies will be those of his own household." This, then, is the issue. He is like a sword upon which everything is split into two parts: either for Him, or against Him. That is what this is about now. If the father becomes a Christian, and his wife, or son, or children do not want to become Christian, there is an obvious division. And, of course, that those sinners, pagans, will always attack the Christian. So, here then, is the sword. The sword is only a symbol of unrest and war. Hence, this is what is at issue here.

Furthermore, the Lord says, "He who loves father or mother more than Me is not worthy of Me. And he who loves son or daughter more than Me is not worthy of Me." That is, if the son becomes a Christian, but out of love for his parents who remained pagan says, "Let me remain pagan, too," it is obvious that he is not worthy of God's love. For, salvation is in the Lord Jesus Christ, and the one who prefers to remain in sinfulness, and thus to be ruined along with his parents and his people, in that sense—that man, of course, will lose his soul, and he is not worthy of God's love. That is, then, what this is about.

Moreover, a word on this: "He who finds his life will lose it, and he who loses his life for My sake will find it." What I repeat all the time is that a Christian man has to pay attention that, if he has to lose his life, even this is better than losing one's soul. Also, that even the smallest effort out of love for our neighbors, and out of love for God, will not go to waste, because even if one gives a glass of water to the thirsty, his reward will not go to waste. However, likewise the evil done unto other people will not go to waste. Let us beware of evil, and endeavor to do good. God bless you!

ON BUILDING A HOUSE UPON A ROCK

Sermon at the Divine Liturgy on June 22/9, 1996,
in the patriarchal chapel of St. Simeon the Myrrh-Gusher in Belgrade

"'Therefore whosoever heareth these sayings of mine, and doeth them, I will liken him unto a wise man, which built his house upon a rock: And the rain descended, and the floods came, and the winds blew, and beat upon that house; and it fell not: for it was founded upon a rock. And every one that heareth these sayings of mine, and doeth them not, shall be likened unto a foolish man, which built his house upon the sand: And the rain descended, and the floods came, and the winds blew, and beat upon that house; and it fell: and great was the fall of it.' And it came to pass, when Jesus had ended these sayings, the people were astonished at his doctrine: For he taught them as one having authority, and not as the scribes. 'Ye are the light of the world. A city that is set on an hill cannot be hid. Neither do men light a candle, and put it under a bushel, but on a candlestick; and it giveth light unto all that are in the house. Let your light so shine before men, that they may see your good works, and glorify your Father which is in heaven. Think not that I am come to destroy the law, or the prophets: I am not come to destroy, but to fulfil. For verily I say unto you, Till heaven and earth pass, one jot or one tittle shall in no wise pass from the law, till all be fulfilled. Whosoever therefore shall break one of these least commandments, and shall teach men so, he shall be called the least in the kingdom of heaven: but whosoever shall do and teach them, the same shall be called great in the kingdom of heaven.'"

Matt. 7:24-29, 5:14-19

The word of the Lord is always such that His teaching is not given only for the mind and for speaking about it, for talking, but it is given so that people can live by it. Even here, these words of His mean precisely that. He likens every person who listens to His words and keeps them to a wise man; for such a man is like that wise man who built his house upon a rock, upon a firm foundation, and the winds and waters cannot destroy it.

Hence, wise before the Lord is the person who knows and does this. And foolish before Him is the one who listens to these words of His and knows them, yet does not fulfill them.

The meaning is the same for the words in the following passage, "Let your light so shine before men, that they may see your good works and glorify your Father who is in heaven." Thus, it means that people should not only listen to our fine words, by those who know how to express these words well; rather, they should see our good deeds. This is higher—what primarily saves us, and attracts other people. For, even the most beautiful words, if they are coupled with opposite actions, turn people away from the truth. And good deeds speak for themselves, even if we are not good with words, as the Holy Apostle Paul says about himself, "Even though I am untrained in speech, yet I am not in knowledge" (2 Cor. 11:6). Therefore, to show our faith by our words, when the time and occasion allow, but also with our actions, and for that, any time and occasion are always appropriate.

May the Lord help us to be wise servants and handmaidens of His, and to build our house upon a rock, the rock of faith that we know and act upon. God bless you!

ON SPIRITUAL SEEING AND HOW TO KEEP OUR HANDS DURING PRAYER

Sermon at the Divine Liturgy on June 23/10, 1996,
in the church of the Holy Apostle
and Evangelist Mark in Belgrade

"For where your treasure is, there will your heart be also. The light of the body is the eye: if therefore thine eye be single, thy whole body shall be full of light. But if thine eye be evil, thy whole body shall be full of darkness. If therefore the light that is in thee be darkness, how great is that darkness! No man can serve two masters: for either he will hate the one, and love the other; or else he will hold to the one, and despise the other. Ye cannot serve God and mammon. Therefore I say unto you, Take no thought for your life, what ye shall eat, or what ye shall drink; nor yet for your body, what ye shall put on. Is not the life more than meat, and the body than raiment? Behold the fowls of the air: for they sow not, neither do they reap, nor gather into barns; yet your heavenly Father feedeth them. Are ye not much better than they? Which of you by taking thought can add one cubit unto his stature? And why take ye thought for raiment? Consider the lilies of the field, how they grow; they toil not, neither do they spin: And yet I say unto you, That even Solomon in all his glory was not arrayed like one of these. Wherefore, if God so clothe the grass of the field, which to day is, and to morrow is cast into the oven, shall he not much more clothe you, O ye of little faith?"

Matt. 6:21-30

In the name of the Father, and the Son, and the Holy Spirit! We have prayed on this day, and offered up the bloodless sacrifice to Him Who said, "...unless you eat the flesh of the Son of Man and drink His blood, you have no life in you" (John 6:53). Likewise, He also said, "He who eats My flesh and drinks My blood abides in Me, and I in him… and I will raise him up at the last day" (John 6:56, 54). Hence, what is necessary for our spiritual life, our immortal life and deification, is the Holy Communion of the Body and Blood of the Son of God in the form of bread and wine. However, we have to strive to be as worthy as we can of this greatest Mystery of our faith, because the Apostle Paul cautions all of us: "For he who eats and drinks in an unworthy manner, eats and drinks judgment to himself, not discerning the Lord's body" (1 Cor. 11:29). Furthermore, he says, "For this reason many are weak and sick among you, and many have fallen asleep. For if we would judge ourselves, we would not be judged" (1 Cor. 11:30-31), that is, if we would strive to cleanse ourselves from sin as much as we can.

Similarly, in the Holy Gospel, the Lord says, "The eye is the lamp of the body. If your eyes are healthy, your whole body will be full of light. But if your eyes are unhealthy, your whole body will be full of darkness." Just like in the physical sense, we see this world with the eye, and see where we are going, there is also an inner, spiritual eye. With these physical eyes we see this physical world the same as the other living beings, the way bees or mosquitoes see it, too. However, I say, we have an inner eye, the spiritual eye through which we alone perceive this world, its essence and meaning. Bees and other living beings do not have this. And this spiritual eye is our heart. The Lord says, "Blessed are the pure in heart, for they shall see God" (Matt. 5:8). Thus, only the one who has a pure heart will be able to see God. And our heart will be pure if we strive to cleanse it from sin. The devil plants evil, sinful thoughts into our mind and heart. If we strive with all our might and strength to chase these thoughts away from us, then our heart will be pure. But, if the devil finds in us his helpers, and we dwell on these sinful thoughts, if we feed them, heat them up, and they develop and grow into sin, we ourselves will be responsible. Many times we, and especially unbelieving people of this world, say, "Show us God, and we will believe." They do not understand, then, that the heart is this mirror, this eye through which God can be seen. And what must our, and their, heart be like, how darkened with sin, that the Almighty and All-Pure God cannot be mirrored nor seen in it! Therefore, we should keep this in mind.

Let us strive to fulfill our faith with holy and honorable deeds, and thereby to become closer to God, and be worthy of our ancestors, who knew this and did this even in this world; and so, they entered the Kingdom of Heaven, which is our true fatherland and home. Likewise, we should know that the true meaning of our life is this: with our holy Orthodox faith, and our life here according to that faith, to earn that everlasting world, blessedness in the other world with the blessed heavenly powers, and our blessed fathers and mothers, in the vicinity of God, in the communion of God's Church, which is in glory. I always say this to myself, and to you, brothers and sisters, for we are bound to leave this world, and stand before the Righteous Judge. The unbelievers reproach us how we Orthodox priests not only warn people, but we scare them, scare them with death. This is not so. We only present truth, brothers and sisters, both to ourselves, and to all those who have ears to hear. We will depart from this world. The unbelievers know this, too, but they do not know, or they do not want to know, that the soul is immortal, and that it goes before the face of God to receive either eternal blessedness, or eternal torment. And we should know this, in order to be those who know what they are doing. I place this onto your souls and heart.

Furthermore, I want to say this. Often in church, during prayer, we do not know what to do with our hands: whether we should keep them as they are, or turn them the other way, as the faithful of other denominations do. In the ninth century, around the year 820, the Roman Pope Nicholas I in a letter to Bulgarians, justifies the Western way of holding hands during prayer, as you know, clasped in front of you. In this way, he wanted to justify this posture as it relates to the Orthodox who cross their hands on their chest. Hence, when we stand in prayer, we should know to keep our hands crossed. True, when one has to chant, or to sing with the choir, then it is a little harder to keep the hands crossed on the chest, because the chest area needs to be free, so that they can intone the songs and readings more clearly. However, when we are standing in church and quietly praying to God, or when we quietly respond to the priest's petitions, and especially when we are praying in our home, we should have our hands crossed on our chest. This is not my teaching; I would like to remark that there is a confirmation from the ninth century that the Orthodox held their hands in this manner. We have nothing against other Christian denominations acting differently; as for us, since the issue is already being discussed, we should know how to do this. And how you will act depends entirely on you. It is not, of course, the most important thing, but in these little details a man shows himself, and the faith shows itself.

May the Lord and all His Saints, and the Holy Evangelist and Apostle Mark, help us to fulfill God's will in everything, and thereby to be worthy of the gifts He has bestowed upon us, so that, when we come before our holy ancestors, I repeat this always, we may straighten ourselves up before them; may they recognize and acknowledge us as their own, and may their and our Lord recognize and acknowledge us. God bless you and grant you every good thing!

ON THE TALENTS

Sermon at the Divine Liturgy on September 22/9, 1996,
in the church of St. George in Bezhania

"For the kingdom of heaven is as a man travelling into a far country, who called his own servants, and delivered unto them his goods. And unto one he gave five talents, to another two, and to another one; to every man according to his several ability; and straightway took his journey. Then he that had received the five talents went and traded with the same, and made them other five talents. And likewise he that had received two, he also gained other two. But he that had received one went and digged in the earth, and hid his lord's money. After a long time the lord of those servants cometh, and reckoneth with them. And so he that had received five talents came and brought other five talents, saying, 'Lord, thou deliveredst unto me five talents: behold, I have gained beside them five talents more.' His lord said unto him, 'Well done, thou good and faithful servant: thou hast been faithful over a few things, I will make thee ruler over many things: enter thou into the joy of thy lord.' He also that had received two talents came and said, 'Lord, thou deliveredst unto me two talents: behold, I have gained two other talents beside them.' His lord said unto him, 'Well done, good and faithful servant; thou hast been faithful over a few things, I will make thee ruler over many things: enter thou into the joy of thy lord.' Then he which had received the one talent came and said, 'Lord, I knew thee that thou art an hard man, reaping where thou hast not sown, and gathering where thou hast not strawed: And I was afraid, and went and hid thy talent in the earth: lo, there thou hast that is thine.' His lord answered and said unto him, 'Thou wicked and slothful servant, thou knewest that I reap where I sowed not, and gather where I have not strawed: Thou oughtest therefore to have put my money to the exchangers, and then at my coming I should have received mine own with usury. Take therefore the talent from him, and give it unto him which hath ten talents. For unto every one that hath shall be given, and he shall have abundance: but from him that hath not shall be taken away even that which he hath. And cast ye the unprofitable servant into outer darkness: there shall be weeping and gnashing of teeth.' When the Son of man shall come in his glory, and all the holy angels with him, then shall he sit upon the throne of his glory: And before him shall be gathered all nations: and he shall separate them one from another, as a shepherd divideth his sheep from the goats: And he shall set the sheep on his right hand, but the goats on the left. Then shall the King say unto them on his right hand, 'Come, ye blessed of my Father, inherit the kingdom prepared for you from the foundation of the world: For I was an hungred, and ye gave me meat: I was thirsty, and ye gave me drink: I was a stranger, and ye took me in: Naked, and ye clothed me: I was sick, and ye visited me: I was in prison, and ye came unto me.' Then shall the righteous answer him, saying, 'Lord, when saw we thee an hungred, and fed thee? or thirsty, and gave thee drink? When saw we thee a stranger, and took thee in? or naked, and clothed thee? Or when saw we thee sick, or in prison, and came unto thee?' And the King shall answer and say unto them, 'Verily I say unto you, Inasmuch as ye have done it unto one of the least of these my brethren, ye have done it unto me.'"

Matt. 25:14-40

In the name of the Father, and the Son, and the Holy Spirit. We have prayed to God, one in the Holy Trinity, brothers and sisters, at this Divine Liturgy, in this temple where our honorable and pious ancestors prayed before us; we have served the Divine Liturgy of the Body and Blood of Christ, the greatest holy Mystery of our faith. For, in every holy Mystery and prayer we receive singular grace of God, His help for growing in all that is good—whereas in the holy Mystery of the Eucharist we receive Him, the Son of God, our Lord Jesus Christ in the form of bread and wine. For it was He Who said, "He who eats My flesh and drinks My blood abides in Me, and I in him" (John 6:56). Moreover, this—the holy Mystery of Communion, therefore, is that holy Mystery that brings us into the most wonderful bond and union with the Son of God, and with all Orthodox in the world. On the other hand, the Apostle Paul cautions us to be watchful of how we approach the holy Mystery of Communion, "He who only eats and drinks [as if it were ordinary food], eats and drinks judgment to himself." And then he says, "If we would pay attention, we would not be judged; this way, though, there are many who are sick, and many have even died" (cf. 1 Cor. 11:29-31). If we would examine ourselves, then we would be worthy of Holy Communion. Usually, we are between the two inevitabilities: if we do not partake of Holy Communion, we cannot have life in us; if we commune unworthily, same thing. None of us are worthy of that greatest Mystery. Even the Saints considered themselves unworthy; however, we should strive to be by fighting against sin, against evil within us. This is what is most important.

We have acquired a new brother in service today, a new deacon in service to God, the holy Church, and the Orthodox people. The term deacon in Greek means precisely that, to serve. As the Lord Jesus Christ says, "Whosoever will be chief among you, let him be your servant, for even the Son of Man," that is, He Himself, "did not come to be served, but to serve, and to give His life as a ransom for many" (Matt. 20:27-28).

In today's Gospel reading, you heard Christ's parable of the talents, how God gave one five talents, another two, and the third man one. To each according to his strength, provided that they work with that money and multiply it, and when He comes, to give Him an account and the surplus. And you know, as you have heard, what the first two did: the one who received five talents worked hard and earned another five; the one who received two, earned two more. And both of them heard from the master those most important words, "Well done, good and faithful servant; you have been faithful over a few things, I will make you ruler over many things: enter into the joy of your lord." Although the first one earned five, and the other only two, yet according to their strength and how much was given to them, both of them have doubled their gift. Whereas the third one who received one talent buried his master's money thinking: I know my master is a hard man; he gathers where he has not scattered seed, and reaps where he has not sown. And when the master came and asked to settle an account with him, he then said, "Lord, I knew you to be a hard man, reaping where you have not sown, and gathering where you have not scattered seed. And I was afraid, and went and hid your talent in the ground. Look, there you have what is yours." And you heard the words of the master, "You wicked and lazy servant, you knew that I reap where I have not sown, and gather where I have not scattered seed. Why have you not at least deposited my money with the bankers, and at my coming I would have received back my own with interest. You have not even bothered to do that much." And then he said, "Take the talent from him, and give it to the one who has ten talents. And cut the unfaithful servant in half."

This, brothers and sisters, is about all of us. God has given us gifts, to some more, to others fewer. However, everyone through one's efforts can acquire the same reward, to hear the same words from the Master, if one endeavors. The effort, then, with regard to what is good, is what exalts us before God. This should be an admonishment on this word of the Lord both to me, and to these priests and deacons, especially the latter, since their title means "servant." By serving our neighbor, we will acquire a reward from Him, and an acknowledgement that we are diligent and wise stewards of His. Let this, then, brother Vladimir [the newly-ordained deacon], be an ever-present word before your spiritual eyes; may you, by your service as a deacon, and if you are made worthy of a higher rank, by your service acquire greatness before God—both you and myself, and every Orthodox Christian. That is the most important thing.

Furthermore, we are all co-workers of Christ. We should do what we can, because God has gifted us with His talents, so that we can multiply them and be of use to our neighbors. However, there are challenges that our times dictate that surpass our powers; according to the word of the Lord that we have read at the ordination today, and each time at the ordination into any priestly rank, God's grace is always what heals the infirm, and supplements the insufficient. This is also a consolation for us priests and pastors; while God expects from us more than we are able to do, He has given us strength, and He knows how strong we are; likewise, He puts before us the tasks of this time, and He knows how great they are, and whether they surpass our strength. If they are greater than our strengths, He, according to His words, will add of Himself to supplement what we are lacking. This is a consolation for us, our stability, not to extend ourselves, as St. Basil the Great says, to that which is above our strength, but also not to be satisfied, or make excuses for ourselves, with what is below our strength. To do what we can, no more, no less; more than that, if it is needed, will be done by the Almighty God, as He has done unto our ancestors.

May the Lord help us as well, who today represent the Serbian people and the Orthodox faith, to be worthy of our name, the Orthodox name of the Orthodox Serbs.

ON THE WORDS OF THE LORD: "THEREFORE BE WISE AS SERPENTS AND HARMLESS AS DOVES"

Sermon at the Divine Liturgy on January 16/3, 1997,
in the patriarchal chapel of St. Simeon the Myrrh-Gusher in Belgrade

> "Behold, I send you forth as sheep in the midst of wolves: be ye therefore wise as serpents, and harmless as doves. But beware of men: for they will deliver you up to the councils, and they will scourge you in their synagogues; and ye shall be brought before governors and kings for my sake, for a testimony against them and the Gentiles. But when they deliver you up, take no thought how or what ye shall speak: for it shall be given you in that same hour what ye shall speak. For it is not ye that speak, but the Spirit of your Father which speaks in you. And the brother shall deliver up the brother to death, and the father the child: and the children shall rise up against their parents, and cause them to be put to death. And ye shall be hated of all men for my name's sake: but he that endures to the end shall be saved."
>
> Matt. 10:16-22

To truly be human in this world is like being a sheep among the wolves, because "the whole world lies in wickedness" (1 John 5:19). I have said it before, and will reiterate, what you should remember well: a sheep among wolves is in danger from two sides. First, to be harmed, that is, torn apart by the wolves. This is not why the Son of God sends you. The other danger is for the sheep to perceive and conclude that it cannot survive among the wolves in any other way except as a wolf, and to become a wolf itself: to sharpen its teeth, to learn to howl, to turn its hooves into claws, and from a sheep to turn into a wolf. Christ does not send us for this either, but for this: by our faith, and our life according to that faith, to entice the wolves into becoming the sheep of Christ, if they want it.

To be free of both dangers, Christ gives us a solution and says, "Therefore be wise as serpents and harmless as doves." Wisdom will preserve you so that the wolves do not harm you, or tear you apart. And harmlessness, goodness, will keep you from becoming wolves yourselves. On the other hand, this means that we can develop our intellectual, rational capacities more and more, endlessly, under the condition, though, that we simultaneously develop goodness within us, because goodness then will provide us with balance. The eyes are of this world, observing what, together with us, both flies and bees also see with their thousand eyes. However, with our mind we see what they cannot see, and these are the inner, spiritual realities and eternity.

Nonetheless, the mind is cold. Sometimes it cuts right through the heart, or next to the heart. Goodness, on the contrary, is warm, but blind. To reiterate, our people have a saying: "Good and foolish—brothers." That is, if someone is only good, but of little wisdom, everyone can not only use him, but also make fun of him, trip him up.

We are in danger of man developing the mind, but forgetting goodness, or considering it something for lesser, lower people; thus, he can ruin, of course, his own and the lives of his neighbors. For, all these big criminals, swindlers, have an advanced mind and often great capacities, even academic, well-developed. And evidently, goodness, as I said, is insufficient and lacking.

Here, then, is the solution for a Christian man. To develop our God-given mind, which differentiates us from all other living beings who only have instincts. We have instincts as well, but we have a mind that we were endowed with by God, and by which He has exalted us. We also have a heart, and will, and freedom.

May the Lord teach us and help us to always have and develop both the mind and goodness, to His glory, to the benefit of our family, our nation, and all of mankind, and for our salvation and theirs. God bless you!

ON MEMORIAL (SOUL) SATURDAY

Sermon at the Divine Liturgy on March 1/February 16, 1997, in the patriarchal chapel of St. Simeon the Myrrh-Gusher in Belgrade

> "Verily, verily, I say unto you, He that heareth my word, and believeth on him that sent me, hath everlasting life, and shall not come into condemnation; but is passed from death unto life. Verily, verily, I say unto you, The hour is coming, and now is, when the dead shall hear the voice of the Son of God: and they that hear shall live. For as the Father hath life in himself; so hath he given to the Son to have life in himself; And hath given him authority to execute judgment also, because he is the Son of man. Marvel not at this: for the hour is coming, in the which all that are in the graves shall hear his voice, and shall come forth; they that have done good, unto the resurrection of life; and they that have done evil, unto the resurrection of damnation. I can of mine own self do nothing: as I hear, I judge: and my judgment is just; because I seek not mine own will, but the will of the Father which hath sent me."
>
> John 5:24-30

Today, on Meatfare Sunday, the holy Church holds a memorial service for all the departed throughout the ages: our fathers, brothers, and sisters.

We are one in Christ, one Church whose head is Christ, and we are all the mystical body of the Church, the Body of Christ. Part of this Church of Christ is also the Lord as the Head of that Church, the Mother of God, all the holy Martyrs, and other Saints in the Church triumphant, and likewise we, the living, who are still in the Church militant. Part of this Church, as I said, are all those who have reposed in the Lord, too. And it is our duty, if we can even say for love that it has a duty, to remember our departed, because we are a community; we remain that even after their death, and our own when it comes; the communion remains with his and our God, with all the Saints, and with all our departed.

Praying for the departed, both today and always, let us not forget that this hour awaits us as well, and to strive even now, because we do not know when that hour will come, and to be worthy to come before the Son of God, so that we may hear His voice, "Come, ye blessed of my Father, inherit the kingdom prepared for you from the foundation of the world" (Matt. 25:34). Let this be an admonishment to us today, and a counsel unto ourselves and everyone today.

May the Lord remember His departed servants, who in faith and in life according to faith, departed this world. May He help us as well to keep in mind this hour of our coming before Him, the Righteous Judge, so that we would live with this faith, life according to that holy Orthodox faith. God bless you!

ON THE WEDDING IN CANA OF GALILEE

Sermon at the Divine Liturgy on May 5/April 18, 1997,
in the patriarchal chapel of St. Simeon the Myrrh-Gusher in Belgrade

> "And the third day there was a marriage in Cana of Galilee; and the mother of Jesus was there: And both Jesus was called, and his disciples, to the marriage. And when they wanted wine, the mother of Jesus saith unto him, 'They have no wine.' Jesus saith unto her, 'Woman, what have I to do with thee? mine hour is not yet come.' His mother saith unto the servants, 'Whatsoever he saith unto you, do it.' And there were set there six waterpots of stone, after the manner of the purifying of the Jews, containing two or three firkins apiece. Jesus saith unto them, 'Fill the waterpots with water.' And they filled them up to the brim. And he saith unto them, 'Draw out now, and bear unto the governor of the feast.' And they bare it. When the ruler of the feast had tasted the water that was made wine, and knew not whence it was: (but the servants which drew the water knew;) the governor of the feast called the bridegroom, and saith unto him, 'Every man at the beginning doth set forth good wine; and when men have well drunk, then that which is worse: but thou hast kept the good wine until now.' This beginning of miracles did Jesus in Cana of Galilee, and manifested forth his glory; and his disciples believed on him."
>
> John 2:1-11

With this miracle, the Lord set a beginning to all the other miracles He performed, always for the sake of people's needs. This miracle as well, of turning water into wine, the Lord did not perform so that people could get drunk, but because it was obvious they were poor people, and it was possible that the wine would run out at the wedding. First, He did this to help them out in their trouble; second, we already know by now what the Lord as God had known, and for what purpose

He had created wine, and did not forbid it for his disciples and Christians. It is that wine in small quantities has the effect of nourishment—it goes immediately into the body, into the blood, burns up quickly in the organism, and provides heat. So when we use it reasonably, the way we should, then it is to our benefit. One thing is that it provides heat as nourishment; also, it releases into our organism finished components, not only alcohol, but tannin as well, and acids, and other components. If we use Christ's teaching as we should, it will react within us as good wine, that is, it will give us much needed and necessary strength.

That the Lord told His mother, "Woman, what have I to do with thee?" in our language, for our present manner of speaking, sounds harsh, to address one's mother with the word "woman." However, in their time, this term represented an expression of respect to call one's mother "woman." God bless you!

ON CHRIST'S CONVERSATION WITH THE SAMARITAN WOMAN

Sermon at the Divine Liturgy on May 25/12, 1997, in the church of St. George in Bezhania

"Now Jacob's well was there. Jesus therefore, being wearied with his journey, sat thus on the well: and it was about the sixth hour. There cometh a woman of Samaria to draw water: Jesus saith unto her, 'Give me to drink.' (For his disciples were gone away unto the city to buy meat.) Then saith the woman of Samaria unto him, 'How is it that thou, being a Jew, askest drink of me, which am a woman of Samaria? for the Jews have no dealings with the Samaritans.' Jesus answered and said unto her, 'If thou knewest the gift of God, and who it is that saith to thee, "Give me to drink;" thou wouldest have asked of him, and he would have given thee living water.' The woman saith unto him, 'Sir, thou hast nothing to draw with, and the well is deep: from whence then hast thou that living water? Art thou greater than our father Jacob, which gave us the well, and drank thereof himself, and his children, and his cattle?' Jesus answered and said unto her, 'Whosoever drinketh of this water shall thirst again: But whosoever drinketh of the water that I shall give him shall never thirst; but the water that I shall give him shall be in him a well of water springing up into everlasting life.' The woman saith unto him, 'Sir, give me this water, that I thirst not, neither come hither to draw.'"

John 4:6-15

We have prayed to God, brothers and sisters, on this Sunday, the day of the week of the resurrection of the Son of God. On this Sunday we commemorate the evangelical event when the Lord Jesus came to Jacob's well, and asked the Samaritan woman for a drink of water. First, let us be edified about one thing: the Lord grew thirsty according to His human nature, and it also says that He was tired when He sat down by the well. He experienced this according to His human nature, because divinity is out of reach of fatigue, thirst, and hunger.

From these and other words of the Gospel we see, brothers and sisters, that heretics are falsely teaching that God had only one nature, only the divine one, that is, that the divine nature was so immense that it completely destroyed, so to say within, the human nature, and that He remained only God. They say it would be the same as if we took a glass of water and poured it into the sea, the ocean. This ocean, with its immensity, would swallow up, enclose this water, so to speak, so that it would not exist. This human logic with regard to divine things, is obviously too shallow, short, and insufficient. If the Lord says, "I am thirsty," how can we humans say, "No, Lord, You are not thirsty, because You are God." We know that He as God is not thirsty, but as man He is. When the Evangelist here says that He is tired, should we tell the Evangelist that we know better than him that Christ is not tired? And so on. Even on the cross, He suffered and died according to His human nature, but He is one person—the God-man suffered. Suffered, of course, by His human nature.

Moreover, in this event we see the Lord speaking with a woman, and as we gather from the following words, with a sinful woman. At that time, no teacher in Israel, nor in other nations, would have dared to speak with a woman, and to expound on such lofty things as the Lord had brought up to that Samaritan woman: that the Lord is spirit, and that one ought to pray to Him in spirit and truth. Furthermore, that people will not pray to God only on that mountain, nor in Jerusalem, but across the whole world. At that time, both in the East and the West, as St. Gregory the Theologian says, men passed and enacted laws, and they secured for themselves that which they forbade women. Certainly, even today we now have the demands of feminism and that female lobby, whereby they do not ask that we be one in Jesus Christ, but that we be the same. And you see it yourself, and know, where this has led us. What a terrible moral fall exists among women and men alike. So we do not acknowledge, as St. Gregory the Theologian says, this difference in demands and attitudes. What the Lord prescribed is equally valid both for men and women. "Blessed are the merciful...," not only male, but female as well. "Blessed are the pure in heart..." and so on.

Therefore, every commandment of God relates equally both to husbands and wives. There are differences, of course, not only physical, but also psychological, but they are not such that they make men higher, and women lower beings, unworthy of the heavenly kingdom. True, according to the word of the Apostle, and according to the Bible, Adam was created first, and then the woman from his rib. However, according to the interpretation of the Holy Fathers, it was so that none of them would become prideful. God created the woman from the same nature that Adam had, so that they know they are one in Christ Jesus. And then, the love that exists should be such as is becoming to beings created by God. Not an urge toward irresponsible pleasure, nor a tendency toward sin, to what is contrary to God, toward adultery, fornication, and other misfortunes of sin; rather, an aspiration toward respecting the person of one in the other, and preserving the honor of the soul. "... neither fornicators, nor idolaters, nor adulterers... nor revilers, nor swindlers will inherit the kingdom of God" (1 Cor. 6:9-10).

The Lord had foreseen this, as God He saw that this woman "had five husbands, and the one you are with now is not your husband" (John 4:18). May the Lord Who sees our thoughts and our hearts, Who likewise sees our deeds, help us, so that our mind, heart, and vision, our hands and everything are clean from sin on the path following Him to the Kingdom of Heaven. "Where I am, there will my servant be also" (John 12:26). And He is in the Kingdom of Heaven, where we should strive to go by our faith, and our life according to that faith, in honor and holiness. God bless you and grant you every good thing!

ON NOT RESPONDING TO EVIL WITH EVIL

Sermon at the Divine Liturgy on June 20/7, 1997, in the patriarchal chapel of St. Simeon the Myrrh-Gusher in Belgrade

> "Again you have heard that it was said to those of old, 'You shall not swear falsely, but shall perform your oaths to the Lord.' But I say to you, do not swear at all: neither by heaven, for it is God's throne; nor by the earth, for it is His footstool; nor by Jerusalem, for it is the city of the great King. Nor shall you swear by your head, because you cannot make one hair white or black. But let your 'Yes' be 'Yes,' and your 'No,' 'No.' For whatever is more than these is from the evil one. You have heard that it was said, 'An eye for an eye and a tooth for a tooth.' But I tell you not to resist an evil person. But whoever slaps you on your right cheek, turn the other to him also. If anyone wants to sue you and take away your tunic, let him have your cloak also. And whoever compels you to go one mile, go with him two."
>
> Matt. 5:33-41

The Lord cautions us not to swear by anything, but to have such love of truth amongst ourselves, and such trust that we are telling the truth, that it is enough to say, "yes, yes," or "no, no." Admittedly, on important occasions, the Church allows for oaths to be taken so that one can come to the truth more clearly, especially in court. We know it from Holy Scripture as well, where it says that the Lord swore "by Himself." Hence, the issue here is not to avoid taking an oath, even when there is a necessity or a need, but for us to try, as I said, to be truth-loving; for, God is the Truth, and the devil is falsehood and the father of lies. In that sense, we should be lovers of truth.

Also, here's another lesson that bears repeating. In the old Mosaic Law it was said, "an eye for an eye, and a tooth for a tooth" (Exod. 21:24). That was a higher degree of justice than the one they had had before. Lamech, who had two wives, said that he had killed a man for wounding him, and a young man for bruising him (Gen. 4:23). Then came the Mosaic Law that said: one cannot do that, but to give an eye for an eye, a tooth for a tooth, and a hand for a hand (Exod. 21:24-25); as much as it had been done unto you, that much you could do unto others in return. Now comes the word of the Lord that we should do even more, so that the initiative would cross from the evil side over to us. So He says not to resist evil with evil. This does not mean to avoid resisting evil in general; that would be passivity, the destruction of the difference between good and evil. Rather, not to resist with evil; we cannot respond to wrongdoing by wrongdoing. For the Apostle Paul says, "Do not be overcome by evil, but overcome evil with good" (Rom. 12:21). This is the meaning of these words of Christ, as I said, not the literal meaning. For even He, when He was on trial, and when a servant slapped Him, did not turn His other cheek to him, but He said, "If I have spoken evil, bear witness of the evil; but if well, why do you strike me?" (John 18:23).

I think you know what this is about. Let us be ready to do more than the evil is asking, if there is any prospect that the sinner might be restored, that he might understand. In any case, let us not be passive, but take the initiative with regard to good. Certainly, there are many evil ones who have become Christian, because Christians were fulfilling that word of Christ by showing how much they love their enemies, how much they strive for them to repent as well, and to understand that they are sliding into ruin.

May the Lord help us to have the love of truth among us as well; likewise, out of that love for our neighbor to love even our enemies, in the sense that we pray to God, but also show it with our own lives, so they might understand that they are falling into spiritual ruin, into eternal torments, and so they might repent and be saved. God bless you!

ON THE CONVERSATION WITH THE SADDUCEES

Sermon at the Divine Liturgy on August 21/8, 1997,
in the patriarchal chapel
of St. Simeon the Myrrh-Gusher in Belgrade

> "The same day came to him the Sadducees, which say that there is no resurrection, and asked him, saying, 'Master, Moses said, If a man die, having no children, his brother shall marry his wife, and raise up seed unto his brother. Now there were with us seven brethren: and the first, when he had married a wife, deceased, and, having no issue, left his wife unto his brother: Likewise the second also, and the third, unto the seventh. And last of all the woman died also. Therefore in the resurrection whose wife shall she be of the seven? for they all had her.' Jesus answered and said unto them, 'Ye do err, not knowing the scriptures, nor the power of God. For in the resurrection they neither marry, nor are given in marriage, but are as the angels of God in heaven. But as touching the resurrection of the dead, have ye not read that which was spoken unto you by God, saying, "I am the God of Abraham, and the God of Isaac, and the God of Jacob?" God is not the God of the dead, but of the living.' And when the multitude heard this, they were astonished at his doctrine."
>
> Matt. 22:23-33

Sadducees were rationalists, that is, they relied only on their reason, not realizing that God in the Holy Scripture revealed to us only as much as we can understand, and as much as we need for our salvation, but that there are truths that surpass our limited mind. So, in order to humiliate Christ, and to show Him as guilty before the people, they invented an incident—according to the Mosaic Law, if a man was married, and died without children, his brother was obliged to take his wife; the child who would be born out of this union would be registered under the name of the deceased brother, so that his progeny would not cease, and so that it would also partake in that glory when the Savior comes. From these words of the Sadducees, it was obvious that the woman was barren, and that it was pointless, after she had been with the first and the second one without producing any children, that she should be taken by the others, too. However, they made this up, as I said, to show how pointless it was. It is clear that one man could have had more than one wife even according to the Mosaic Law. In fact, this was due to the difficulties they had in those times, when a lot of men would die in battles, and there would be many more women left—what would have happened to them. That is another matter, though. God through Moses decided that one man could have more than one wife. Of course, it was not possible for one woman to have several husbands at the same time. Evidently, this way one could not be sure who the father of the child was, if a woman had more than one husband: whether it was the child of one or the other husband. Christ also says that they "do not know the Scriptures or the power of God; for at the resurrection people will neither marry nor be given in marriage."

Procreation and marriage are bound to this world. In the other world they neither marry nor are given in marriage, but they are like angels. That is, a husband will recognize his wife, and a wife her husband, and the children will recognize their parents. However, a husband will not recognize his wife by these earthly relations, but by the love that actually joined them together in this life.

Yet they, the Sadducees, did not believe in angels either. And Christ explained this to them, speaking about angels, even though they had not asked. Namely, when Moses, having escaped from Egypt, was watching the sheep of his father-in-law Jethro, he saw a bramble bush that burned, but was not consumed by fire, and having come to see what it was, he heard a voice from the bush, "Take off your sandals, for the place where you are standing is holy ground. I am the God of Abraham, the God of Isaac, and the God of Jacob" (Exod. 3:5-6). In this way, God consoled Moses by showing that the Jewish people would not perish as slaves in Egypt; indeed they were as if in flames of fire, but they would not be consumed by it. Moreover, the miracle of the bramble bush that burns, yet is not consumed by the flames, is at the same time a symbol, a sign of the Holy Mother of God who received the Son of

God and gave birth to Him; she was a burning bush that was not consumed by the flames of divinity.

Therefore, let us have this in mind that God is the God of Abraham, the God of Isaac, and the God of Jacob. God is not called a God of millions, but as we can see, a God of one in a generation of all of mankind: the God of the holy Abraham, and in the second generation the God of the holy Isaac, and in the third generation of the holy Jacob. Let us strive, brothers and sisters, that God may be called our God, too, by our being His genuine sons and daughters. God bless you!

ON THE SCRIBES AND THE PHARISEES

Sermon at the Divine Liturgy on August 25/12, 1997, in the patriarchal chapel of St. Simeon the Myrrh-Gusher in Belgrade

> "But woe unto you, scribes and Pharisees, hypocrites! for ye shut up the kingdom of heaven against men: for ye neither go in yourselves, neither suffer ye them that are entering to go in. Woe unto you, scribes and Pharisees, hypocrites! for ye devour widows' houses, and for a pretense make long prayer: therefore ye shall receive the greater damnation. Woe unto you, scribes and Pharisees, hypocrites! for ye compass sea and land to make one proselyte, and when he is made, ye make him twofold more the child of hell than yourselves. Woe unto you, ye blind guides, which say, 'Whosoever shall swear by the temple, it is nothing; but whosoever shall swear by the gold of the temple, he is a debtor!' Ye fools and blind: for whether is greater, the gold, or the temple that sanctifieth the gold? And, 'Whosoever shall swear by the altar, it is nothing; but whosoever sweareth by the gift that is upon it, he is guilty.' Ye fools and blind: for whether is greater, the gift, or the altar that sanctifieth the gift? Whoso therefore shall swear by the altar, sweareth by it, and by all things thereon. And whoso shall swear by the temple, sweareth by it, and by him that dwelleth therein. And he that shall swear by heaven, sweareth by the throne of God, and by him that sitteth thereon."
>
> Matt. 23:13-22

We are called, brothers and sisters, to be witnesses of the Son of God, and of His faith in this world, by our Orthodox faith and our life according to that faith; this is the duty of all of us, especially us priests, or I should say, first and foremost of us priests. For this reason, the Lord cautions us, "Woe to you, scribes and Pharisees, hypocrites! For you shut up the kingdom of heaven against men." This is done by faulty, wrong and unchristian faith; thereby we scandalize those who are not Christian, and we become a wall, so to say, which those who would want to become Christian cannot pass; looking at us, they form a perception of what Christianity is, yet they cannot fully grasp what it is because of us and our actions. Thus, we certainly ruin our own souls, but furthermore, we throw ourselves even deeper into the fires of hell, by scandalizing others as well. We do not enter the Kingdom of Heaven ourselves, and we do not let others enter.

Likewise, the Lord calls hypocrites those Pharisees who present themselves as pious, but in fact devour widows' houses; they are ready to sell widows' houses to raise their own standard of living.

If we strive to win over one unbeliever to become a Christian, but do not instruct him, both with our faith and our life, to be a true Christian as is becoming, thus making him the son of hell twice as great as we are—woe unto us.

And so on, all those other words with regard to the temple, and fussing over trifles that are of no consequence, whereas we leave off what is truly important.

May the Lord help us as well, who today represent the Orthodox faith and the Serbian people, and the Orthodox priesthood, to be up to the task and sincere witnesses of our faith in the Son of God, and our life according to that faith, for these two are what saves us, and this is what will help the salvation of all our neighbors who want to hear and see the truth. God bless you!

ON THE SCRIBES AND THE PHARISEES
SECOND SERMON

Sermon at the Divine Liturgy on August 25/12, 1997,
in the patriarchal chapel
of St. Simeon the Myrrh-Gusher in Belgrade

> "Woe unto you, scribes and Pharisees, hypocrites! for ye pay tithe of mint and anise and cummin, and have omitted the weightier matters of the law, judgment, mercy, and faith: these ought ye to have done, and not to leave the other undone. Ye blind guides, which strain at a gnat, and swallow a camel. Woe unto you, scribes and Pharisees, hypocrites! for ye make clean the outside of the cup and of the platter, but within they are full of extortion and excess. Thou blind Pharisee, cleanse first that which is within the cup and platter, that the outside of them may be clean also. Woe unto you, scribes and Pharisees, hypocrites! for ye are like unto whited sepulchres, which indeed appear beautiful outward, but are within full of dead men's bones, and of all uncleanness. Even so ye also outwardly appear righteous unto men, but within ye are full of hypocrisy and iniquity."
>
> Matt. 23:23-28

Both these words, and the ones we heard yesterday [*see the previous sermon*—T.N.] are an admonishment to the scribes and the Pharisees as hypocrites who falsely presented themselves as pious, but were in fact using piety only for their own base interests. Certainly, in the times that we have passed through, it was difficult to show real piety because of our enemies, who were powerful, and wanted to destroy faith in any way possible. Let it not be so now, when things are much easier, that we show our faith in the manner of these Pharisees! The Lord cautions us in another place not to show ourselves and our piety before people, but in secret before God, Who sees what is done in secret, but will reward us openly (cf. Matt. 6:6).

The Mosaic Law ordered to give a tenth, but of the fruits of the earth, from what man had sown, and what he had labored for, and from the cattle; and here the Pharisees gave a tenth of mint, a spice, and a herb, and of dill and cumin, yet they left what was more important in the law—justice, mercy, and faith. Then the Lord says the following, "These [justice, mercy, and faith] you ought to have done, without leaving the others undone." Those things that should be done are more important than the ones that should not be left undone.

Likewise, speaking of cleaning the outside of the cup and dish. The inner purity is more important, and once it is achieved, it will give value to the outside as well. And then in the end, "Woe to you, scribes and Pharisees, hypocrites! For you are like whitewashed tombs which look beautiful on the outside but on the inside are full of the bones of the dead and everything unclean." You see in yourself, and in me, and other people, how we make an effort on the outside to be not only polite, but lavishly dressed—and what other things do we do! It is not a matter of not paying attention to cleanliness and respect when we go to visit someone, to show with our clothes our respect for them, or when someone visits us. The point is not to misrepresent ourselves, while inside it is like a whitewashed tomb, full of the bones of the dead, and impurity. People of this world adorn themselves on the outside, and disregard what is most important, what makes us human—justice, mercy, and faith, truth, and love.

This is what we should pay attention to!—for "[t]he king's daughter is all glorious within," as it says in Holy Scripture (Ps. 45:13). May our soul be like the daughter of the Heavenly King, and her beauty all glorious within! God bless you!

ON THE TRUE FAITH

Sermon at the Divine Liturgy on May 21/8, 1997,
in the chapel of St. John the Theologian in Belgrade

> "Now about the midst of the feast Jesus went up into the temple, and taught. And the Jews marveled, saying, 'How knoweth this man letters, having never learned?' Jesus answered them, and said, 'My doctrine is not mine, but his that sent me. If any man will do his will, he shall know of the doctrine, whether it be of God, or whether I speak of myself. He that speaketh of himself seeketh his own glory: but he that seeketh his glory that sent him, the same is true, and no unrighteousness is in him. Did not Moses give you the law, and yet none of you keepeth the law? Why go ye about to kill me?'
>
> Then said Jesus unto them, 'Yet a little while am I with you, and then I go unto him that sent me. Ye shall seek me, and shall not find me: and where I am, thither ye cannot come.' Then said the Jews among themselves, 'Whither will he go, that we shall not find him? will he go unto the dispersed among the Gentiles, and teach the Gentiles? What manner of saying is this that he said, "Ye shall seek me, and shall not find me:" and "where I am, thither ye cannot come?"
>
> John 7:14-19, 33-36

In the name of the Father, and the Son, and the Holy Spirit. Celebrating today, brothers and sisters, the Holy Apostle and Evangelist John, the patron Saint of the students of this Faculty of Orthodox theology, I pray to God and all the Saints, to help the teachers, students, and all of us, to be worthy of the teaching that the Lord Jesus Christ addressed to all the nations, and the Holy Apostles. They are the ones who preached His message, lived by it, and gave their lives for this faith, for the Son of God, and for all that He spoke and did, whereby He gave us the strength to walk on His path, on the condition that we take up our cross and follow Him.

The Holy Apostle and Evangelist John is the disciple "whom the Lord loved" (John 13:23). Certainly, the Lord loved all the Apostles, and all people in the world. Out of this love, He ascended the cross, and suffered death in order to grant salvation to all, if they adopt it with the right faith, and life according to that faith. Never forget the words of the Holy Gospel of John, "How can you believe," he says, "since you accept glory from one another but do not seek the glory that comes from the only God?" (John 5:44). Indeed, desiring to be praised by people, surely out of vanity, what else, we thereby prevent ourselves and others from seeking that real glory, which comes from God. For, even when they are well-intentioned and wise, people are not able to grasp everything, and they can be misguided, not to mention those who, with their own interest in mind, praise or scold someone. However, before God we cannot present ourselves as better than we are by dishonesty, injustice, or any other such thing. He sees even our thoughts; He hears our words, and sees our deeds; even when we do things in darkness, He will repay us all according to our merits, for He has endowed us with great gifts, and expects from us to respond to these capacities that He bestowed upon us when He gave us our freedom. In the book of Revelation, the Lord says in the end, "He who is unjust, let him be unjust still; he who is filthy, let him be filthy still; he who is righteous, let him be righteous still; he who is holy, let him be holy still. And behold, I am coming quickly, and my reward is with me, to give to every one according to his work" (Rev. 22:11-12). "Yes, I am coming soon," says the Lord (Rev. 22:20).

Come, Lord Jesus, and before that help us to be with You and You with us, whatever may happen in this world. Even if we should lose our lives, let us not depart from You and Your ways. That is the chief thing to know and to apply in our lives at all times. This is the meaning of the teaching that the professors and teachers impart here; this is the meaning of the teaching that each of you students should accept; thereby we should witness now, in this time, the Son of God, and His teaching. God bless you and grant you every good thing.

ON THE HEALING OF THE LEPER

Sermon at the Divine Liturgy on October 21/8, 1997,
in the patriarchal chapel of
St. Simeon the Myrrh-Gusher in Belgrade

> "And it came to pass, when he was in a certain city, behold a man full of leprosy: who seeing Jesus fell on his face, and besought him, saying, 'Lord, if thou wilt, thou canst make me clean.' And he put forth his hand, and touched him, saying, 'I will: be thou clean.' And immediately the leprosy departed from him. And he charged him to tell no man: but go, and shew thyself to the priest, and offer for thy cleansing, according as Moses commanded, for a testimony unto them. But so much the more went there a fame abroad of him: and great multitudes came together to hear, and to be healed by him of their infirmities. And he withdrew himself into the wilderness, and prayed."
>
> Luke 5:12-16

Leprosy is a severe contagious disease, and in its advanced stages the skin falls apart, and parts of the human body fall off. Even in the Mosaic Law it was decreed that lepers must live outside residential areas, on dumps, and people who could or wanted to would bring them food. Moreover, they had to wear jingles on their feet, and when they passed anyone, they had to say, "Unclean, unclean," so that the person would step aside to not catch the illness. If it happened that they were cured, they would wash themselves, come to the temple, and bring a sacrifice for their cleansing—a male or female dove.

This disease still exists today in India. Only, it is difficult over there, in such highly populated areas as Indian towns and cities are, to separate oneself and thus preserve oneself from infection. Christ as God heals even this disease, as we see.

Nevertheless, it says, "He withdrew Himself into the wilderness, and prayed." The Son of God has the need to converse with His Heavenly Father; that is what our prayer is as well, and should be: a conversation with our Heavenly Father. There are three kinds of prayer. First, those in which we glorify God, second, those in which we thank Him for all the good He does for us daily, and third, those in which we ask for the things we need.

May the Lord hear us and grant us whatever we are asking for our own good, and for the good of all people. God bless you!

WHO IS THE GREATEST

Sermon at the Divine Liturgy on January 2/December 20, 1998, in the patriarchal chapel of St. Simeon the Myrrh-Gusher in Belgrade

> "And he came to Capernaum: and being in the house he asked them, 'What was it that ye disputed among yourselves by the way?' But they held their peace: for by the way they had disputed among themselves, who should be the greatest. And he sat down, and called the twelve, and saith unto them, 'If any man desire to be first, the same shall be last of all, and servant of all.' And he took a child, and set him in the midst of them: and when he had taken him in his arms, he said unto them, 'Whosoever shall receive one of such children in my name, receiveth me: and whosoever shall receive me, receiveth not me, but him that sent me.' And John answered him, saying, 'Master, we saw one casting out devils in thy name, and he followeth not us: and we forbad him, because he followeth not us.' But Jesus said, 'Forbid him not: for there is no man which shall do a miracle in my name, that can lightly speak evil of me. For he that is not against us is on our part. For whosoever shall give you a cup of water to drink in my name, because ye belong to Christ, verily I say unto you, he shall not lose his reward.'"
>
> Mark 9:33-41

The question of primacy, of the greatest one, is in fact, the question of pride, and we have inherited this pride from our parents. The Lord answers His disciples and teaches them that the one who wants to be the first has to be the last, and being the last means to be a servant to all; that is the one who will be the greatest. The organ that is the most important one is a servant to all the other ones. The brain and the heart are the two most important organs in the human body precisely because they serve all the other organs and parts of the body. The brain affects the function of many organs in the body—it coordinates them and serves them. Therefore, like the heart, it is more important than all the rest, and the greatest among them.

In the eyes of Christ, the one who is the master and the king will not be the first, nor the greatest; God's measures are different. The first before Christ is the one who is a servant to all, because Christ says of Himself even, that the Son of God did not come to be served, but to serve and to give His life "as a ransom for many" (Mark 10:45).

Furthermore, the Lord teaches His disciples about who is with them, and who is against them. He tells them not to forbid those who cast out demons in His name, even though the person is not their follower. Later, the Lord will say something quite different in principal, a criterion stronger than the first one He had set. That is: The one who is not with Him, is against Him (Luke 11:23, Matt. 12:30). The first, milder one, was valid at the beginning of His preaching. As His end on earth drew closer, and as the Apostles advanced and became stronger in His teaching, so the word regarding who was against, and who was with Christ, became stronger and more specific. God bless you!

AFTER THE FALL OF WESTERN SLAVONIJA

On Saturday, May 6, 1995,
on the feast of St. George the Great-Martyr,
after the Liturgy in the church of St. George,
His Holiness, Patriarch of Serbia Paul served a *moleben*—a prayer service to the new Serbian martyrs. The next day at noon, in the great church of St. Sava in Vrachar, the *moleben* was served again for the new victims of Croatian aggression.
The Patriarch addressed the people after the prayer service.

In the name of the Father, and the Son, and the Holy Spirit! The day after tomorrow, God willing, brothers and sisters, we will depart in order to serve the Divine Liturgy and pray to God, one in Holy Trinity, in Moshtanitsa Monastery on the feast of the Burning of the Relics of St. Sava. Right before that day, we have gathered here, brothers and sisters, to serve a *moleben* in the temple of our spiritual father, whose holy relics were turned into ashes in this precise place. The bonfire that was set ablaze here is the greatest beacon of the nation that knows, and even of those who did not always have eyes to see, so that at least from here they would see their destiny. Our people especially did not recognize those who, hiding behind the great powers of the world, prepared the extinction of St. Sava's nation. From the time of Vrachar, 400 years ago, to Pakrats and Okuchani only four days ago, there existed one Jesuit plan—by fire and sword to kill and exile all that is Serbian, not only in Western Slavonija. After hundreds of thousands killed in war, the war whose fiftieth anniversary is being commemorated now, the turn came again for another pogrom on May 1st, 1995, this time in Western Slavonija, a region that managed to survive even in the Second World War in the Independent Croatian state, that quisling creation. Now they are pounded to dust by the heir to that Ustasha state, the one that the whole world today recognizes.

As for many others, likewise for me personally, nothing remains of what used to exist when I came into this world. The church where I was baptized was demolished. Someone was particularly eager to erase every trace, the birthplace and origin, of the present Patriarch of Serbia. However, our real fatherland, our collective memory as a Christian people, we carry them with us as our cross. Christ tells us, "Whosoever wants to follow me, let him take up his cross," (Matt. 16:24) therefore, it is our fate to carry the cross.

Deaths and defeats are difficult beyond measure, but they are passing, even when it seems to us that they tend to pass too slow. Salvation comes only to those who acknowledge the far reach of God's justice, for they know His word, "I will never leave you, nor forsake you" (Heb. 13:5).

Therefore, we pray to Him, our Savior, that amidst this evil that has befallen us we would not debase ourselves as a people, and as humans. As always, when Serbs were going through the worst, let us summon the last bits of strength left in us, so that we do not lose our spirit, that we are not caught by despondency and disappointment. For, this is precisely the goal of those who wish to break us, to beat us down, and to destroy us to such a degree, so that Serbs would turn against Serbs. But let us lift up our heads, my brothers and children in Christ, I beseech you in a fatherly manner; let us stop now the mutual accusations; let us not justify ourselves by blaming others, when we know where the evil comes from, and where it can come from still. No one's accountability can be hidden; everything will fall into its place, and in its own time. May this decisive moment help us to snap out of it.

We have gathered here to pray for the repose of the souls of those who died in this most recent Ustasha attack; for the healing of the wounded, for the salvation of the imprisoned and abused, for the care of the exiled and unfortunate, and for all the victims of this half-century war that has been waged in our country under the guise of peace, only to manifest itself in its real appearance and terror now. We will pray near Yasenovats on Wednesday, on the feast of St. Sava. For it is not a coincidence that there was an invasion of Yasenovats at this time, in order to obstruct our *moleben* that had been announced, as well as the memorial service to those who died at the hands of evildoers on the biggest place of suffering of the Second World War. The world media turn their heads and refuse to see this even after the fact. We were invited and expected to come to this commemoration. We had to withdraw, because the capture of Yasenovats means a repetition of the crime right before our eyes, and in the face of the whole world. We will pray close to this holy place under which lie more murdered people than some of the present European countries have. We will serve a funeral service for the dead, not to call for revenge or hatred, but to caution the living, those from whom the crimes were hidden, or who did not believe there had been any crimes. For this reason, we will also pray for our enemies, who think that they are victors if they repeat their crimes. We will pray for them, for they do not know what they are doing, and what misfortunes they sow for their people, who will not have peace until their brothers' blood begins to cry out from the earth. Hatred will poison and seek out people, unless the divine truth leads them out of darkness, and frees them of the unclean powers of which they are servants, unless they sincerely repent, not before us, but before the living, and all-seeing God.

May the Resurrected Lord save all of us, and all people of goodwill, because we are all the children of God. Christ is Risen!

The day before, at the moleben, *the Patriarch also said the following:*

Even in these misfortunes that have befallen us, through our own fault, but also through the fault of other nations, Europe and America, too, the only thing that remains for us as an actual consolation, and not only a consolation, but a real help—both to us and to those who are fighting in this war, and dying each day—is this: to truly be the people of God. To preserve ourselves from everything that is evil and sinful, for if we keep away from that, God will be with us, and we will survive as the people of God, regardless of the sacrifices.

Patriarch Paul serves liturgy in Prizren
as the Bishop of the Diocese of Raška and Prizren

THE SERBIAN PATRIARCH PAUL (PAVLE)
A SEEKER FOR A DIGNIFIED SOLUTION TO THE TRAGIC FATE OF KOSOVO AND METOHIJA

The following excerpts are a testimony of Patriarch Pavle's struggle, lasting several decades, to find a dignified solution to the tragic conflicts in Kosovo and Metohija.

When I came to Kosovo as the Bishop of Raška and Prizren (1957) I saw another aspect of the ordeal of the Serbian people. When Old Serbia was turned into the Autonomous Region of Kosovo and Metohija, the Serbs were suddenly reduced to a minority in their country, as they had been in the Turkish times. Already in my first episcopal reports I pointed out repeatedly that, although the Serbs were in authority, Kosovo was in fact controlled by the Albanians. In World War II most of their people welcomed the Italian occupation as their liberation, for the Albanians from Albania were then united with those in Kosovo, Metohija and western Macedonia for the first time. Great Shipnia was created, but, in spite of the fact that it lasted, as an Italian protectorate, only as long as the occupation lasted, it has continued to live in the consciousness of the masses, enticed by their leaders, as an achieved national goal that ought to be preserved. Led to believe that the circumstances were only temporarily changed, they only waited, and to a large extent lived to see, the recovery of what had been lost. Warnings were reaching me to take care what I write in my regular reports to the Holy Synod, for they also came into the hands of the secular authorities, but it was becoming increasingly apparent that somewhere, in some place it had been decreed that Kosovo and Metohija should be no longer Serbian. It was becoming obvious in various ways that the behavior of the ordinary people was concordant with that, although the elderly ones condemned the violence and greed of those seeking to seize their neighbors' houses and lands. There were among

Paul as a boy, a student, and a bishop

these some who were conscious of their Serbian origin and who sensed that something leading to no good was being hatched...

It is well known that numerous Albanians used to visit, sometimes even in greater number than Serbs, the relics of St Stefan Dečanski seeking relief for their troubles. Once, standing in the monastic yard, I happened to overhear the conversation between an Albanian, who was coming out of the church with his mother, wife and sick child, and a young man who had come from Montenegro and happended to be there. He asked the unfortunate father: "What do you want from our

Enthronement of Bishop Paul, 1957;
group photo in front of Church in Prizren

Procession around the Dečani Monastery, 1964

Saint?"—"I have come neither to your Saint nor to our Saint," replied the Albanian, "but to God's Saint. And as he is God's Saint, he is both yours and ours. For if the Saint thought the way I and you think, neither you nor I would come to him." The youth remained silent, and the Albanian came up to me to ask a blessing for the child...

It is evident that not only Albanians are to blame for this situation in Kosovo. They were supported and incited not only by the republics of the former joint state, Yugoslavia, but also by the outside world. But what I found the most regrettable was the complicity of the politicians from our people.

The Orthodox Church always appeals for peace and justice among men, reminding its member that we were not asked before our birth whether we wanted to be born in this or that nation, in this or that religion, in this or that religion. But it does depend on us whether we shall act as righteous men or not, and we are responsible before God for all our deeds."

I shall tell you the true story of an event which happened in Kosovo eighty years ago.

In 1979 I ordained a young priest in Uroševac in Kosovo. When the laying on of hands and the Liturgy were over, we met in the church hall for a moment of rest and talk. Someone mentioned the words of

Procession around the Dečani Monastery on the occasion
of changing the vestments of the Holy King, 1964,
with Bishop Paul of Raška and Prizren.

Christ: "He that endureth to the end will be saved." An old man said in connection with that: "I remember the Turkish rule. Ours was a large joint family household with more than sixty members. The times were grim. The Albanians abducted a girl, we overtook them and retrieved the girl. They killed first one and then another member of our family. We avenged the murders. But hardly a week passed when an oppressor and his suite quartered themselves on us. We had to treat them as guests and to feed and tend their horses. What we prepared for our family was eaten by others. Our family elders went to the priest and said:

> Father, we are on the verge of killing all the people in the house, including ourselves, to stop once for all these torments. Or shall we flee to some place in Serbia? But, then, how are we going to feed sixty mouths on the journey? Or shall we turn Turks, like so many around us? The priest replied: Brothers, I am a little above you, and the pressure I have to bear is even greater. But I beg you to endure.

Patriarch Paul visiting Los Angeles, 1994

A year or two, and freedom will come. They said: But, father, that is what we have been listening to for more than five hundred years, and yet nothing has come out of it! If we knew that it would come even in fifty years, we would muster our last strength and endure! And the priest said: That is what I, too, beg you!

Patriarch Paul in public transportation

And then the old man ended his story: "That was in 1910, and freedom came in 1912. If we had given in then, we would have lost in two years all that we had been holding on to for five hundred years."

The essence of the story is this: There would have been no trace of Serbs in Kosovo if they had not cherished the hope that they would remain on their fathers' land and if they had not summoned up, week by week, the tenacity and resolution to endure and survive. At present, too, you can hear speculations on the loss of Kosovo, but the modest Serbian houses and the Serbian shrines are still standing there. This shows how many difficult years has weathered the most valuable contribution which the Serbs were able to make, and which they did make, to the common treasury of man's achievements.

Each war is a disaster, and the civil war as it was in Croatia, Bosnia and Herzegovina and Kosovo is the worst disaster of all. In the civil war, the enemy is the neighbor, fellow-citizen, even a relative in the case of mixed marriages. There is much we have to repent for, both we and Albanians, there have been great disaster and atrocities. Forgiveness comes after repentance.

Patriarch Paul walking on a street in Belgrade

The future of the Serbian nation—not only in Kosovo and Metohija, but wherever it dwells—will depend on whether it acts in full accordance with what is holy and honest, righteous and evangelical. Both the present and the future can be built on Truth alone.

Truth must be hampered, and it cannot be replaced by ingenuity in the affair of national and state importance, or, for that matter, in any other affairs.

It has been alleged that I am subverting, together with some others, the unity of Yugoslavia with the aim of establishing a Greater Serbia. But I am saying today again: if the setting up of our independent state and its preservation and progress were possible only at the cost of crime, I would rather wish that not only Greater Serbia, but also small Serbia and all the Serbs including myself may vanish than accede to anything unrighteous and inhuman. That is what the Covenant of Kosovo and the commitment to the Kingdom of God means to me.

Patriarch Paul, 2005